Tracking Consciousness Before Birth and Beyond

Jaroslav Vlcek D.Sc.

FriesenPress

Suite 300 - 990 Fort St
Victoria, BC, V8V 3K2
Canada

www.friesenpress.com

First Edition — 2017

Book cover design:
Back cover: Jaroslav Vlcek
Front: Jaroslav Vlcek and Joshua Maloon

Illustrations: Pen drawings in the 1st part of the book by Lubomir Vlk

ISBN
978 1 4602 8503 9 (Hardcover)
978-1-4602-8504-6 (Paperback)
978-1-4602-8505-3 (eBook)

1. PHILOSOPHY

Distributed to the trade by The Ingram Book Company

Tracking Consciousness Before Birth and Beyond

Jaroslav Vlcek DSc.

Synopsis

Tracking Consciousness Before Birth and Beyond is based on the author's recollection of his conscious life before birth. In the first part of the book, the author narrates his memories in a poetic form. In the second part, he explains and analyses the narrative from an adult viewpoint and shows its relationship to the scientific and empirical knowledge of life. In the third part, entitled *Return,* he discusses in depth the various events taking place during his prenatal period, such as conception; recognition of food as a source of energy and body building substance; starting the heart; building the brain and body; power of the life force; tree of life; the unborn child's inherent intelligence in the timing and execution of its birth and other experiences in this pristine prenatal existence.

Going "beyond" contains the author's theory of the beginning of life on Earth, based on the quantum concept of the sun's energy as its life force and the awareness of that energy as consciousness. Building on the Lamarck's and Darwin's theories of evolution, Dr. Vlcek views evolution as a creative process fuelled by consciousness, spirit and innate intelligence. Basically, he suggests that a lifeform can make changes to its DNA based on its life experience. "If that were not possible, neither would genetic engineering be," he says.

The author regards consciousness, a universal force, to be the key to life. He sees life as being made up of variable length journeys, which can be viewed as quantum events (objects) possessing wave and particle characteristics. Every life journey, short or long, physical, mental, emotional—when terminated by consciousness—produces a result of that journey ("particle") that is added to the brain/mind and personality of the individual at that time. He believes that personality is mortal, whereas the soul, connected to the eternal flame of life in the heart, is immortal.

Table of Contents

Part 1

Journey into the World

Foreword

The unique opportunity to write a foreword to this collection of poems ushered in a familiar feeling of tentativeness as I conceived thoughts and ideas, molding them together to express myself in this new role. I realized that this was a metaphor for my own biological conception.

In the last fifteen years of my pioneering work in the field of cellular consciousness, thousands of people from different countries have shared their personal experience of reliving their lives from preconception through, to, and beyond birth.

Prenatal memories during therapy sessions are classically expressed through movement and sound. In this delightful book, Jaroslav Vlcek has transformed this preverbal world into the more familiar adult world of language through his exquisite poems.

In my clinical practice, artistic people may create one or two paintings, drawings, or poems expressing their cellular consciousness, but Professor Vlcek's poems cover the whole realm of growth from the first poem *The First Journey* (ovulation, conception and implantation) to the last poem *Into Light and Space* (birth). In the twenty-seven poems comprising the collection, Professor Vlcek has, in an unprecedented way, not only exposed his personal life circumstances, but has brought to light scores of biological and psychological events that open doors to new insights and understanding of prenatal life and its meaning to our existence. We see, for example, such notions as determination of gender by conscious agreement between the two uniting cells; the unborn child's recognition of food as a source of energy and material for building its body; its experience of a state of life's order as its highest sensation; the power of life force; experience of seamless unity with the outside world; its bond to Mother Earth through the luminous tree (placenta); ability to establish communication with its mother; its innate intelligence in the timing and execution of its birth. These are but a few of the fascinating revelations from the author's prenatal life put before us.

These poems will challenge the professional skeptics who still doubt the truth that cellular memories exist. They will resonate for those brave souls who have already journeyed into that magical cellular world of agony and ecstasy and will inspire those spiritual aspirants who are seeking enlightenment through self-realization.

Graham G. Farrant, M.D., F.R.C.,
Richmond, Australia, June 1989

Author's comment: Dr. Graham G. Farrant (1933–1993), a medical doctor in private practice in Australia, did postgraduate work in psychiatry at McGill and Harvard universities. He pioneered cellular consciousness and held international workshops in this area of psychology. His work was to be summarized and presented in his book titled *From Soul to Cell*. Unfortunately, his sudden death in 1993 prevented him from finishing his book.

Prologue

Now and then I travel
a timeless track
through a vibrant space
to a silent cave
to witness my beginning:
then
a dreamless state,
now
a living dream.

Stillness,
deeper than any
I have ever known,
fills the enclosed space.
At first, I cannot see,
then the light of life
dispels the darkness.
I wait...

Though the present
offers but
an endless view,
and the future
is concealed,
I am peaceful
and feel secure.

Now a disturbance
breaks the silence.
Toward the ceiling of the cave
I turn to look:
There in the lining
I see myself stir,
awaken.

The First Journey

I know I am.
Small, as if I fill
no space at all,
I push higher,
gain strength and
scan my surroundings.

Many like me
fill the cave,
lie still,
asleep,
except the one
next to me.

To her I direct my thoughts:

"My energy rises,
pulls me outwards;
I wish to leave,
enter the world below."

She understands:

"When you go,
I will be sad,
may never see you again.
Alone in the world,
how will you find
your way?"

My sister's thought
disturbs me,
tugs against
my urge to leave.
Her intimation
prompts me to seek:

What should I know
before I go?

Outside, high in open space,
I detect a presence.
An invisible Source
knows the order of the world,
and can change it.
I approach and
state my wish.

Unseen,
the all-knowing Source
responds to my thoughts:

"You have grown strong
with energy.
When you leave,
you'll need the power
to know where you are
and
remember your way.
Without it, you will be lost.
But notice where you are
and
recall the way you came,
and you will always know
what to do
and
where to go.
This power
I give you now."

I feel more light,
more energy.
I am ready now.

Above me
in open space
busy beings
move to and fro.
They talk about me,
look for a place
for me to go.

Two agree
to escort me
down to Earth.
I don't know them,
but they know me.
I trust them
as my guides.

My time has come.
In the cave,
a launching slide
is put in place.

Unseen,
the all-knowing Source
directs all.

I am not the first to leave.
Others, not like me,
depart first.

Now I
slide,
lose contact,
begin to fall.
A slow, faultless fall,
as a feather drops,
still in air.

A tunnel contains me.
Outside, night blue space,
dotted with bright lights,
envelops my glide.
In full control
I enjoy my fall,
fall,
fall.

Bump!
I hit something:
an island,
no bigger than I.
Where am I?
Before I turn to see,
I lose my hold,
resume my fall,
now faster
than before.

Outside,
dark blue lightens.
Two figures,
faint shadows
in the dawning light,
move to and fro.

The tunnel
I drop in
begins to curve left,
tapers,
and now I stop.

I land
in a narrow stream,
begin to drift ahead

touching the stream's banks
and shallow bed.

I enjoy my glide,
can see where I am,
remember the way
the unseen Source foretold.

I like the land outside:
on the right a climbing bank,
on the left open land.
Bright patches by day
dissolve into night,
emerge once again,
nourished by the light
that brings them life.

As I move ahead,
slender forms rise
along on the left:
my journey's first companions
greet me on the way.
I expect to see them again
and do
around the next bend.

I've wound my way far,
without a pause;
now tired, thirsty,

I need a rest.
I float
into a small bay,
and touch the beach.

Instantly,
welcoming hosts surround me.
They seem to know
my journey's purpose,
my importance.
They treat me royally,
nurture me,
want me to stay.

But an urge
to resume my journey
moves me on.
I ease into the bay,
find the stream
and drift again
where the current flows.

The stream winds
through a wide plain,
invites me
to trust the way,
to feel at home.
I move with greater ease
as if propelled underneath,
leaping over gaps
my size.
I move fast,
faster.

Confident in my travel,
I wish to know
wherefrom comes the call

that urges me
to move on.

My centre is darker,
denser,
covered by a veil.
Careful, I look in,
discern a design:
a white, neatly folded
sacred human form.
I understand the sign
and the purpose
of my journey.
It is
to deliver the sacred form
on time.
This is my mission,
my destiny.

Outside,
crossing a rise,
I feel my timing is right.

Farther downstream,
a pool
in front of a dam
blocks my way,
forces me to stay,
and spend the night.

By day
I fret to go.
The longer I wait,
the more I hate
the pool,
the dam.

I want to charge,
and break it.

I lunge.
Just then
the dam cracks,
opens.
A torrent
sweeps me down.
Speeding,
bouncing

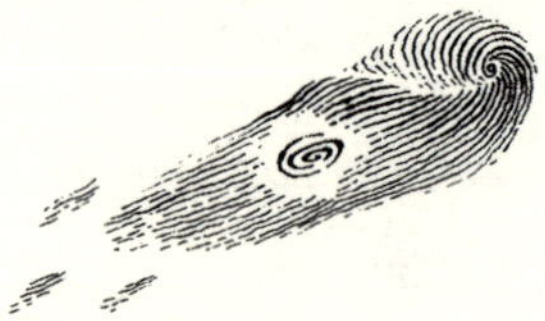

through a narrow gulch,
I can hardly note
and remember
the way.

At last,
widening into a valley,
the stream curves right,
opens and spreads,
its current drops.

Like a boat with little wind,
I sail slowly downstream.
Again I have time
to look where I am,
be in command
of my journey's run.

The ride is peaceful,
full of pride—until,
across to the right,
a disturbance
sharpens my sight.

Quick and energetic,
strange entities
race toward me,
like a group of riders
in pursuit.

Steadily, they close the gap.
Who are they?
What do they want?

Not hostile,
they sense my concern:

"We come from the being
friendly to the one
you come from."

I believe them,
can recall at times
another's presence near.

The spirited intruders
unsettle me,
especially the closest
shows serious interest,
is determined
to stay.

I don't mind
—if it is right—
to receive the stranger,
but first

I must seek
advice.

I send a message up;
slowly it rises.
At last,
the answer comes:
The visitor may stay.

The stranger,
now my guest,
moves to my left,
clings more and more
as we ride along,
slowly taking hold.

The closer I am
to my friendly guest,
the more I am possessed,
absorbed by its bold intent,
excited by its energy.
I want to feel it,
be it.

Consciousness leaves my body,
moves toward the visitor.
Is it the same me?
I lose my identity.
I am no more.

. . . .

Now I,
the friendly guest,
the active partner,
press against
my receptive host.

The surface caves,
draws me in.
Inside,
I reach the centre,
begin to spread,
extend,
permeate
the liquid substance.

Dissolved,
suspended in fog,
my role met,
who am I?
What's next?
I wait.

I still know that I am.

Now only
a point of consciousness,
I rise,

hover over a countryside
in need of warmth.

Below I spot a cottage;
within it a humble room,
where a boy sits before a girl:

"I wish to apologize
for being aggressive.
I surrender victory.
You can be the leader now
as you were before."

She replies:

"I am satisfied
with what happened
between us.
I want you
to continue to act,
lead the way."

Solemn, the boy vows:

"I accept your wish.
I'll act and lead outside.
You will live inside me,
a silent inner companion.

Every night in secret
we will share my day,
celebrate our union.
The purpose of my life
will be to live for you,
my life's inner mate."

Back from where I rose
with a known purpose

and surge of life,
building must be done:
move logs
join them with others,
create new designs.
No time to stop.

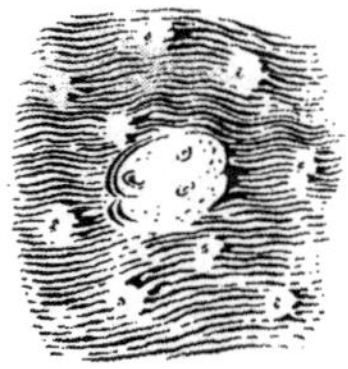

Now, there are
two rooms in my house:
the closer one,
from which I come
and a new one
in front of
the pass-through wall.

I practice crossing,
visiting the new room.
I will store there
my new life experience.

Dazed,
still exhausted
losing myself,
blinded by uniting,
I keep the promise
and set out on the way
with my life's mate.

A while, the course runs
level and straight.

With effort I move ahead.
At the end of day,
I turn to my inner mate
to share my experience.
She is glad.
Our life is
as we planned.

Now the course
runs sharply down
to the left.
I slide down a steep slope,
land at an open door.

A large chamber lies ahead.
This place, I sense,
holds what I seek,
invites me
to enter,
settle down.

I enter,
feel the surface:
hard to yield!
Move to another spot,
again too firm.
Try yet another;
It also lacks
what I seek.

Growing weak
I speed up,
search round and round,
circle the chamber,
helpless,
no place to settle down.

Tormented,
almost spent,
finally I land
in a small crevice
where the floor
and roof meet.
Success!
Implanted!
I will live!

Outside, three beings
rest on grass.
Exalted,
I call to them:

"Look at me!
I am new,
I am one of you."

They do not hear or see.
Only the one
who harbors me
knows,
somewhere inside,
I have arrived
and smiles

with a spark of life
at another,
across to the right.
They both smile.

Where I have landed,
strange entities live.
They frighten me,
especially the tall one
straight ahead,
wants me gone.
Afraid,
I lower myself,
burrow in
and wait.

Touching Stars

The wall-like surface
I have landed on
draws me closer.
Moved to find
what's behind the wall,
I focus where I touch,
begin to make it soft.
The substance seems familiar,
responds to my wish
to dissolve.

I work hard and long.
At last I succeed,
bore a hole
into a deep tunnel.
As I descend,

drop deeper,
I cannot see its end.

At my left,
an object
catches my interest.
As I look closer,
it seems
to lack something.
I want to keep it,
but first move deeper
and find more
of the same.

The tunnel turns left,
now follows
a horizontal course,
opens wide
into an enclosed space
where glistening particles
swim in the dark
like stars at night.
I like them,
lure them,
take them
back with me.
As I turn,
they follow.

Now inside me,
I touch one.
It fills me with light.
I feel more alive.
I touch another,
yet another

and each time
resonate with light.

This light
leads me far
into the universe,
to the stars
I came from.
I am delighted
to be with them
again!

Alas, a star fades,
loses the light
it gave me.
Another star grows dim.
Many shed their light
as they attach to me.
The light of the stars
does not last!
My space darkens,
I need more stars
to keep
the joy of life.

Meantime,
grown strong and tall,
I raise my head,
look around,
stare in the direction
of the hostile dweller
that did not like me here.
Impressed by my size,
he grants me victory.
I am the leader here
now!

I turn back to the tunnel,
supplier of light and life
and tap
the never-ending stream
of delightful bits
that bring me bliss.
I have no concern
no special task.
My wish is
just to be
the way I am,
complete.

Ring of Protection

A noise below
catches my attention.
The lively ones there
all act the same.
They urge me:

"Why don't you laugh,
do what we do?
We always follow
the lead from above."

I don't want to heed
their advice,
I want to live my life
as I like.

Facing the disturbing crowd
I need to protect myself,
build a shield
against their noise:
First I grow more body
between me and the laughter,
then, turning left,
I build around
until I close the ring.
Inside I feel safe
from others.

A new independence
returns me to peace.

When I want
I can still hear the ones
that laugh below.
I enjoy turning there,
in and out.

Mati

Deep inside the linings
I touch the being
that harbors me,
feel my life's connection.
I want to build a bond,
share my deepest feelings
with my nurturer,

my protector.
My life depends on her.
I want to tell her
I am grateful,
but must be careful
not to turn her
against me,
for I could not
survive alone.

A long time
I have known this being,
but not this way.
Before,
I was a part of her,
now we are disconnected.
I am her guest.
She nourishes me.
She is Mati.
She does not know yet
that I am
a different being.
It is my secret.
One day
I will tell her.

To feel our bond,
I find on my right
a small body,
about my size,
open to my affection.
Often I lie beside it,
touch it gently,
grow fond of it.
We spend much time
exchanging warm feelings.

My Inner World

From the sanctuary
within Mati
I sense the world outside:
land, open space.

We move from place to place.
Mati bends,
her quick hands
work the ground.
Her moving, touching, doing
bring the outside into me.
Bit by bit,
with pictures
I build my inner world.

As I unite with the world,
I feel again the union
with my inner mate
when we united.

Each time Mati moves
I add a new piece
that connects
with my previous whole,
seamlessly.

I know
there is more
beyond my current whole,
land I'll reach one day
make my own.
It, too, will merge
with my present whole,
seamlessly.
I delight in the vision:

The world and I
are one.

I love to have it so
as I grow bigger

Hungry Birds

A wild commotion
draws my attention
to a flock of birds outside.
They shriek,
fight,
demand.
What's wrong?
I want to help
quiet the angry flock.

My wish spins a dream.
It carries me
deep into my past,
an ethereal space,
a peaceful place
where everything
happens according to
an exact law,
the world of
elemental existence
where I had
my beginning.

There,
in a farmyard
I see myself
being assembled:

A little unit,
glittering
rare,
precious matter,
my first substance.

Invisible elementals
inhabit this subtle world.
They helped create me
also know the birds.

As I listen
to their silent voices
I remember:
They gave me
the finest substance
they could find.
With it I carry
their highest virtues,
their aspirations.
I am the bearer
of their expectations
of a better life.
They made me
their leader.

I appeal to them now
"Can you help the angry birds?"
Slowly the answer comes:
"Listen to them,
then tell the one
who harbors you
to feed them."

I send the message to Mati.
Shortly after
she feeds them,

they quiet.
I feel
I have helped the birds
and
satisfied the elementals.
Peace restored,
I thank the subtle world.
In a while I too sense
increased wellbeing.
Satisfied,
I fall asleep.

Another day,
same time,
the birds are back;
They shriek,
fight,
demand.

Again I ask Mati
on their behalf.
She gives them
what they need.
They quiet.
Shortly later
I too feel
satisfied.

Day by day
after the birds are fed
I too get nourishment.
Grown used to it,
I am grateful to Mati
for feeding the birds
and my wellbeing.

Under the Apple Tree

On Sunday afternoons,
warm days after work,
Mati and the One
who is always near
come to sit and rest
under the apple tree
by a creek.

They sit quietly,
speak little
in low voices.

I sense their warm feelings
toward each other
and me.

The tree above us
forms a ceiling of protection
for our love trinity.

Submerged in this
quiet ambience of love,
I turn within, enjoying
a deep peaceful state.

Aware of the warm,
softly glowing
pink space, I fall into
a dreamless sleep.

Upward Bound

As each day passes,
I feel a change coming.

I get more excited,
ready myself for action,
I want to grow.

The moment has come.
I move,
add to my base,
rise,
spiral up,
steadily grow higher.

I am busy building
without time to rest,
but now I must stop,
go back to where I started,
tell my base
it remains
a part of me.

I am proud of my size,
my creation,
return,
resume building.

Where the supplies come in
I stand,

examine each carefully,
then decide:
if I like it
make it part of me.
Without ceasing, I sort,
choose,
direct new supplies
where they belong.

With each substance I absorb
I learn more
about the busy outside:
water runs,
creatures fly,
leaves flutter in air.
Everything under the sun
vibrates.
The outside
quivers with life.
They all tell me:
we are!
Mati brings me that!

The matter I taste now
delights me,
the best yet!
I want to find
where it comes from;
is there more?

I hesitate.
Never have I gone
that far
outside my body.
I must be careful,
remember the way.

Little by little,
out I move
follow the winding path,
then turn down
to a deep hollow.
The elementals here
are busy
making the delights
I have been looking for.
The supply is rich.
I sense
it will never end.

Satisfied,
I find my way back.

Flame and Friendship

My interest now
is held
by a place above me
where
a lively source
sparkles with energy,
scintillates with light,
exudes joy of life.

I am drawn more and more
by its dynamic force,
its pulsating liveliness.

It seems that
it wants to tell me:

"I am your friend.
I am inviting you

to join me.
I will teach you
what I know.
You can be
like me."

I hesitate,
feel
I am not able
to accept the invitation.
I need more time
to grow
stronger.

Time passes.
My friend keeps
urging me:
"Try it."

Slowly
I begin to
feel the strength,
gain the courage
to try and join
the friend.

Now ready,
I have decided:
With all my strength
and will,
I strike a spark.
Flame engulfs me,
my whole body
lights up
and
instantly

I leap
to my friend.

We embrace
and start dancing,
turning around,
joyfully celebrating
our friendship.
I listen to the rhythm
and try
to follow my friend
in this dance.

Now I know it
and must return
and try to dance
alone.

I strike a spark
but do not jump.
Another,
again I cannot jump.
The third one,
stronger,
this time I jump.
Another spark
and jump,
spark – jump,
spark – jump
in rhythmic harmony
I am doing it
the way my friend
taught me.

I rejoice:
Now I hold
my own flame.

I learn:
this flame
gives me courage
and strength
to carry out any task
present and future.

I will put it to the test:
I need to move down,
find a new,
bigger space
for my growth.
I focus,
the flame ignites, and
instantly
I have courage
to move.

As I carry it out
and lower myself,
my feeling is:
now I have
the strength and courage
to do anything.

Order of Life

Above me arcs a space
where I file
all in proper place:
all that I like
and wish to keep,
all that I do,
all that I am.
The space fills
with transparent files
that fit together
in perfect order.
Most files I put
in the space on the right.
Almost full,
I begin to fill
the room on the left.

Everything I do
and feel
I complete
and
put in its proper place,
maintain a perfect order.
This awareness is
the best state of being
that I know.
I want to retain it
forever.

Near the centre of my head
a stream brings new supplies.
I sit by it patiently,
watch them float in.
If I want to keep something,

I follow it
to its proper place
and thus know
where to find it
when I need it.

Like this one here:
I follow it right,
then up,
a short distance left,
and turn the corner
to reach its file.
I remember
its trail.

My life's journey
stays the same:
to follow and
remember the way,
wherever I go,
whatever I do,
whatever I feel,
whatever I learn.

Journey is my way
to grow,
to know where
I am
and who I am.

I am the maker of perfect order.
To see everything reach its proper place
brings me calm,
poise,
control of my life.
Beyond that state,
knowing all that I am,

there is nothing else
I could be.

It seems life outside
also tends toward
fulfillment of order.

A being walks toward us.
Closer, he hesitates.
Mati asks,
Has he done
what he was told?
He is not finished yet.
Mati is disappointed.
I would like to help
Mati's order be met,
bring the work
to its proper end.
I wish the world outside
to have the order
I have.

Different, Yet One

It's bright and fresh outside,
when Mati and two others

walk along a meadow path,
turning right by a stream.

It is the first time
I observe her.
What is Mati like?
She steps quickly.
Her talk
is loud and fast.
Her energetic pace
feels strange to me.
Mine is much slower;
I am not like Mati.

Mati says something.
The others don't agree;
they stop,
talk back.
Her voice rises
to convince them.

Again
they shake their heads.
Although not alike,
I agree with Mati,
defend her way.
We live as one.

Life Force

Teeming with life,
all my cells
grow,
divide,
multiply.

My body
swells with energy,
bursting,
bounding,
vibrant
like the world outside:
fields of daisies quiver,
bloom into light,
reaching for the sun,
effusing life.

My own inner parts
surge with appetite,
demand constant attention,
all at once.
I can hardly keep up.

An enormous force
thrusts me forward
in space and time.
Its rising flood
builds my confidence,
swells my size.

Forever forward bound,
I can do anything,
meet
every challenge,
leap
every obstacle.
I grow strong,
my future is bright.
I know everything
now
and
what is to come.

My life force clears
a winding path
into a future.
Day by day,
I follow the way
and succeed.
Satisfied, I carry out
my life's design.

Limitless,
my life force
can help
those outside,
like the weak child
in our house.
If it believed
in me,
it could be strong.

Visitor

Every day, when Mati cooks,
a being like her
comes to talk.
Mati likes the visitor,
turns to listen
to be asked advice.
The visitor looks up to Mati,
leans toward her answers,
trying to find
her way in life.

I like the visitor.
Her gentle manner
engenders peace.

I look forward to her visits,
again and again.

Today,
Mati cooks in silence.
The visitor promised
to be back,
but left,
never to return.

She found her way
and went away
with the man
who wanted her
to go with him
into the world.
It was Mati's wish
too.

I miss her.

Tree, Earth and I

Above me
a luminous tree
spreads wide its crown.

Alight with life,
it speaks to me.

As I gaze
into its winding veins,
small particles
thread toward me.
One speck enters me,
rides a half circle,
stops near my centre,
seeking a place.
I will give it a home,
life
within me.

Another grain
slips around a bend,
meanders toward me.
I watch its every turn.
At times it stops,
rests in silent coves,
grows
as it slides close.
This one has much
to tell.
In pictures,
a story unfolds.
Not far off,
I see a stream
widen into a bay,
a speck of life
lodged in its bank.
High water
washes it down,
carries it along
a zig-zagging path

till Mati gathers
and takes it
to the house.
At last it arrives
here before me.

I like its wandering tale,
and,
sorry for its lost home,
invite it
to live in mine.

The world outside
teems
with wandering life,
searching for a place
to settle down.

I listen to their tales.
Each particle I adopt
connects me
to its source,
lastingly.
Bit by bit
the living Earth
feeds me Her matter
and
binds me to Her.
Everywhere inside
I feel Her presence.
Now I cannot
turn back from Her
without breaking the bond
and the pain of separation.
Forever I am bound
to my true mother.

To Earth I owe
my substance.

I discover:
anything I take and keep,
make my own,
connects me forever
to its source.

A new being
comes to us
looking for work.
Feeling his need
to stop wandering,
I wish I could help.

The luminous tree
shares everything with me:
needing life,
needing to know,
needing to be,
I turn to the tree,
my closest friend.
It always gives,
asks nothing
in return.
When I awaken
to start a new day,
the tree
lights up,
greets me with joy.

When Mati and I
listen to the tree,
we are happy.
The tree at my side,
I command my life,

send Mati my love.
When Mati is sad,
needing more life,
to help her,
I want to say:
"Be like me,
look at the tree,
rejoice as I do;
your life can be
as happy as mine."
But she does not
listen to me,
does not share
my joy.
I am sad
that I cannot help.

Unfulfilled Love

Among the beings outside
a stranger arrives.
He works and stays
in our house
at night.
Unlike the others,
he talks little,
does everything well.
Others look up to him,
admire him.

Mati likes him too
and he her.
A smile,
a look
lingers.

Both are drawn
toward each other.
The attraction grows,
they stop,
talk alone.
Mati's mood
grows warm.
Her feeling
attracts me
to him also.

In time, the stranger
starts to insist,
and pressures Mati.
She grows tense.
Determined to prove
his love, he sets a time:
After dark,
by the gate,
he will meet her:
"We can be one."
But Mati
does not come.

Next day,
the stranger departs,
never to return.

I am sad
his love for Mati
found no proper end,
order was not met.
Now I am the one
left to fulfill
his love for Mati,
when I grow up.

Power to Move

From within,
deep in my chest,
rises a power
to command
and
control
all my movements.
I extend my arm
and become
the mover
of that arm.
I am the maker
and
director
of all the movements
my body makes.

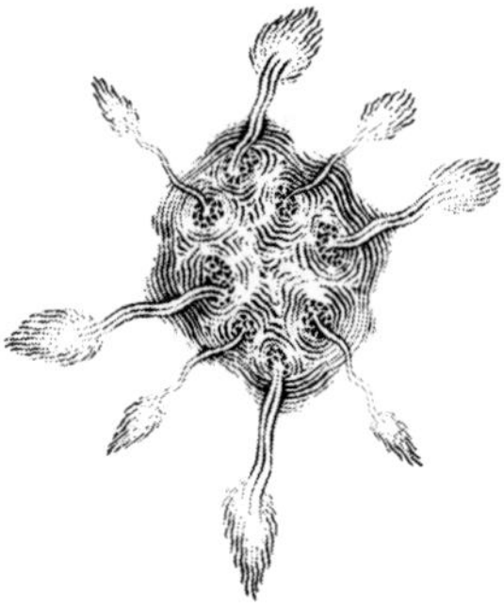

I discover I can choose
which arm
I shall move first.
I try both;
each moves well,
but I prefer the right
to move first.

Slowly my arm ascends.
I feel a deep flow of energy,
in perfect coordination
with the movement.
I can focus this power
in any direction
I wish.

Everywhere
I want to move,
my power
moves me.
It pervades,
controls
my body,
can move mountains,
rotate the Earth,
do everything!

Sounds and Sights of Him

On special days
Mati and I listen.
Sweet vibrations
rise and fill
the room.

A being who
is always near
sits behind the table,
alluring us with sounds.
Ripples of air
stream through the room,
reflect,

curve
toward me.

The waves
flow from everywhere.
One by one
I absorb them,
begin to see:
walls,
corner,
bed,
table.
I even see Him
playing the violin.
Sometimes He sings,
sometimes just smiles,
sometimes sits serious.

Mati's eyes long for Him.
I study the waves.

The sound
holds us three together.
One day,
I wish to know
more about it.

Today
Mati sits silently.
I feel her inner pull
across the room
toward Him.

He plays inviting tunes
to bridge the distance,
draws her close.
I feel her tense

until, at last
she rises
to meet Him halfway
across the room.

The tension ebbs,
subsides
as they get close,
renew their union.

Left out,
no one to cling to,
I lie alone and wish
the future to bring
one like Mati
to meet me,
pull me
toward the union,
someone to be
my own.

When He is around
she watches:
does He approve?
When out of sight
she longs for Him.
He has power over Mati.
When He storms
out the door,
harsh sound jars
my inner peace.
At other times
I feel they celebrate
my presence
as she looks at him
with love.

Light

Centered in my head
I have found a place
that lights up
when I visit it.
The feeling delights me.
I linger there,
enjoy its brilliance.

But now,
instead of one,
two places,
a short space apart,
light up to greet me.
Which shall I visit first?

I have made my choice:
the spot on the right.
From now on
I always go to
the light on the right,
before turning left.
This light shines less bright,
but I want
equal time for both.

Now I know
light and space
await me outside.
Everything there
glows in bright light.
I look forward
to enter it.

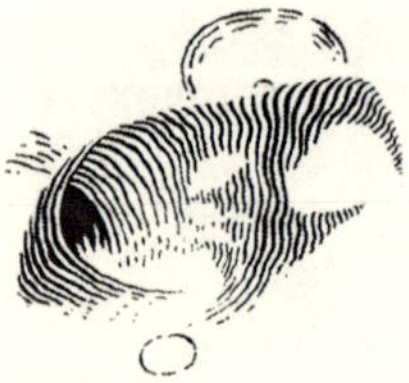

Attacks of Anger

A shooting pain!
Again my body is attacked!
I have learned
the attacks come
when Mati rages
as she does now,
shouting
at a lame woman
with a weak mind
who does not understand
what she did wrong.

Screams!
I cringe inside.
The attackers,
lit up and
linked in chains,
pulsate forward,
stream toward me.
So many this time!

Bracing myself,
I begin to shake.
My body is on fire,
enraged.

All night I wage war,
fight for my life
without stopping.
I must defeat them,
I must survive.

At last,
completely exhausted,
I fall asleep.

I wake up calm.
The battle is over.
I have won.
Now docile, the attackers
have turned
into my guards.
Now they face
the other way,
ready to defend me
against
another angry lot.

Having my guards,
I feel strong.

Place of Silence

A large noisy crowd
has gathered outside.
For a while I stay,
as I often do,
a silent witness.
But their voices rise,
exceed my comfort,
force me to withdraw

inside.
I close my eyes,
roll them upwards
and
turn them
where once
they were one,
near the middle
of my head.
Now the noise is gone.
I like it this way.

I learn:
Unwanted world
can be shut out
by rolling the eyes
to a place
from which they came,
when they still were one,
when I could not hear,
as I do now.

When I reach
that place,
near the middle
of my head,
my life is tranquil.
I want
to remember
it
forever.

Sleep/Wake

As I keep growing,
the space around me
tightens.
More and more
I am part of everything
Mati does.
Today she sits,
her hands fly,
stripping feathers.
Three others
sit across by the wall
doing the same.
They carry a lively talk.

I fall asleep
but not for long.
Mati's laughter
shakes me awake.
Annoyed.
I drift back to sleep
only to have
another burst of laughter
wake me up again.
On and off
sleep/wake!

I grow angry
at Mati and the others.
It's their fault
I cannot
have my rest.

Through the Arm Loop

Wrist and elbow bent,
my right arm
arches up
toward my head.
My left arm
slides across my chest
to form a loop with the right.
My head reaches forward,
tries to squeeze
through the opening.
It holds tight.

The power of movement
stretches my neck.
I push hard,
break open
the arm loop
and rest.

In a while
I repeat the exercise.
Again and again
squeezing through the noose,
my neck grows stronger.

Wellbeing

The liquid surrounding
radiates warmth,
glows with soft light.
I feel good
and comfortable as
I lie,

conscious of
how beautiful my life is.
I have everything
I need.
Peace,
wellbeing.

Not even the life outside
can disturb
my contentment.
I wish to live like this
Always.

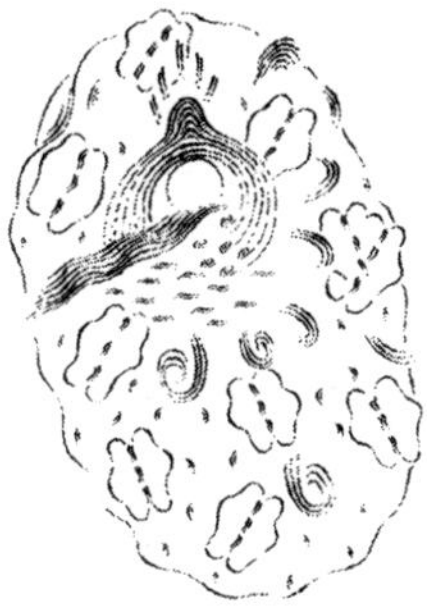

Thoughts

Exciting and alive,
thoughts about my future
gather in my head.

I lie in a trough
that will narrow,
curve to the right
as it takes me closer
to the world outside.

I am absorbing so many
ideas from without.
Each being outside
sends thoughts to me:
Mati,
the One always near,
others
who mill around,
expecting my life
to carry their messages.

The ideas crowd my head,
each one begs:

"Take me,
accept me,
keep me alive
in your life."

How do I know
which ones to accept,
which are right for me?
How do I choose?
I must be careful,
see clearly.
I must have control,
keep the right thoughts,
for each one
will impose itself,
take its share
of my future life.

Like ribbons of light,
thoughts pull me up
to a place
where I can find advice.
I will consult:

the closest in me,
the highest in me,
the lightest in me,
the liveliest in me.
I will choose
the best for me.

Knocking on the Wall

Around me the space tightens.
I must let Mati know that
I have grown big.
I am proud of my size,
all I can do.
I have confidence,
can think ahead
and direct
my future course.

But how do I find a way
to get in touch
with Mati
and tell her
about my need
to begin
to communicate?
The thought
of not knowing
sweeps over me,
elicits a strange
new feeling
how to act.

I can think now,
get ideas

and try them out.
I will find the way.

For several days, I puzzle
where and how
I approach Mati.
First I lean left,
but cannot press close enough
to hear her.
Next above,
she is not on that side.
I turn my head down
and follow with my body.
Being upside-down
seems right.
I am close to the wall.

About four o'clock in the afternoon,
Mati and a few others
chat by the kitchen window.
I make my move:
with my right elbow
I knock slowly
three times on the wall,
listen and wait.
Mati has not heard me.
Again I knock,
again no response.
Now I knock four times,
wait,
no reaction yet.
Mati chats on with her friends;
I grow anxious.
If I cannot reach her,
I am doomed,
my life will end.

Another day at four,
again I try,
knock several times
and pause.
Mati hears me!
She moves inside
to let me know.
I burst with joy.
She tells others
how I am trying
to get her attention.

From now on
we work together.
Every day 'round four
I knock
and Mati moves
a certain way.
In harmony
we commune.
My fears about my life
have vanished.

My upside-down position
is pleasant.
Closer to the ground,

I enjoy the bounce
when Mati walks.

Force of Change

Welling within me,
a strange new energy
pervades my body,
pulls me out of here.

Mati walks along a sunlit road,
I can feel the bumpy air.
She rests beside a tree
on a sunny bank,
gazes down the road ahead.

Little by little
my future unfolds:
I sense a big change coming.
Soon I'll leave this place
for another,
farther along
my journey's path.

My home has been good,
I feel sad to leave.
So much here
I will miss:
the tree,
abundance,
friendships.
But I cannot resist
the force of change
urging me on
when the time comes.

Time and change
always go together.

The force of change,
I sense,
flows into everything.
I feel it in my cells.
Everywhere outside
nothing stays the same.
Moving energy spins
inside every particle.
Each being there
also knows this force
and the sadness
it leaves behind.

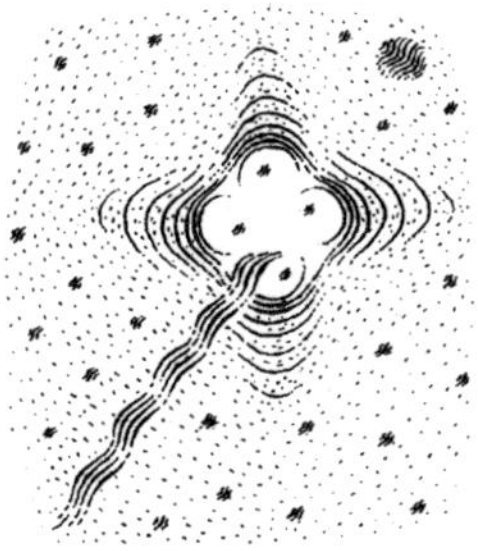

Preparing to Leave

Only a few days left
before I move out,
enter
the world of light and space.
I must prepare.
Inside me awakens a force
whose enormous power

will grow,
explode,
propel me out.
I feel its tension build,
can hardly hold it back.

At night, during sleep,
I make the first move,
enter an empty room,
feel around
and find a door.
It is shut.

Next day I practice
stretching my neck,
feel the propelling force.

At night, I enter
another empty room
with a closed door
that points ahead.
The night after,
I find yet another
empty room
and closed door.
Another night,
another room,
another door
I cannot open.
How many rooms,
how many doors
must I try
to find the way out?

Still my energy rises,
tension floods my senses,
vibrates my body

with breaking force.
I speed up the search.
This night,
at last,
I find the right door.
I know
it is the one
to lead me out.
In the morning
I will be born!

Into Light and Space

Dawn!
This is the day
I will open the door,
move out
into the world
where light and space
abound.

Outside
all is still awakening
as I gather tension
and strength
to meet the task ahead.
My first step:
Announce that I am ready.

Arms crossed and folded
tight against my chest,
shoulders curved in,
I tense my body,
stretch my neck,
and with my head
press against the door.

After a moment's rest
I push with greater force.
Nothing happens yet.
I stop and wait

Next time,
with all their might,
my legs
thrust me forward
to hit the door.
It stays shut,
but I sense a response:
Mati seems to know
what I am up to,
but is not ready yet.

I am!
My spirit soars.
Like a king
I want to command,
direct everything.

The outside stirs to motion,
but not fast enough for me.
I want to go
now!

With energy renewed,
I lunge forward,

bang my head on the door.
It does not budge.
Again and again
my head pounds the wall
till I am spent.
I have to stop and rest.

Refreshed,
determined,
I ram the door
again and again
in vain.
Wearing myself down,
I cannot struggle on
for long.

When I stop
I hear voices from outside,
Mati's and a woman's
who came to help.
The woman tells Mati
to relax and rest.
Mati is too anxious.

She asks for Him,
wants Him here.
They tell her:
he is hunting a stork.
No! She wants him home.
Someone must find Him,
bring Him back.

As the woman soothes Mati,
my anger at them grows.
I want to scream,
"This is no time to rest!
I must get out!"

I beat my head senseless,
the stress is killing me.
"Let me go!
Let me go!"

One last time, I push.
No use;
Mati will not understand.
I cannot get out.
My journey will end.
I am doomed.

Life energy spent,
stuck in this place of terror,
I can do nothing
but die.
Defeated,
I accept my fate.

I succumb to the end-of-life wish,
turn away,
let go
of my body.

With only my soul consciousness
I stagger
onto a wide plain,
find a river,
lie down on its bank
to die.
Fog rolls over me.
I feel
an unending space.

What's that?
Is someone calling me?
I stir;

I am not dead yet.
Regaining life consciousness
and
with a newfound strength,
I must go back
where I left
and try again.

I find the door,
thrust forward—
A change!
An opening
around my head!
Harder, harder I push.
Widening,
the gap grows
and now
out slides my head.
Now my arms,
still crossed
reach the opening,
elbows first.
I push out to my waist.
Sharp pain!
I stop.

The woman tries to help.
With hands around my neck,
she twists it right and left.
I want to yell:
"Let go of my neck!
It hurts!"

Each time I try
to push myself out,
the pain knifes.

It's too strong,
I cannot cross it!
I squeeze my abdomen,
still I cannot bear the pain,
I am caught.

But I must get out!
Pushing with legs,
again I try,
but can't get
past the pain.
I must find a way!

Above, the woman
grabs my arms and pulls.
I squeeze my middle
as much as I can,
the pain wrenches,
knifes my abdomen.
I strain to stop it
in my head
and finally
succeed
in blocking the pain.

Past the painful point
I slide.
I am out!
Joy springs up
in me
and everyone.
I have made it,
arrived
into the world!

Gasping for air
I open the throat,

wheeze in
the first big gulp of air.
I will live!

A small regret
enters my head,
to return,
to where I came from
but ecstasy
turns me forward.
I am born!

Part 2

Through the World

Introduction

The collection of poems on the preceding pages tells the story of a prenatal life, a period that the majority of people find difficult to remember. That is to say, it is not part of their postnatal conscious living memory. Yet, it is the most fundamental and significant part of the human life journey. We only need to remind ourselves that, during a span of some nine months, a marvelous biological system is developed that can function for almost a hundred years. A miraculous creation indeed! It would be very difficult, even impossible, to design and develop a mechanical system of similar complexity that could last that long. In view of this intriguing phenomenon, we ought to be inspired and curious to find out and learn more about our prenatal existence.

Science has amassed through observation a considerable amount of data and knowledge about the physical side of the development of the prenatal child but has been unable to tell us hardly anything about its life experience. This is because science is unable to observe and measure consciousness, which is at the forefront of our experience of life. Consciousness is an inherent property of all living forms and a component of the life force. It is under the direction of the self, soul or whatever else we choose to name the "I" in "I am." Every living organism requires at least some level of consciousness, together with memory and intelligence, in order to cope with life and the environment in which it expresses itself.

Consciousness is already present in the cell. Despite being very small, the cell is biochemically already a sophisticated system. We know that even single-cell organisms have the ability to cope with the environment they live in.

Memory is the track that consciousness leaves behind. All of us are familiar with memory that is stored in the brain, but we know little about the kind and mechanism of memory stored in the cells. Where there is life, there is consciousness; where there is consciousness, there is memory; where there is memory, life becomes continuous. Thus memory, based on consciousness, maintains the continuity and contiguity of life.

We will deal with the phenomena of consciousness and memory more deeply in part 3 of the book. At this time, it will suffice that the reader accepts the idea that the prenatal being is conscious from the very beginning of its individual life, as stated in the first verse of the first poem *The First Journey* with the words **I know I am.**

In this second part of the book, we will examine and explain the content of the poems from an adult point of view. The explanations will be simple. Normally, poetry does not need an explanation. In our case, however, the commentary and analysis of the poems is necessary to provide the reader with clarification of the content and put the intended meaning into a familiar form for adult comprehension. At the same time, especially if we find an event and its meaning interesting or important, we will attempt to enlarge upon and emphasize it by pointing out its relation to the knowledge and experience we have from other areas of the study of human life, such as biology, psychology, philosophy, religion, mythology and folklore, etc. Hopefully, this investigation will inspire in the reader a greater trust and belief in prenatal life.

The memory tracks of a prenatal child correspond to its real-life experiences. On the basis of that, we could say that the prenatal memory is real and credible but, in the sense of its understanding and interpretation, unclear and not easily understood when we compare it to postnatal memory, which is based on our sensory and mental powers and is logical and verifiable. Prenatal memory is written in the language of life—*light*. We will return to this topic later.

We can imagine the reawakening and reliving of our prenatal memory as a recording played back in sequential order like that of a video or movie.

Awakening the memory of prenatal life has primarily a personal value. However, some events are common to all of us; they transcend our personal meaning. These transpersonal experiences—conception, starting the heart, building the body and memory, starting the communication with mother before birth, and the birth itself, are experiences we all underwent and thus are of interest to everyone. We can talk about them generally.

To communicate the prenatal memory in words seems impossible, since there were no words at that time. Yet, the verbal form of communication, though imperfect, is the one with which we are most familiar. For this reason, the whole presentation is of necessity metaphoric. It is also for this reason that I have chosen simple words and kept them to a minimum. I think of prenatal life as a truly poetic existence. That led me to use the poetic form. It is, however, not a form that we are accustomed to in poetry. The collection could be more properly called an epic poem, a prosaic poem or poetic prose. However, for lack of a better term, I shall refer to the collection of poems as the *Poem.*

The use of asterisks. Asterisks will be used to bracket the quotations from the poems that contain the ideas discussed in the text. Asterisk in Greek means "little star". In the poem *Touching Stars,* the embryo recalls **The light [of the particles] leads me far into the universe, to the stars I came from. I am delighted to be with them again.** The use of asterisk to refer to the prenatal child appears natural.

The First Journey

The poem *The First Journey* offers an opportunity to look into the secret and magical happening of the first three key events at the beginning of human life: ovulation, conception and implantation. We could call it the cellular phase of our life.

I know I am The biographical story begins with the awakening of a tiny lifeform, an egg, in a small *cave* (the ovary) with a feeling of energy and an intention to push up and leave (beginning of ovulation). In the **I am**, the "*I*" stands for the self, soul or whatever we may wish to call the subject of self-awareness; "*am*" denotes the state of being a conscious living being. The consciousness that's active here is the pure basic form of consciousness that connects us with the source of life everywhere. This has a huge importance for us. It is the basic consciousness (energy) without an identity of who we are. It is extremely difficult to reach this identity-less state in adult life.

The egg "sees" (is conscious of) many like itself, still lying asleep, except the one next to it, that appears like a sister and seems also to be awake. The egg cell addresses "her" and tells her about its intention to leave, **to enter the world below.** The neighbouring cell expresses sadness at its decision to leave. Of interest to us is the communication between the ovulating cell and its neighbour. Embryologists tell us that during ovulation one or more of the other egg cells also "wake up," later to form a so-called *yellow body,* whose function is to help hormonally during pregnancy.

This episode involving the cells bears a similarity to a wedding custom of bride and bridesmaids. We might see its origin in prenatal memory. Even the throwing of the bouquet by the departing bride to the next bride-to-be (next egg cell to ovulate?) bears a similarity. Flowers symbolize the "blooming" state of the life force.

Alone in the world, how will you find your way? The ovulating cell is moved to seek an answer to its "sister's" disturbing question.

High in open space, I detect a presence, an invisible Source It is hard to say what the invisible Source (that gave the ovulating cell the advice of how not to get lost in the world) could have been. Was it a real (namely, parent) or an imaginary being, God, a supernatural power or a strong concentration of natural energy? For us, what is more important is this seemingly simple advice, one of the greatest truths of life: in order not to get lost, we have to remember where we came from and where we are going (consciously follow and remember the way). Forgetting the life journey leads to the fragmentation of life and uncertainty of knowing who and where we are and where we come from. It is interesting to note that in Hinduism forgetting life events is considered a sin.

As adults, we would say that to remember our way, we need some form of orientation ability based on sensory organs and consciousness. The cell does not have the sensory apparatus, but it has its genetic prescription in its DNA to which the embryo has access through the "*I am*" consciousness (discussed later). A gene may exist that the journeying cell can "illuminate" (become conscious of), which will enable it to monitor its movement. From the poem, we learn that the cell can recognize the direction in which it is moving (up and down, left and right, forward and backward and also the speed of moving). It recognizes the existence of space. It may be aware of the gravitational force. Its path is also influenced by its energy and mass by Einstein's theory of relativity. There are other factors, for example physiological ones, at play as well.

Beside spatial orientation, the cell receives information about its surroundings via consciousness. A memory track of its journey is laid down. Thus, not to get lost, we only need to be focused on and be conscious of our journey and rely on it. Many people who live close to nature do so.

I feel more light, more energy. I am ready now The sensation of more light (energy) always accompanies increased consciousness, which leads me to believe that consciousness plays the most important role in orientation.

The first among the tarot cards (Figure 1.)—which C.G. Jung considered to be archetypes—bears the number 0 and the name The Fool. It portrays a young person standing on the edge of a precipice, ready to jump. In the right hand, on a stick over the shoulder, he has a bundle with food; in the left, a flower. At his feet is a leaping white dog. Timothy Leary, who looked at the tarot as representing stages of life, called it a symbol of a newborn.

Our interpretation will explain this symbol in terms of the ovulating egg as follows: The number zero is also the shape of an egg. The young person about to leap off the precipice symbolizes the egg about to drop into the oviduct. The white dog represents the cell's orientation capability based on consciousness, crucial to its survival described above, and the flower a blooming level of its life force (energy) and readiness. The bundle with food will be explained later. Finally, the white sun in the upper right corner of the picture denotes the pure consciousness *I am*. The Fool? It often seems overly adventurous or foolish to set out on a journey into the unknown. Some would even say today that it may not be such a great idea to drop into the world, given its condition.

Figure 1. The Fool

Above me, in open space, busy beings... talk about me... two agree to escort me down to Earth It is difficult to explain the activity taking place in a seemingly other-worldly realm where some ethereal beings prepare a 'baby' for a journey to earth. What comes to mind are the 'thought forms' of the parents thinking and talking about wanting a baby. The visionary poet and artist William Blake painted an angel who is accompanying a baby to earth with a message: "Go and love without the help of anyone on Earth."

Many people believe in the existence of angels and similar astral beings. Scientists might consider the possibility of concentrated energies, which create conditions especially suitable for life.

The next two stanzas of the poem describe the egg cell leaving its place in the ovary and the beginning of its fall under the direction of the all-knowing Source. The egg describes the departure as a sliding movement at first, then *_a slow, faultless fall_*. Before the egg leaves, it mentions some other cells *_not like me_* that depart ahead of it. Our explanation would be that these other cells are nursing cells whose function is to feed the traveling egg during its journey, symbolized by the bundle of food on the shoulder of The Fool.

A tunnel contains me. Outside, night blue space, dotted with bright lights, envelops my glide. It appears that the ovulation took place on a clear night, full of stars. Although we might be sleeping, our body still receives information about the weather outside through subtle channels of perception of which we are normally not aware

*_Bump! I hit something, an island no bigger than I_* The egg was probably falling the wrong way and was intercepted by one of the cilia (whip-like objects) whose purpose is to catch the falling egg and direct it to fall in the right direction, if it does not fall that way.

*_I land in a narrow stream, begin to drift ahead_* The narrow stream would be the mucous surface of the oviduct. The land outside contains landforms in the valley where the mother lived.

*_Slender forms rise along on the left: my journey's first companions_*. The rows of rising slender forms can be explained as the cilia that line the oviduct. Their purpose is to enable the egg to move ahead. By rising (as they are stimulated), they create a furrow through which the egg moves. This act/action could remind us of the inspection of a guard of honor that is afforded to a head of state on its visit to a foreign country. The egg and its important role in life are recognized by other cells as such a "dignitary."

After a long journey, the egg feels *_tired, thirsty_*. It floats into a bay where *_welcoming hosts surround me... nurture me._*. The entities that host the egg and offer it nourishment are the nursing cells that preceded it during ovulation and are depicted as a bundle attached to a stick on the right shoulder of The Fool (Figure 1.). They also know the egg as a "royal" cell.

They [the hosts]... want me to stay... But an urge to resume my journey moves me on The egg feels that it cannot stay with the hosts, since its inner voice urges it to keep moving forward. It appears that the journey is very important to it.

We find a close similarity to the above sentiment in the words of the poet Walt Whitman in *Song of the Open Road.*

> However sweet these laid-up stores,
> however convenient this dwelling
> we cannot remain here...
> However shelter'd this port
> however welcome the hospitality ...
> we are permitted to receive it but a little while....

Further in the same poem:

> no sooner you arrive...settle yourself to satisfaction,
> before you are call'd by an irresistible voice to depart...

In the following part of its journey, the egg cell moves through a wider area and seems to be moving faster, being helped by the cilia that push it along from underneath.

I wish to know wherefrom comes the call that urges me to move on... My centre is darker, denser... Careful, I look in, discern a design: a white, neatly folded sacred human form It was known by its discoverers that the color of the DNA molecule is white. What is remarkable, however, is the finding by the egg cell that the call, urging it to continue its journey, was hidden within the *sacred human form.*

To quote Walt Whitman again:

> keep on, there are divine things well envelop'd,
> there are divine things more beautiful than words can tell.

The poet has a deep impression about what one can find on the road. What more beautiful and divine than a sacred human form?

How would it be possible for the egg to perceive a human form? We could begin by asking a more familiar question: How does an architect "see" a house when he or she is looking at its plan? To understand the cell's perception, we have to consider the interaction between its consciousness and the DNA. If we think of the DNA as a memory (a blueprint), then the cell would simply re-enact the "human form" as a memory recall.

The purpose of my journey is to deliver the sacred form on time Our egg cell, now aware of the sacred content it carries and its need to keep moving, realizes the purpose of its journey and the mission in its life. While the mother is climbing a hill, it feels that its timing is right. Timing and synchronicity are obviously very important during conception.

Farther downstream along its journey, the egg cell arrives at a pool formed in front of a dam that **blocks my way, forces me to stay, spend the night.** In the morning, the egg becomes agitated **I want to charge, break it [the dam].** We can think of the "dam" as a temporary obstruction (mucus accumulation?) of the flow. Suddenly, the dam cracks and opens, sweeping the egg into a rapid stream that eventually subsides and opens into a wide, slow moving flow **I sail, like a boat... in command of my journey's run... The ride is peaceful, full of pride.**

Suddenly, a disturbance makes the egg turn its sight to the right: **quick and energetic, strange entities race toward me... like a group of riders in pursuit... Steadily, they close the gap.** Not hostile, the "riders" inform the egg that they come from someone close and friendly to the being that harbors it. The egg **can recall, at times, another's presence near.**

What happens, following this, is the most important moment in human life: conception. It begins by the egg becoming aware of one of the sperms (*strangers*) that is closest to it and **shows serious interest, is determined to stay.** The egg is not sure whether it can receive the sperm and sends **a message up... the answer comes: the visitor may stay.** It is not certain where the message travels to and who answers it. My feeling would be that it travels into the brain of the mother. The egg knows its mother from the past and is thus able to communicate with her. This event may remind us of the behavior—in adult life—of a daughter who may consult her mother about meeting a suitor.

All of us would like to know how the event of our own conception unfolded, how our individual and independent life began. For an easier understanding, we will divide conception into three phases or steps: (1) meeting and acquaintance of the sexual cells, (2) their merging and loss of identities and (3) the rise of a new human being and their identity.

Phase 1. The egg recalls: *The stranger, now a guest, moves to my left, clings more and more as we ride along, slowly taking hold.** The sperm joins the egg and makes contact with the egg's left side. There are different customs among various cultures about which side the woman occupies on the side of the man. In ancient Egypt, the woman stood on the right side, like the egg in our case.

As they travel together, the egg is fascinated by the energy of the sperm to the point of being possessed by it: **Consciousness leaves my body, moves toward the visitor... I lose my identity.** The egg loses its awareness of being an egg (its identity) but retains the memory of its origin and journey. It still has the consciousness *I am* that connects it to the source of life.

It might be of interest to us to know what happened "psychologically" to the egg when its consciousness left its body and "moved" into the sperm. We can observe in small children—when their attention is strongly focused on some object—being startled if we disturb them, as if they are not present where they are physically but are where the object is. The fascination of the egg with the sperm and its energy, during which its consciousness embraced the sperm, is the ultimate degree of attraction and desire for oneness, a feeling that is rarely experienced to such a degree in adult life. It may resemble a hypnotic state (because of the loss of identity) but differs from it in that it does not involve control over the subject.

Phase 2. The identity and role of the egg terminated, the energetic sperm with its consciousness now enters the "stage" and takes on the leading role: **Now I... press against my receptive host. The surface caves, draws me in.** The sperm penetrates the egg, dissolves, and like the egg, loses its identity **My role met, who am I?** but not the memory of its origin and journey, and not the basic consciousness *I am.*

In a close and active relationship between two individuals, only one of them can assume a leading role at any given time. The other has to follow and, though it may seem passive, is also "active" when it agrees voluntarily. Psychologically, both roles are equal.

Phase 3. The rise of a new being and its identity. This phase is dramatic and veiled in mystery. It begins with a critical feeling of uncertainty: **What's next? I wait.** The union of the two cells, each having life consciousness, sets out to seek its identity and a direction in life. First, its consciousness rises **to gain a wider view**, hovers above a countryside and finds a cottage with a boy and girl in it. The boy kneels before the girl, apologizes for his aggressive behavior, surrenders his *victory* and asks her to resume the role of the leader. She is **satisfied with what happened** and asks him to continue to lead. He accepts her wish to be the leader and promises to share his life with her. The boy then makes a commitment to her: **The purpose of my life will be to live for you, my life's inner mate.** The union of the spirits of the egg and sperm discovered its identity and the direction for its future life. The male spirit will incarnate, and the female spirit will live inside him as his spiritual mate.

At this time, it might be helpful to clarify the term "identity." By identity we understand our conscious identification with what we are or wish to be, that which defines our life role at a given time (in part 3 we will find how the identity arises, using the quantum theory). Without identity, not to know or feel who or what we are, we would be in a state of life's uncertainty and vulnerability, even crisis. On the other hand, in this vulnerable state of no identity, our basic consciousness "*I am*" has access to deep levels of our psyche, including the subconscious.

The result of finding one's identity—through the identification with someone or something—also establishes our oneness with what we identify ourselves with.

The science of embryology places the beginning of our current life at the time when the fertilization of the egg takes place. The chromosomes of the two reproductive cells combine to give rise to a new DNA, and everything settles down and leads to a new self-sufficient and self-determining first cell called the zygote. It teaches us also that the physical gender of a new human being is determined by the presence or absence of the chromosome Y in the sperm.

Science gives us a descriptive, objective view of the biological processes that take place but does not tell us about life the way we know it, as a subjective conscious experience. The purpose of this writing is to reveal this conscious experience in early life.

To be able to understand the psychology of conception, we have to view the union of the two reproductive cells as a union of the male and female spirits, also called the male and female principles. These cells were created by the male and female beings and were thus imbued with their spirits (principles). Although we believe that spirit exists, we are usually not conscious of it. We can only say, based on our experience, that it is a form of energy similar to consciousness. Its existence can be compared to that of a particle in physics, which scientists are unable to study directly but can observe its effect. We also know that energy is indestructible.

The poem describes the search for identity by the union of the sex cells as a conscious journey. We can see it as a journey of the basic consciousness *I am*. This basic life consciousness, according to the poem, finds a scene of two young people of the opposite sex deciding to stay together. They decide who is going to lead in life and what will be the nature of their relationship, including the purpose of their life together. The question arises: How real are these beings? We can say that they are as real as our dreams, ideals[1] or thoughts. We will interpret the episode of the 'boy and girl' as an archetype[1] (ideal form) of the roles of man and woman entering a marriage, from the man's perspective. We will regard them as spiritual forms.

If we accept the idea of the archetype, where would the consciousness of the cell union find it? The most natural place would be in the union of the parents. This is also supported by my personal recollection

1 The concept of archetypes (Plato's ideal forms) was advanced by C.G. Jung. He saw them as universal patterns of thought and models of life, being part of collective consciousness, and symbolizing prominent personality traits, human roles and relations.

of a newborn cell (a result of cell division) in my body that got its identity from the life I was experiencing at that time.

In prenatal life, its basic life consciousness *I am* connects the cell union with all of life.

As we mentioned above, another way for the cell union to find its identity would be in the union of the parents. This is possible because of the basic consciousness *I am*. It further strengthens the idea that we are connected to our ideals at all times, whether we are conscious of it or not.

In summary, we can say that conception is a most significant life event, a beginning of new life that not only contains the biological drama of renewal and reproduction but offers also an insight into the mystery of life itself. It has a profound impact on our adult life.

In the subsequent part of the poem, the cell union that has taken on a male identity narrates: **Back from where I rose with a new purpose and surge of life, building must be done... create new designs. No time to stop.** What takes place is probably the joining of the chromosomes and formation of the new DNA molecule and creation of the first human cell, the zygote. From this point on, we can talk about it as having a self/soul and identity.

Now there are two rooms in my house: the closer one from which I come, and a new one... behind a pass-through wall. We are told about the first cell division that took place. It gave rise to a new cell, which the consciousness of the elementary life unit could enter by moving freely through the cell wall (empirical evidence of the aware consciousness being "mobile" and nonlocal). The self/soul will store its **new life experiences** there. This gives the new cell its identity, establishes its oneness with the self/soul and becomes the cornerstone of its memory. We have here the beginning of the growth of an organism.

Intuitive idea: Energy (consciousness) passing through a cell wall has been experimentally verified in physics. It is referred to as quantum tunneling. (See Subchapter 5.3 in the third part of the book.)

I keep the promise, and set out on the way with my life's mate... At the end of the day I... share [with her] my experience... Our life is as we planned. Now, a multi-cellular embryo describes its journey toward the womb. It remembers its promise to share its experiences with its inner feminine spirit as they planned during conception. The cells of the embryo would, at this time, still be undifferentiated stem cells.

A large chamber lies ahead... invites me to enter. The embryo enters the womb and feels instinctively that it is the place to settle down. It begins to feel the surface but finds it hard to attach to. It moves to another place that is too firm; it tries yet another, but that one is not suitable either.

I speed up, search round and round, circle the chamber helpless... almost spent, finally I land in a small crevice... Success! Implanted! I will live! The embryo describes a traumatic experience in trying to find a place to attach itself to the wall of the womb. At the end, it succeeds and locates one in a crevice and declares that it will live. The degree of difficulty to implant in the womb—described here as life and death struggle—seems surprising. Apparently, this is not uncommon according to the work of the British psychiatrist R.D. Laing and others who identified patients exhibiting the effects of implantation trauma that became a lifelong burden on their psyche.

Shortly after it has attached itself, the embryo announces its arrival to a group of three people outside **Look at me! I am new, I am one of you.** It may be interesting to note that the freshly implanted embryo declared itself to be a human being and a new member of the human family. The embryo tells us that it came among humans as one of them when it implanted in the womb. This might help us to resolve the ongoing discussion about our beginning as a human life.

Only the one who harbors me knows somewhere inside I have arrived, and smiles with a spark of life at anothe. Embryo's mother noticed that something inside her "arrived" and looked at her husband with a smile. Both of them "understood" that they would be having a child. This event took place on a country meadow near my home in Czechoslovakia around May 25, 1924. In those days, women were still quite natural and conscious of becoming pregnant. They did not require pregnancy tests.

In the last stanza of the poem, the embryo becomes aware of some unfriendly entities, probably polyps, which also inhabited the womb and would, naturally, have felt threatened by a stranger arriving in their midst.

Touching Stars

After implanting and proclaiming itself to be a newly arrived member of the human family, our heroic embryo devotes its attention and effort to find out **what is behind the wall** where it landed. It begins to make a hole into the womb wall by dissolving it. It is hard work, but the substance is familiar to it, and eventually the embryo manages to "bore" (dissolve) an opening that leads into a dark tunnel. It starts to descend in it. On the way down the tunnel, it finds an elongated object that lacks something. **I want to keep it but first move deeper and find more of the same** It's not clear what the object and others like it are. They lack some vital part or property, most likely energy.

The tunnel **opens wide into an enclosed space where glistening particles swim in the dark like stars at night.** We could think of the tunnel as being the beginning of the umbilical cord and the enclosed space the beginning of the placenta.

A question arises: who or what is traveling through the tunnel? If the umbilicus and placenta were extensions of the anatomy of the body of the embryo, it would be a free movement of its conscious self through its body, which we already know being possible from the description of the division of the cells. From the way the embryo describes the journey, we are not fully sure in this case.

At the end of its forward travel, the embryo discovers a space filled with scintillating particles. It likes them and wants to keep them. On the way back, it succeeds to lure them into its body. This would indicate that it does not consider the placenta to be part of its body.

Now inside me, I touch one. It fills me with light. I feel more alive. I touch another, yet another and each time resonate with light... this light leads me far into the universe, to the stars I came from. I am delighted to be with* *them again. In this highly significant episode from its prenatal life, the embryo describes the connection between energy, first perceived as light, and later experienced as life. The following words from *Mary Poppins Comes Back* by P.L. Travers: *"I come from the sky and its stars, I come from the sun and its brightness"* resonate with the experience of the embryo described above.

We all experience energy that makes us more alive, but we have lost the memory of seeing it as light that originates in the sun and stars. This light is captured by plants and, after undergoing a series of complex transfers and transformations, it gets to our cells. Life is energy, and we experience this energy as light. This fact will help us understand consciousness discussed in part 3 of the book.

A star fades, loses its light it gave me. Another star grows dim... The light of stars does not last! My space darkens, I need more stars to keep the joy of life. As the energy of the sun was being transferred from the scintillating (food) particles to its body, the embryo saddened and realized that it needed this energy to maintain "its joy of life".

I stare in the direction of the hostile dweller... it is impressed by my size... grants me victory. . . I [the embryo] am the leader here now. Embryo returned to the unfinished business of the unfriendly dweller in the womb, resolved who is the "boss" and thus rid itself of its initial anxiety and fear.

Shortly after, the embryo returns to the tunnel to **tap the never-ending stream of delightful bits that bring me bliss. I have no concern... My wish is just to be the way I am: complete.** A wonderful statement about wellbeing when all our needs are met! When that happens, we feel *complete*, which implies that "being complete" is a natural and perfect state.

Ring of Protection

In this poem, the embryo asserts its psychological independence from its mother. It seems that the organs or tissues below it are enjoying a laugh and are urging it to laugh with them: **Why don't you laugh... We always follow the lead from above.** The embryo does not want to laugh; it follows no instruction or lead from above to do so. This shows that the embryo lives its own life, independently from its mother/keeper. It does not participate in her feelings, if it does not want to. On the other hand, her own body cells follow her "lead" and share in the laughter.

Facing the disturbing crowd, **I need to protect myself, build a shield against their noise.** The embryo proceeds to build a layer of cells around itself that will act as a shield (ring) of protection. The mother's nervous system does not reach the embryo, and thus she cannot influence it directly as she can her own cells. By adding a layer of cells around itself, the embryo creates a "buffer" zone.

Intuitive idea: Tumors, such as those formed by cancer, may just be the body's defense against "toxic" conditions, which could be physical and emotional.

Sensitive people, when they find themselves in negative surroundings, often talk about creating a circle of protection around them. This may have its origin in prenatal memory.

When I want I can still hear the ones laughing below. Although the embryo built a protective layer around itself, it did not cut itself off entirely from participating in the life of its mother. It would participate only on its own terms—further proof of its free will and independence.
The embryo turns its attention to its mother who offers it protection and nurturing accommodation, and becomes aware of its life dependence on her.

I touch the being that harbors me, feel my life's connection. I want to build a bond, share my deepest feelings... My* Mati...[*my*] *life depends on her... I am grateful but must be careful not to turn her against me for I could not survive alone. It appears that the embryo is aware of its life connection with its mother and her role in its survival. It is grateful for that but also feels that it needs to be careful and maintain a close and friendly relationship with her for its survival. It recalls, **A long time I have known this being... I was a part of her, now we are separated.... She nourishes me, she is Mati. She does not know yet that I am a different being... One day I will tell her.** The embryo recalls the time when it was a part of its mother's body (as an egg cell in her ovary) before it separated during ovulation. Although the poem does not describe the life of the egg cell in the ovary prior to ovulation, we could assume that it was an inactive, waiting existence in a state of quiet readiness, something like a seed. As a seed, it had only dormant consciousness. It is interesting to find that the embryo is aware of its mother's unawareness of it as a separate being. It intends to tell her sometime in the future.

My Inner World

Mati bends, her quick hands work the ground. Her moving, touching, doing bring the outside to me. Bit by bit, with pictures I build my inner world. The embryo describes the creation of an image of the outside world from the outdoor physical activity of mother. It creates this inner world from the movements of her body, her legs and arms as she works. She also uses her eyes and other senses as well as her mind.

We found in the analysis of the poem *Touching Stars* that the embryo perceived life energy as light. The mother's physical activity, which required life energy within the various body moving parts, accompanied by her sensory input and mind activity (also an energy-requiring process) were probably picked up by its keen consciousness (awareness of energy), thus providing the embryo with the ability to "see" the outside world (further explanation will be found in the third part of the book). Rather than speculate about the physical nature of the process, let us turn our attention to what the exercise of creating an image of the outer world meant to the embryo's life psychologically.

As I unite with the world, I feel again the union with my inner mate While constructing an image of the outer world, the embryo is drawn back to its experience of conception and the feeling arising out of the merging of the original two selves: the egg and sperm. Their unification laid down a tendency for the embryo to merge with (be part of) everything, such as, in our case, the world. We could generalize and say that *merging or becoming one with everything is an inherent property of life.*

It is also worth noting that **(every) new piece... connects with my previous whole seamlessly.** This suggests that the embryo's process of perceiving something—in our case, forming a composite view of the outside world characterized by a "seamless" contiguity among all the images—awakens in us a feeling of oneness of all things, stationary or moving. This is further elaborated by the embryo. **There is more beyond my current whole, land I'll reach one day, make my own. It too will merge with my present whole, seamlessly. I delight in the vision: the world and I are one... I love to have it so.** The embryo looks into the future when it will encounter more of the world and continue to add it to its current size. It delights in the prospect of being one with the whole world.

Hungry Birds

In this important, mystical poem, the embryo learns about its physical beginning and its role in nature. It travels far into its past where spirit (energy) and matter have their first meetings, into the world of elementary forces, the place of its physical and spiritual origin. What leads it to undertake this journey is the disturbing behavior of a flock of hungry birds, probably farm chickens. For grownups, it would seem like a common daily occurrence on the farm, but in the embryo, it awakens a strong feeling **What is wrong?**

The embryo's wish **I want to help quiet the angry flock** carries it through a fog-like ethereal space into its deep past, as if in a dream. The embryo perceives this world as **a peaceful place where everything happens according to an exact law, a world of elementary existence** What the embryo was experiencing was most likely a journey into its unconscious realm. Out of this realm came the first matter for its body. This "matter" probably came via the sperm cell. The physical makeup of the egg is determined much earlier in the life of the woman, whereas the production of the sperm cells in a man is an ongoing process.

In this passage, we are moving into an invisible physical domain where we do not have firm ground under our feet. It is a fluid world without limits, a world of fine vibrations, elementary particles and energies, a world we know about indirectly from scientific evidence. Life in this world is dynamic, subject to precise physical laws and is propelled by the purest life forces. In this world, the embryo had its beginning in a farmyard. It recalls *_being assembled: a little unit, glittering, rare precious matter, my first substance_*.

This first substance was given to the embryo: *_invisible elementals inhabit this subtle world. They helped create me, also know the birds._* We are being told that this world of essential existence is inhabited by living elementary forces ("elementals"), which we may think of in a physical sense as being very small charges of energy that facilitate chemical reactions and the creation of compounds. These elementary forces *_gave me the finest substance they could find. With it I carry their highest virtues, their aspirations. I am the bearer of their expectations of a better life. They made me their leader_*.

We are encountering events that give rise to thoughts and questions about the origin and roots of life. We will all agree that we had to begin somewhere as a particle of matter, but the idea that we could have been given (with this "matter") certain human characteristics, social standing and role would be difficult to accept. One of the possibilities for the origin of such a memory could be connected with the formation of the DNA by the uniting reproductive cells. Here, the greater probability of the bearers of such a memory would be the sperm cells that are "assembled" a relatively short time before conception. Their DNA would have been imbued (inspired) with the spirit of the father at that time. This carries some logic, but we would have to work out the connection with the workings of the elementary world as described by the embryo. In any case, a fascinating possibility!

I appeal to them now, "Can you help the birds?" Slowly the answer comes: "Listen to them, then tell the one who harbors you to feed them. The elementary forces or energies—living elementary entities (elementals) to the embryo—appear to inhabit the elementary world. Their role apparently lies in creating the living matter for all the living forms from the simplest to the most complex, such as the human. They seem to know the lifeforms and their needs. Thus, they know the answer to the embryo's question about the hungry birds: the birds need food. *_I send the message to Mati... she feeds them, they quiet... I feel I have helped the birds and satisfied the elementals._*

The embryo learned how to recognize and deal with the need of other living organisms. This connected it with its own feeding.

Among the world religions, Hinduism and Buddhism believe in the existence of benevolent or angelic supernatural entities or lower-class deities called *devas*. In Hinduism, devas represent forces in nature (divine energy) that are responsible for and assist in the creation of all living forms. They are described according to their Sanskrit name as "beings of brilliant light." The embryo is aware of their energy (light) and their creative ability. They inspired and motivated it to understand the universe and become one with it. They gave it the spiritual energy it needed to understand what it should do.

An example of the idea that the quality of matter can influence the standing or role of an individual member in a community is shown among the bees, which are able to create a queen by feeding one of them royal jelly.

Under the Apple Tree

Tired after working on the farm during summer, the parents enjoy a quiet rest sitting on a bench under an apple tree. The embryo senses their quiet mood and also their warm feelings toward each other. It perceives the three of them (the couple and the tree) as a love trinity, with the tree forming a protective ceiling. It is still very early in its life when its waking consciousness is weak, as if looking through a veil: **All I am aware of is a warm and softly glowing light space, deeply satisfying.** The embryo sinks into a dreamless sleep.

We can all reach a dreamless state of consciousness in adult life through very deep relaxation and surrender, a state of perfect health.

Upward Bound

In this poem, the embryo describes an intensive period of growth: **I ready myself for action, I want to grow... I move, add to my base, rise, spiral up, steadily grow higher.** Starting at its base (feet?), adding matter, the embryo elongates in a spiraling way. Could we theorize that the embryo is gradually awakening genes following the DNA spiral?

I am busy building... now I must stop... tell my base, it remains a part of me. The embryo makes a very important statement about maintaining the wholeness of its body by always returning its consciousness to the starting place of growth. It is constantly aware of its whole body: **Where the supplies come in I stand, examine each carefully, then decide: if I like it I make it part of me.** The embryo watches over the incoming flow of nutrients, sorting and examining them. It retains those which it "likes." What is its criterion for "liking"? We can think of it in the same way as what we like as adults: something that awakens in us a feeling of familiarity, something that tastes good, is pleasant to hear, nice to touch or smell, etc. The embryo does not have sensory organs, but it has their prescriptions in the DNA, or it may, at this stage, be aware of the tissues from which they develop. While this makes some sense, it is not convincing. There is probably a simpler explanation: *We like something because it is like us*. We may notice that the word 'like' is used to denote both a similarity and also, as a verb, to be fond of, to enjoy something. The embryo keeps what is like it, which presupposes that it must know the makeup of its body (more on this in the third part of the book) and keeps adding to it the same or similar substance with which it is already familiar.

The embryo keeps growing, adding fresh substance **I learn more about the busy outside: water runs, creatures fly, leaves flutter in air... The outside quivers with life. They all tell me "we are"** While Mati moves outdoors, the embryo learns about the life outside. It is struck by the dynamic nature of the elements and lifeforms that all seem to say "we are." This is the same declaration as **I am** expressed by the egg at the beginning of the first poem *The First Journey* and signifies the conscious awareness by the various lifeforms and nature's elements of being alive.

The matter I taste now delights me... I want to find where it comes from... I hesitate, never have I gone that far outside my body... Little by little, out I move, follow the winding path... to a deep hollow... The elementals here are busy making the delights... The supply is rich. I sense it will never end... Satisfied, I find my way back. Curious about a particularly delightful substance, the embryo sets out on a journey to find where it is coming from. It moves very carefully, mindful of moving away from its body (centre of the conscious self). The winding path would suggest that the embryo is moving through the umbilical cord. It finds the place where the elementary forces are assembling the delightful substance. It is not certain what the body part is where the substance is being made by these elementary forces. The embryo returns with the feeling of a rich supply that will never end.

In the above episode, the embryo is looking for the source of a nutritious substance and checking on its never-ending supply. This is prototypical to all life and has earned a place in mythology, religion and literature. For example, in mythology it is depicted symbolically in the tarot card called The Moon. In religion, it is a reoccurring theme in the Bible, and in literature it appears, for example, in the poetry of Rumi, who writes of going to a "place of sweetness where the flow never dies."

Flame and Friendship

In this very significant poem, the embryo describes the awakening of its heart to action. The heart is the most important physical organ in our body, and its activation is one of the key events in prenatal life. Medical science can give us evidence of the start of the heart through ultrasound imaging but is unable to describe what the embryo is experiencing. While the physical role of the heart is obvious and well understood, its psychological role is hidden. Its importance will be clear in the following passage.

The embryo's attention is drawn to a place above it, where a radiant, energetic source pulsates with life. It would not be difficult to guess that this **source sparkles with energy, scintillates with light, exudes joy of life...*

*I am drawn more and more by its dynamic force, its pulsating liveliness.** is Mati's heart that is inviting the embryo's (still sleeping) heart to join it: **I am your friend, will teach you what I know.**

At first, the embryo does not feel strong enough to accept the invitation of the friend. It feels that it needs more time to grow.

Time passes... my friend keeps urging me "try"... Slowly I... gain the courage... With all my strength... I strike a spark... my whole body lights up... I leap to my friend. After a period of growing stronger, the embryo describes how it created a spark that put its whole body on fire and, at that moment, "jumped" to its friend—Mati's heart.

The heart is a muscle requiring an electric impulse (spark) of appropriate strength to move. It may remind us of a car engine. The car engine also works by using electric spark, and its movement is caused by the combustion of a fuel mixture. One may wonder whether the invention of the car engine was inspired by the heart.

What "jumped" and joined Mati's heart? Was it the embryo's consciousness directed by its true self (soul)? In the spiritual teachings of Eckankar, this event would be called "soul travel." Although "travel" implies movement, no movement of the soul takes place. Rather, it is the soul's spiritual awareness of things—in our case of the heart—where it is not subject to the limitations of time and space. In the third part of this book, we will learn about the quantum nature of consciousness (light), which can be in two or more places at the same time.

Our explanation is that the "movement" described above is a natural ability of the basic life consciousness *I am* to communicate with all forms of life. By becoming aware of the Mati's heart, the embryo established the heart-to-heart communication through its basic consciousness *I am* directed by the self (soul).

We embrace and start dancing, turning around, joyfully celebrating our friendship. I listen to the rhythm... follow my friend in this dance. Even today, we may see two close friends embracing—in some cultures also turning around— when they meet. Dance likely had its origin in this event.

After experiencing the friendship and learning the rhythm of the Mati's heart, the embryo's consciousness refocuses on its physical heart trying to make it work on its own: **I strike a spark but do not jump. Another,* *again I cannot jump. The third one, stronger, this time I jump. Another spark and jump and so on... spark–jump, spark–jump in rhythmic harmony**.

We are born with legs, but have to learn to walk. We are born with eyes, but must learn to focus and converge them to see three-dimensionally. So it is with our other faculties as well as the heart. The prenatal child had to learn to make its heart perform rhythmically by coordinating the electrical impulses with the heart's muscle movements.

I rejoice: now I hold my own flame. I learn: this flame gives me courage and strength to carry out any task, present and future Having succeeded in making its heart beat regularly, the embryo has learned that it now possesses a flame (courage) and strength to carry out any life task.

With this knowledge, the embryo puts its new ability to the test. It needs to move in the womb to create more room for its growth. It focuses on its flame, which gives it the courage. It carries out the move. Having succeeded, it affirms **now I have the strength and courage to do everything**.

Based on the embryo's experience of starting its heart, we could say that the heart has two main psychological attributes:

- Heart is the place from which we start a friendship.
- Heart is the seat of courage and strength and a starting place of action.

Because of the heart's prominence in our life, both its friendship aspect and its courage and strength aspects will be briefly explored through examples from mythology, religious symbolism, rituals and common beliefs about the heart. These examples will serve as a support for the prenatal memory of starting a heart and the above conclusions drawn from it.

The association between the heart and the feeling and expression of friendship and love is universal. Such expression as "sweetheart," to "win or break one's heart," etc. are commonly used. So are the images of the heart as a symbol of love. We often see an icon of a woman holding a heart, which personifies female friendship. Saints have often been painted with an open heart to symbolize pure love.

The heart as an instrument of courage, strength and power has also been expressed in many different ways, such as "man's true strength lies within his heart" or "heart is stronger than sword," etc.

Flame, fire and light (of the heart) have long been used as symbols of life force, deity, purification (destruction of evil) and authority. Threatening forces or entities, for example in dreams, are often said to be warded off or dispelled by light and flame.

From Greek mythology comes the legend of Prometheus, who was chosen by the reigning god, Zeus, to create people. Prometheus is thus considered to be the father of mankind. Prometheus fell in love with his creation and wanted to help people by giving them fire. The myth is not quite clear as to how he got the fire. Some state that he stole it from Zeus, who wielded the power of lightning, but it is also said that Prometheus lit a torch using the light of the sun. In any case, Zeus did not want people to have the power of fire, believing that they could challenge his authority. He resented this act so strongly that he punished Prometheus by nailing him to a rock.

In view of our knowledge about the heart, our interpretation of this well-known myth will be that Prometheus put the spark (fire), which he took from the sun, into the hearts of people. This gave the people courage and power to challenge the supreme power of Zeus, who felt threatened and became angry. We would understand the electrical impulse to the heart to be the sun's energy. Finally, let us remind ourselves that the element of love (Prometheus and people) is also brought out in this interpretation. Both aspects of the heart, flame and friendship, are represented in the myth.

In the ancient Olympic Games, brave men performed feats of great strength, skill and bravery under the Olympic flame, which is a symbol, according to our interpretation, of the fire of the heart. In the modern Olympic Games, the country hosting the Olympics will send its athletes to light and carry a torch from the "mother" flame in Olympia, which is then used to light the flame in the host country. The Olympic flame burns for the duration of the games. In this ritual, we have both the symbolism of the flame's strength and courage, as well as the passing of the flame from the mother's heart to the incipient heart. Greece is the "mother" country of the games, the hosting country the "incipient heart." Also, the modern Olympic Games were conceived with the ideal of promoting friendship among nations. Ideally, the Olympics are a celebration of the heart.

Figure 2. Dancing Shiva

In Figure 2, we are looking at the psychophysical as well as the spiritual/religious aspect of the heart represented by the symbol of the Dancing Shiva from the religious roots of Hinduism. This powerful symbol, in the form of a small statue, combines not only the physical aspects of the heart—namely, the flame, beat, rhythm (dance) and action— but also expresses its subtler spiritual and religious aspects and values.

A student of Hindu philosophy will understand the symbolism of dancing Shiva on the basis of its religious meaning, which embraces the beliefs of reincarnation of the soul and its eternal life. Our interpretation will be worldly, yet it will point in the same direction as the message indicated by the deeper, more religious view.

We will interpret Shiva's dance as follows: Lord Shiva dances within a circle of flames that represent both the electrical impulses to the heart (flames) and the spiritual light of life. He holds one such spark in the hand of the extended left arm. In the hand of the extended right arm, the dancing god holds a hand drum, denoting the heartbeat and the rhythm of life. The circle of flames symbolizes the continuity of life. Shiva's right leg stands on (controls) a mystic demonic creature, called Tripurasura, that represents forgetfulness, which leads to fear.

The position of the inner right hand in Eastern traditions is a gesture of fearlessness, while the inner left hand is in a position signifying the act of teaching. This left hand points to a raised left leg, which is said to signify freedom or release from fear.

We have here the symbolism of the physical action as well as the spiritual values of the heart. We also have a teaching lesson by god Shiva, who shows us how we can gain release from the uncertainty of life caused by forgetfulness (fear) through the correct attitude and action of the heart. When this lesson is learned and applied, our life becomes a joyous dance and a spiritual journey. The afterlife will take care of itself.

Because the symbol of dancing Shiva represents the creative energy of the heart and its role as the starting point of all action, it is used by the students of yoga for personal transformation and spiritual growth.

The start of the heart activity is the key event in our life. For the prenatal being, it lays down a foundation for the unfolding of physical activity. This capability of using and controlling the movement of its muscles and body facilitates its ability to be born. From this moment on, a fetus is no longer a passive creature, developing more or less automatically. Now, it can decide and express its life as it wills with the help of its actions. With the commencement of the heart action, the first developmental stage ends, and the prenatal child begins to live an active life with the goal of being born. This new being carries its own flame and has the courage to act. The starting of the heart is a heroic deed and forms the basis for a successful and self-confident life.

Hidden in the safe haven of its mother, the prenatal being now expresses its fervent life force and fast growth. The term "embryo" is no longer suitable. Understandably, we do not have a common word for this kind of being. "Fetus" sounds foreign and academic. From now on, we will refer to the prenatal child in our story variably as the preborn or fetus, later also child, birthing child and baby.

Order of Life

In this poem, we learn how the preborn child built its brain and began to use it as a memory bank. More importantly, we will learn how the preborn became aware of a natural pattern of order that its life follows.

Above me arcs a space where I file all in proper place... all that I do, all that I am The preborn describes how it files everything it experiences in an arching space on top, presumably its head. The experiences might include its feelings, views of itself, the occurrences around it—everything that enters its consciousness. Each experience is a transparent file, and all the files are fitted together in a proper place (presumably, genetically provided) and order to form a whole. First, it puts more files in the space on the right (the right hemisphere of the brain) and, when full: **I begin to fill the room on the left [the left hemisphere].** It would indicate that the right hemisphere is older, perhaps more basic or rudimentary than the left in terms of its evolution and content.

Everything I do and feel I complete, maintain a perfect order. This awareness is the best state of being that I know. I want to retain it forever. This is a powerful statement by the preborn about the way its life is experienced and organized. It tells us that everything it does or feels, it completes (brings to its end), and then deposits the memory of it in its head. It regards this process as the best state of being and wishes to keep it forever.

We would interpret the "best state of being" to be the best feeling one could have about one's life. The question "How are you?" would prompt the answer "Everything is as it should be—in order."

Figure 3. Order

According to the preborn, our life consists of a sequence of conscious experiences of various events, actions, thoughts, feelings, etc., each forming a segment of a life experience of certain duration. At the end, we deposit the result of each experience as a memory in the brain and body. This memory record contains only that of which we were conscious, considered important and accepted as our truth. When we accept something, it becomes part of us and influences our attitude and actions toward what we do next. We could say that our life grows like a tree, each experience adding to the previous whole.

The University of Toronto (my place of work), has in its emblem the motto: *Velut arbor aevo,* which, loosely translated, means: *May it grow like a tree.*

The following stanza of the poem illustrates the process: The preborn sits by a stream at the centre in its head where the supplies float in. It watches them and, if it wants to "retain" any one of them, it follows it to its proper place. This would indicate that the filing of memory follows a predetermined path. If we want to retrieve the memory, we need to be conscious of where we filed it and "revive" the path to it.

Since the location is known beforehand, it would mean that the brain is already prewired and has a genetically determined network with places for filing various kinds of memory. This would fit with our knowledge of the structure of brain and neuroscience. The preborn then gives an example of a path it (we don't know what it was) followed to its memory location: **My life's journey stays the same: to follow and remember the way, wherever I go, whatever I do, whatever I feel, whatever I learn... Journey is my way to grow, to know where I am and who (I am).**

The above is a key discovery by the preborn about the meaning of its life journey: everything in its life follows a journey, not only physical, but also everything it does, feels, learns, etc. Journey is the unborn child's way to grow, to know where it is and who it is.

I am the maker of perfect order... (it) brings me calm, poise, control of my life... knowing all that I am, there is nothing else I could be. The preborn tells us that it follows the Order of Life that organizes its life. It realizes that the Order of Life results in the best and truest way to live. If we applied it, we would know our complete life journey, all that we are, and have no unfinished business or ambition. Simple, logical, true!

In the Bible (John 14:6), we find the following statement by Christ: "I am the way, the truth and the life." The preborn says the same: The journey ("the way") is my way to grow ("the life"), to know who I am ("the truth"). We may note also that almost all biblical stories incorporate the format of a journey. Each has a definite ending, and each question is answered in an exact manner: **It seems life outside also tends toward fulfillment of order.** A preborn sees the life outside as following the same order it has.

In the next stanza, the preborn gives an example of a life situation where order was not met. It concerns a worker who has yet to finish the task given to him by Mati. She is disappointed. Her life's order has not been met (has not reached its proper end). The preborn would like to help and wishes the world outside to have the order it has.

The *Tao* ("The Way") is the basic principle of the old philosophical Chinese teaching known as Taoism. The Tao is the natural order of things, often compared to a river. It flows through every living thing. There is a similarity between the *Tao* and the Order of Life described by the preborn. We will return to this topic in the third part of the book.

Since we find a close connection between religious teachings, the philosophical thoughts and way in which the prenatal being experiences life, we could consider the prenatal life to be a spiritual existence or, vice versa, we could say that religion has its roots in prenatal life.

Different, Yet One

The preborn has an opportunity to observe the behavior of Mati in company with two other women. It wonders **What is Mati like? She steps quickly. Her talk is loud and fast. Her energetic pace feels strange to me, mine is much slower. I am not like Mati.** The preborn describes Mati's manner of moving and talking as much more energetic than its own. We might wonder about the ability of such an "undeveloped" human being to compare itself and Mati on the basis of different "energy." At the same time, we recall that the preborn has demonstrated a very keen sense and awareness of energy.

The preborn is conscious of an argument between Mati and two other women over something. Mati is trying unsuccessfully to convince them of her viewpoint. The preborn sides with Mati although it does not know what the argument is about: **Although not alike, I agree with Mati, defend her way, [because] we live as one**.

Though it is not like Mati, its feeling of unity (oneness) with her is, obviously, very important to the unborn child. The unity in this case refers to unity of all life.

Life Force

This poem describes the preborn's intensive physical growth: *All _my cells grow, divide, multiply. My body swells with energy._* The preborn experiences a state of high energy generated by fast growth. We will refer to this energy as the _life force._ The preborn also becomes aware of the same force in the world outside in describing fields of daisies reaching for the sun with their open blooms. We can see a similar image in the open mouths of baby birds in a nest reaching for food when a parent bird appears.

We know from biology that most of the energy our cells need is supplied by mitochondria, semi-autonomous organelles, which are the power plants of the cells. They form one of the essential links in the long process of energy transfer from the sun to the human organism.

*_An enormous force thrusts me forward in space_* The preborn experiences life force as a power that moves it forward, accompanied by a feeling of confidence and an overall increase of the power of life: *_I can do anything, meet every challenge, leap every obstacle._* We would agree with the preborn that a feeling of strength and high energy is accompanied by confidence and adds to the success in anything we do. However, the fetus carries this confidence even further. It feels that it knows not only the present (in which it is a full participant) but also *what is to come*. It is an interesting observation and raises the question: how is this possible? We can explain it in terms of inertial movement, a definition we know from physics. It may work like this: if we are conscious of the energy that is directed toward an action but do not think about the result and stay in the moment, we may be able to "predict" the result on the basis of our psychological experience of the flow of life force and its inertia. This is an important topic, and we will return to it in the third part of the book.

Day by day I follow the way and succeed... I carry out my life's design. This statement by the preborn suggests that its life follows a design that appears to be part of the life force. We know that the plan or design, as far as the human body is concerned, is contained in the DNA. But is that sufficient to realize it? What if something in this fragile process goes wrong? We have evidence that there are damaging factors that can adversely affect the life of an unborn child during pregnancy. The DNA may not provide an instruction on how to deal with "accidental" failures and repair itself. The science of genetics acknowledges it in the definition of mutation. A role in this process can be played by consciousness and will be further explained in part 3.

*My life force can help those outside... if [the weak child in my house] believed in me, it could be strong.** We have here an idea that the life force, when fully realized, has a potential to influence (restore) health in others. These are some of the claims of therapeutic methods based on increasing and balancing the body's energies. The Bible has many examples where Christ would heal the sick, if they believed in him, simply by his presence and touch.

Visitor

In this short episode, we are reading about the unborn child observing and experiencing meetings between Mati and another woman who visits to consult her about a life decision. The woman wants to reach a decision as to whether she should go with a man who wants her to be his life partner. The visitor *looks up to Mati, leans toward her answers in trying to find her way in life.** The preborn does not understand the conversation; it only perceives that the woman asks questions and listens to Mati's answers attentively. Like Mati, the preborn likes the visitor: *I like... her gentle manner... look forward to her visits again and again*.

The preborn feels the friendly emotions of Mati toward the woman and looks forward to her visits. It is sad when she goes away: *Today Mati cooks in silence. The visitor promised to be back, but left, never to return.** The woman decided to follow the man who wanted her to go with him on a journey through life. It was Mati's wish, too. The preborn misses her.

This episode illustrates the prenatal child's capability of sharing in the life of its mother through her chemistry of good feelings she has toward another person. Feelings of friendship and love are contagious.

The Tree, Earth and I

Everyone had an opportunity to experience of being attached to the "*Tree of Life*" (placenta) in our prenatal life. In this significant poem, the preborn devotes its attention to the reception and assimilation of matter that becomes its body. It also describes the tree of life as a giving friend that speaks to and shares its secrets with it.

The unborn child describes a luminous tree alight with life: **As I gaze into its winding veins, small particles thread toward me. One speck enters me... stops near my centre seeking a place. I will give it a home, life within me.** The preborn sees the placenta as a tree-like structure radiating light. The light comes from particles of matter charged with life-giving energy. We have come across the image of lighted specks of matter for the first time in the poem *Touching Stars.* In the current poem, we are learning about the preborn being able to observe these particles of matter that float to it from the placenta, each looking for a place to settle in. The preborn invites them to live, have a home inside it. What a wonderful way to view the process of transferring the matter from the body of mother Earth into our bodies!

Another grain... meanders toward me... At times it stops... grows as it slides close. This one has much to tell The preborn observes the winding path and arrival of another particle inside its body. This one brings a story about its origin and journey. The story is told in pictures. The preborn relates:

I see a stream widen into a bay, a speck of life lodged in its bank. High water washes it down, carries it along a zig-zagging path, till Mati gathers and takes it to the house. At last it arrives here before me... Sorry for its lost home, I invite it to live in mine. We are led again into the secret and magical world of the elementary life. The speck of matter—we don't know what kind of matter—seems to be alive with an elementary consciousness and thus a memory. It reminds us of the journey of the egg. Because of that, we could speculate that the speck of matter could have been a "speck of living matter," such as a single cell or a cluster of cells detached from a living organism like a plant.

The world outside teems with wandering life, searching for a place to settle down. We learn that the world we live in is in constant motion, where everything is traveling, looking for a place to settle down, a home. It does not tell us what causes the motion or what constitutes "home."

I listen to their tales. Each particle I adopt connects me to its source lastingly. The preborn reveals to us that everything is connected, and the connection is manifest when we accept something and make it a part of us. In so doing, we also become connected to that thing's origin. But that "thing" also originated somewhere before and so on and so on... perhaps all the way to the Big Bang. This points toward the unifying principle before and beyond everything, including the universe. Mind cannot understand this. A more powerful faculty is consciousness, discussed in the third part of the book.

Bit by bit the living Earth feeds me Her matter and binds me to Her. Everywhere inside I feel Her presence. Now I cannot turn back from Her without breaking the bond and the pain of separation. Forever I am bound to my true mother. To Earth I owe my substance. The preborn generalizes this feeling: By accepting the matter of the earth, the unborn child feels a lasting bond. The preborn realizes that it would not be able to break that bond without the pain of separation. Unwanted or forced separation is felt by all life, especially by a child, as painful and has a strong negative effect on subsequent life.

Anything I take and keep... connects me forever to its source. The unborn child accepts this binding relationship with the earth because it is aware of the substance. Later on, we will look at the reciprocal relationship of how the earth feels about the creation of human beings.

The sentiments expressed by the preborn in the above discussion could be adopted as a starting point in the study of ecology.

Later, the preborn gives an example of a human being who is wandering, also looking for a home. He was probably an unemployed farm worker seeking a job. The fetus, who has given a home to particles of matter, also feels the need of this being and is sad that it could not help him to stay. This episode also explains the ancient custom of offering hospitality to traveling, homeless beings.

Needing life, needing to know, needing to be, I turn to the tree, my closest friend. The preborn turns its attention again to the tree (placenta) and reflects on it as a source of life and existence. The tree satisfies its need of life. By this we understand that the placenta provides the necessary nourishment. The tree also satisfies its need to know. After we satisfy our basic need to live, we are interested in knowing about the world we live in. The last need, _to be_, is more of a spiritual nature. We have a need to reflect on our self or soul, the _I am_ that can be linked to happiness and meaning of life.

*_I turn to the tree, my closest friend. It always gives, asks nothing in return_* is a definition of friendship, the way we ideally know it. *_When I awaken... the tree lights up, greets me with joy. When Mati and I listen to the tree we are happy._* In this short statement the preborn expresses its joy of being connected to the lit-up tree of life that greets it each morning and feels the same joy when both Mati and it "listen" to the tree (placenta). This would indicate that mother communicates with the fetus chemically through placenta.

The tree at my side, I command my life, send Mati my love. When our needs are met and we feel joy and command our life, we are ready to send love to others and set in motion the realization of our common goals. The tarot card that expresses this state of being is The Chariot. The horses of the charioteer (the preborn) are represented by the placenta.

*_When Mati is sad, needing more life... I want to say... "Look at the tree... your life can be as happy as mine" But she does not listen to me_* We are reminded about the tendency of the fetus to help others if they do not feel the happiness it has. This time it is Mati who appears to be stressed and sad, probably from too much work. The preborn wants her to look at the tree and be happy. A pregnant woman has other things to worry about in her life beside her main role of bringing a new life into the human family. So, from time to time, she has to disconnect from her main role to attend to these matters. Her duties might be burdensome and exhausting. The preborn considers that as not being "healthy" and wants to help.

The resemblance between placenta with its umbilical cord and the shape of a tree is remarkable. We have numerous photographic and artistic illustrations of this. An artist has a keener, often deeper view of life. The illustration chosen here is a painting of the "Tree of Life" by Gustav Klimt (see Figure 6 in part 3), a painter of a century ago.

It shows the placenta not only as a tree, but more significantly, it shows particles of matter, as described in the poem moving through its winding veins. Sitting in the tree is a mythical bird that symbolizes knowledge and wisdom. Not shown in this illustration are an embracing couple on the right and a young curious female on the left witnessing the act of creation. We are not quite certain what the painter had in mind, but these symbols indicate that the tree represents a movement of matter and energy and has to do strongly with the female aspect. We will say more about the illustration in the third part of the book.

In the painting, we also see three tree-like forms of a placental organ, called cotyledon, where the exchange of nutrients takes place. If we think about it in terms of energy transfer, the cotyledon is transferring the energy of the sun—encapsulated in the nutrients—to the unborn, just as a tree in nature captures the energy of the sun to feed its body, leaves and fruit. The memory of prenatal life is obviously deeply rooted in our subconscious.

In many cultures around the globe we find the symbol of the tree in connection with human life. There are also many customs that incorporate the tree as their main motive.

One of the most popular and widespread customs is the celebration of Christmas by a lit-up tree. The custom originated in Central Europe, where it was connected with the birth of Jesus. Family members place their gifts, referred to as gifts from "Little Jesus", under the tree. In the Christmas tree, we see an obvious connection with the luminous tree (placenta) described by the fetus. Little Jesus represents the prenatal child, and the gifts can be thought of as the particles of matter it receives from the tree of life (placenta) or gifts that people bring to a newborn child. Thus, we could explain the symbolism in this custom as a celebration of prenatal life and the arrival of a new child. It is a further proof that prenatal life is a conscious existence though its memory trace in adult life usually resides in the subconscious.

Other examples of the tree as a symbol can be found in mythology, religion, folklore and rituals. The best known among Christians is the legend of Adam and Eve, and the Tree of Knowledge of Good and Evil in the Garden of Eden. When Adam and Eve broke God's rule and ate fruit from that tree, they were expelled from Paradise and became mortal. On the basis of prenatal life experience, our explanation would be as follows: Adam and Eve represent the spirit forms (male and female principles) of man and woman. In their spiritual states they had a lasting life. By ingesting the earthly matter in the form of an apple, they became connected with and bound to earth, hence had to leave Paradise. We could say that our mortal life is an incarnation patterned on that idea or, conversely, our life gave rise to that legend. In any case, we "owe" our life to Adam and Eve.

From the Indian mythology comes a symbol of the Tree of Coexistence, featuring animals in its crown, some of whom prey on and hunt those sitting next to them. This may suggest that there exists only one life which manifests itself in different forms and that a transition of one form into another is natural.

The ancient tradition of celebrating the 1st of May by erecting a maypole has a variety of tree connections. In Central Europe, the tree is a birch, which, at that time of the year, features fresh new foliage. The tree is decorated with ribbons held by young maidens who dance around it. It is a fertility ritual. To us the tree symbolizes the tree of life or placenta.

While attending bonsai (the art of miniature trees) exhibits, I often noticed, especially among first-time visitors, how their faces lit up when they saw these marvelous artistic tree miniatures. I believe that those visitors were subconsciously recalling their memory of the placenta from their prenatal life.

Unfulfilled Love

The fetus follows and experiences an unfolding friendship between Mati and a new worker on the farm who demonstrates great work skill and flawless behavior: *_Mati likes him... A smile, a look lingers. Both are drawn toward each other._*

The preborn participates in the developing relationship and befriends the newcomer: *_Mati's... feeling attracts me to him also._*

The relationship deepens, and the newcomer becomes more determined to express his attraction to Mati: *_After dark by the gate he will meet her... "We can be one." But Mati does not come... the stranger departs, never to return. I am sad his love for Mati found no proper end; order was not met. Now I am the one left to fulfill his love for Mati when I grow up_*.

We are witnessing here the application of the Order of Life as discussed earlier. According to this law, every action that we start must be carried out to its completion. In this example, we have the case of a relationship that was doomed to fail, and a love that could not find its proper end. It continued in the man. It could have been resolved if both Mati and the man had accepted the situation and were able to bring it to an end by dissolving the emotional ties and forgiving their feelings. It is not easy to do. Love can be a powerful and sometimes agonizing experience.

Let us return to the fetus who is aware of Life's Order as the highest form of its existence and takes it upon itself to bring the man's love to its "proper end," to complete it. There is a psychological disorder known as the Oedipus complex, patterned on a Greek myth, which is marked by a grown child's unnatural love attachment to the parent of the opposite sex. It is thought to be caused by an unconscious sexual desire for that parent, which stems from childhood and arises from the child's competition for love with the same-sex parent. Based on the experience of our prenatal child, we could also say that the roots of this disorder could reach into the prenatal period and could mean nothing more than a tendency toward a natural fulfillment of Life's Order. When the child grows up and gains more experience, its "duty" will naturally drop off and free it from its obligation.

Power to Move

In this poem we learn about the fetus becoming conscious of the movement of its limbs and body. It becomes aware of the source of power that executes the movement. *Deep in my chest rises a power to command and control all my movements... I am the maker and director of all the movements my body makes.*

The fetus feels proud and excited by being able to make physical movements and be in charge of them. To us it may seem automatic and obvious, but to an unborn child, the movement of its limbs for the first time is a great discovery.

The unborn child discovers that it has a choice in which arm to move first. It finds that both arms move with the same ease, but it prefers to move the right first. This might be an indication that the choice of which arm to move first is related to right/left-handedness, which may be inborn (acquired before birth). In what follows, the fetus details its experience in executing the movement of its arm: *Slowly my arm ascends... I feel a deep flow of energy in perfect coordination with the movement. I can focus this power in any direction I wish*.

Evidently, the preborn separates the intention to move its arm from the energy that makes it move. First, it becomes aware of the limb it wants to move, then it observes as the power of movement carries it out. It is important to realize that the arm movement the fetus describes here is a free movement. There is no intention to move the arm in a direction as we normally do after birth. At this stage, the preborn just enjoys the feeling of free motion, like we may experience in a free-moving dance. We all remember such dances as children. We could say that the first movements of the fetus are spontaneous and part of the genetic makeup.

Everywhere I want to move, my power moves me. It pervades, controls my body, can move mountains, rotate the Earth, everything. We are made to move. The preborn describes how the power of movement will carry out any motion it wishes to give to its body and its limbs. It feels that its body is "possessed" by this force. Einstein would say that this enormous energy is contained in every atom of our body. This would suggest that the unborn child may be aware, as Einstein was, of atomic energy.

Keeping in mind human anatomy and physiology, we could say that the unborn child became aware for the first time of the energy that enables the muscles to move our body parts. The interesting part of its discovery is the magnitude of this power. The fetus feels that the power of movement is so strong that it can move mountains, even rotate the earth. This statement would imply that the energy or force that the fetus is feeling when moving its limbs is of a magnitude equal to the *strong force* in physics.

Biology explains certain involuntary body motions, such as breathing or heartbeat, as being directed by the autonomic nervous system. Those motions are not the same as the ones described here by the fetus. The motions that the fetus experiences are primal movements that elicit awareness of the energy behind the moving force.

To be conscious of the force of movement is beneficial to our body. Some of the martial arts and other Eastern exercises are based on this principle. It is also slowly making its way into competitive athletics.

Sounds and Sights of Him

On special days, presumably Sundays, Mati and her unborn child listen to appealing sounds: **Sweet vibrations rise and fill the room... A being, always near sits behind the table, alluring us with sounds** The preborn's father plays a violin.

Ripples of air stream through the room, reflect, curve toward me... One by one I absorb them, begin to see walls, corner, bed, table The preborn is telling us that by absorbing these sound waves in a sequence, it can "see" the room and even some furniture in it. To be able to do that, it would have to synthesize the oncoming waves streaming from different directions and arriving at differing times. This would result in a 3D image similar to the bat's orientation in space by its "radar" system that uses ultrasound frequencies; the difference is that the bat generates its own signal (waves), whereas the preborn passively analyses the waves coming from an external source. **Sometimes He sings, sometimes just smiles, sometimes* *sits serious** The preborn recalls the days of rest when its father sits with Mati, who desires him.

The sound holds us three together. One day I wish to know more about it The preborn notices that the melodious sounds keep the three of them together. Its parents enjoy the alluring power of the music, while the fetus is interested in the waves, it would like to know more about one day.

We have an example of the preborn hinting that it would like to do more about its current experience in the future. This may indicate that some of our actions today might have started as a wish in the early, even prenatal life. This is confirmed by the author's own professional life experience.

The preborn describes the feelings between its parents: **Today Mati sits silently. I feel her pull across the room to Him. He plays inviting tunes to bridge the distance, to draw her close. I feel her tense, until, at last, she rises to meet Him... The tension ebbs, subsides as they get close, renew their union.** The preborn is a witness to Mati's loving feelings that give us an insight into the nature of her relationship with her husband. It seems that, at the start, Mati had a feeling of distance (separation) from him, but at the same time, she longed for and was drawn to him. As the music played "inviting tunes," her mood began to soften (evidence of the effect of music on us), and her tension of being drawn increased. Finally, the force of attraction reached its peak, and she rose to meet him in an embrace halfway across the room. Their love union renewed, her tension subsided.

As its parents celebrated their union, the preborn felt left out: **I lie alone and wish the future to bring me one like Mati to meet me, pull me toward the union, someone to be my own.** For the first time, the preborn experiences the feeling of aloneness, the left-out feeling. Its awareness of Life's Order awakens in it a wish to restore the unity with "Mati," or one like her, in the future. Here we again see that the roots of human relationships reach deeply into our past.

In the last part of the poem, the preborn elaborates further on the nature of the relationship between its parents: **When He is around, she* *watches; does He approve? When out of sight, she longs for Him. He has power over Mati.**

This bond of attraction or tension between its parents that the preborn describes could be viewed as a psychological dependency. However, let us not forget the "culture" of that time in which a male played the dominant role "naturally" (men and women were brought up that way). We could almost think of the "macho" man as an archetype. However, that's not the feeling of the preborn, who does not view this dependency as being natural.

When He storms out the door, harsh sound jars my inner peace. At other times I feel they celebrate my presence. I believe there is nothing strange or new for us in this description of the life of a couple.

Light

This poem offers an insight into the process of the formation of the eyes as well as the nature and function of consciousness.

I proposed an idea that consciousness is an inherent faculty of all living matter as a component of its energy and is directed by the highest self or soul. We all know from experience that consciousness can be directed to any part of our body to "illuminate" it for our body intelligence to take a look at and examine. The key word here is illuminate. For the purpose of the current analysis, it would suffice to accept the idea that the function of consciousness is to make a body part, such as an organ, normally invisible to our external eyes, "visible" to our hidden "eye", often called the third eye. In order to do this, it must raise the energy of that part to set it apart from its surrounding so that it could be "sensed" by the third eye, which is sensitive to differences in energy. We could say that consciousness somehow enables contact between an object and a source of energy in a way similar to an electrical switch and a light bulb, or we could imagine that consciousness is a movable source of energy. In any case, these thoughts lead us to start paying serious attention to the role of consciousness in a biological system. We will return to a detailed discussion of consciousness in the third part of the book.

*I have found a place that lights up when I visit it. The feeling delights me. I linger there, enjoy its brilliance** The place the preborn has found and is describing is the original histological tissue from which the eyes were differentiated. This place would light up when visited by the preborn's consciousness. The preborn finds it a delightful feeling (note the association of the word "de-light" with light) and visits this place repeatedly. We can consider this as a confirmation of the above ideas about the function of consciousness.

*But now... two places, a short space apart, light up to greet me. Which shall I visit first?** The development of the eyes has reached a stage where we have the beginnings of two eyes. This poses a dilemma for the preborn in deciding which eye to visit first. We might recall a similar case of having to choose between two arms. The preborn chooses the right eye. As was the case of the arms, a preference is given to the right eye. Although we cannot be sure whether "right" means the same before and after birth, we can consider this choice an indicative of what is known as the *dominant eye.*

Having made its choice, the preborn visits the right eye first, then turns to the left eye. It finds its light less bright. Despite unequal brightness in the two eyes, the preborn likes to treat both eyes equally and dwells on them the same length of time.

*Now I know light and space await me outside. Everything there glows in bright light. I look forward to enter it.** The preborn contemplates the future when it will enter the outside (be born) and looks forward to that time.

Attacks of Anger

Mati's anger, expressed by shouting, has a stressful and painful effect on the unborn child. The preborn describes its experience and reaction to anger: *A shooting pain!... My body is attacked!... The attacks come when*

*Mati rages... shouting... I cringe inside. The attackers, lit up and linked in chains, pulsate forward, stream toward me. So many this time!... I begin to shake. My body is on fire, enraged.** The preborn is a recipient of stress hormones, such as adrenaline, which are being produced in Mati's body during her angry outbursts and flow via the placenta into its body. As adults, we know that the reaction to such chemicals, result of feelings of aggression and fear, is to prepare our body for fight or flight or freeze. We have encountered the ability of the embryo to discern elementary particles in discussing the poem *Touching Stars.* Those particles (molecules?) were also "lit up" with energy. What is remarkable in this case is the preborn's ability to "see" and describe these "molecules of anger" as being charged with very high energy and grouped in chains. A look at a diagram of the adrenaline molecule on the internet reveals its somewhat chain-like form.

All night I wage war, fight for my life... I must defeat them (the attackers), I must survive... At last, completely exhausted, I fall asleep The fight against an unknown enemy required a heavy and exhausting, life-and-death struggle by the preborn. We have to realize that the preborn, being enclosed in the womb, did not have the possibility of fight or flight. It could only shake and fight chemically. To what degree the shaking can actually be expressed in such a crowded space, is a question. The main means that the preborn had at its disposal was a chemical defense, which might take longer than a physical defense.

I wake up calm. The battle is over. I have won. Now docile, the attackers have turned into my guards... now (they are) ready to defend me against another angry lot. Having my guards, I feel strong This passage offers an insight into the nature of the physiological response of our body to a toxic material that enters it. After the struggle with the "poisonous" matter, which may involve physical symptoms, the body develops chemical "antibodies," which will help to neutralize the toxins if a future attack occurs. The preborn sees it as a process of turning the attackers into guards. This would suggest that the process involved, somehow alters the molecule of a toxin into a compound that can cause the toxin to lose its toxicity, for example, by binding to it. Having found a way of neutralizing the poison, the preborn relaxes and feels stronger than before. Interestingly, this process is also reflected in the philosopher Friedrich Nietzsche's popular quote: "That which does not kill us makes us stronger."

Place of Silence

The preborn describes an experience with a noisy crowd outside: **A large noisy crowd has gathered outside. For a while I stay... a silent witness. But their voices rise, exceed my comfort, force me to withdraw inside. I close my eyes, roll them upwards and turn them where once they were one, near the middle of my head. Now the noise is gone. I like it this way.** At this stage of its development, the preborn is becoming more and more interested in the outside and likes to participate in its events. Its perception of sound has also increased. In this episode, it tunes in to an outside crowd of people. Gradually, the sound of the crowd turns into a noise that the preborn finds difficult to bear. It describes a way to shield itself from the noise: * *First I close my eyes, then I roll them upward, then toward each other to become aware of a place where in the past they were still one.**

That place is near the front and middle of its head. Once it becomes aware of the place, it does not hear the noise anymore.

How could we explain this very important and helpful maneuver? One way would be to think that the preborn takes a journey into its past when its eyes were still undeveloped. It was also the time when its sound perception was also nonexistent. This makes a great deal of sense to the preborn. It learns from it.

I learn: Unwanted world can be shut out by rolling the eyes to a place from which they came... when I could not hear as I do now. When I reach that place [in the middle of my head]... my life is tranquil. The explanation is self-evident. The preborn is so impressed by its discovery of the inner place of silence that it wants to **remember it forever.**

We would find the discovery by the preborn also helpful in our adult life, which can be at times too "noisy" for our comfort. This applies not only to sound. We will discuss this important topic in the third part of the book when we will expand on the need for awareness of the continuity of life.

Sleep/Wake

As I keep growing, the space around me tightens. More and more I am part of everything Mati does. The preborn is aware of its increasing body size. With that, it experiences tightness in its enclosure. It is also closer to the mother's body, and through it, to the outside world. It is drawn more to what its mother does.

Today she sits, her hands fly, stripping feathers. Three others sit across by the wall doing the same. They carry a lively talk. I fall asleep but not for long. Mati's laughter shakes me awake, annoyed. I drift back to sleep, only to have another burst of laughter wake me up again. On and off sleep/wake. I grow angry at Mati and the others... it's their fault I cannot have my rest

There are some points we can look at in this episode. In the old days (we are looking at the year 1924), country women used to strip goose feathers to make down blankets, pillows, etc. It was done during the winter months. Usually several women from the neighborhood would get together. It also marked an occasion to socialise, gossip and entertain.

The rapid movement of the abdominal wall during Mati's laughter kept waking up the preborn, disturbing its sleep. As the disturbance kept repeating, it became annoying to it, and even awakened anger at Mati and others at the gathering. For the first time, we find the preborn feeling anger at the happening outside the womb. In the poem *Attacks of Anger,* the preborn became a recipient of Mati's "angry" chemistry that it had to defend itself against to survive. This time the preborn generates its own chemistry of annoyance and anger while its mother is enjoying pleasant feelings connected with laughter. As is the case in *Ring of Protection*, the preborn does not participate in the feelings of Mati. Its needs always come first.

Where did the preborn's feeling of anger come from? I am of the opinion that feelings of wellbeing and survival are part of the innate (instinctive) nature of every organism and thus do not have to be taught. A good example in this category of feelings is love.

Through the Arm Loop

The preborn devises an exercise that will help it during its birth although it is unaware of the purpose of doing so. It moves its right arm, bent at the wrist and elbow, to the top of its head. It slides its left arm across its chest underneath the raised right hand to meet it so that together they form a firm loop. The exercise consists of reaching with its head into the loop and trying to move its head through it: **My head reaches forward, tries to squeeze through the opening. It holds tight. The power of movement stretches my neck. I push hard, break open the arm loop and rest... In a while I repeat the exercise... squeezing through the noose, my neck grows stronger.** The preborn repeats this exercise as if training for a future action.

Obviously, the purpose of this exercise is to strengthen and train the neck muscles for the birth process, which requires squeezing the head through the birth canal. The preborn does not know why it is doing this exercise, which would indicate that it is one of the instinctive motions built into the fabric of human life. This is also confirmed by the preborn's use of the power of movement.

Wellbeing

In this delightful little poem, the preborn reflects upon its life in the womb. **The liquid surrounding radiates warmth, glows with soft light. I feel well and comfortable** It may remind us of a warm, relaxing bath in a softly lit bathroom.

I lie, conscious of how beautiful my life is... I have everything I need: peace, wellbeing The preborn states that it has everything it needs: complete peace and wellbeing. It feels that its life is beautiful.

Not even life outside can disturb my contentment The preborn reflects upon life outside, which cannot disturb its peace. This indicates that it can deal with the disturbances coming from outside by not paying any attention to them.

I wish to live like this always This is a nice wish that will be very difficult to fulfill after birth, but it could remain in our consciousness as an ideal.

Thoughts

This very significant poem reveals the preborn's discovery of thoughts, their nature and the way to deal with them.

Exciting and alive, thoughts about my future gather in my head. For the first time, the preborn becomes aware of thoughts gathering in its head. It calls them "thoughts about my future," meaning that they are directed toward its future life. We will find out later what this means. It describes them as "exciting and alive," which to us would indicate that thoughts are energy circuits that light up neuronal groups in the brain. This would also indicate that, by this time, the preborn's brain is well developed.

I lie in a trough that will narrow, curve to the right as it takes me closer to the world outside. The preborn describes the part of the womb where it is positioned as a trough (trench) which, upon getting narrow and curving right, will take it "closer" to the world outside. It shows that, at this time, the preborn is more aware of the outside world and also that it will be moving toward it. We can explain this "knowledge" of its future location, as we did before, in terms of the inertia of the life force. We may be led also to think: does the life force carries the design of life?

I am absorbing so many ideas from without. Each being outside sends thoughts to me: Mati, the One always near, others... expecting my life to carry their messages. The preborn states that ideas come to it from the outside, from people like Mati, its father and other people. They all send their thoughts to the preborn, which contain messages begging to be accepted: **The ideas crowd my head, each one begs: "Take me, accept me, keep me alive in your life**.

We know from experience that thoughts of people, especially if directed to us and voiced, influence us the moment we accept them. "Accepting" means to start paying attention to them by recalling them.

How do I know which ones to accept, which are right for me? How do I choose? I must be careful, see clearly. I must have control, keep the right thoughts, for each one will impose on, take its share of my future life. It is surprising that, at such an early time in our development, we have to start paying attention to what feeds our mind. The preborn realizes that it needs to be careful and clear and able to control and evaluate which thoughts will be the "right" ones to accept because each one of them will participate in its future life. This bears a similarity to the way of sorting and choosing food particles that the embryo was engaged in when it was building its body in the poem *Upward Bound*. At that time, the embryo was selecting them according to the criterion like/dislike.

In the case of thoughts, the preborn requires a more accurate way of selection: **Like ribbons of light, thoughts pull me up to a place where I can find advice. I will consult the closest in me, the highest in me, the lightest in me, the liveliest in me. I will choose the best.** The preborn reiterates its perception of thoughts as threads of light (having an electrical charge). It describes how they mass up in its body and pull it (its consciousness) up to the place where a decision will be made about their acceptance or rejection. What "place or places" can we think of? The centre of the highest self is usually regarded as being the neocortex. As the place where we are "closest" to ourselves, we would regard the place where our soul resides, which is the heart. The seat of the lightest self (consciousness), we might regard as the third eye, with its place in the prefrontal cortex between the eyes. Finally, as a centre of the liveliest self, we may take to be the pituitary and pineal hormonal glands. An alternative analysis might be offered by considering the three highest chakras (centers of energy) discussed in yoga and Hindu teachings. All this would indicate that the decision in accepting a thought could be a diverse and important process.

It remains for us to address the question of how thoughts that originate outside could be transmitted from those who send them into the consciousness of a fetus. One possibility would be to think of the communication link being the mother. People around her could be asking how she felt, how her pregnancy was coming along, or other customary questions and, at the same time, acknowledging or being conscious of her unborn child. The mother would hear and process the thoughts of the people, and the fetus could somehow sense their "value" from her reaction. This idea appears simple but fuzzy and incomplete because it would account for only the spoken thoughts.

A better hypothesis would involve energy transfer. We have established that thoughts have energy. When we voice a thought, our mind is in a broadcasting mode. We could imagine that the brain broadcasts this energy—for example, in the form of radiation waves, similar to a broadcasting station. The brain of the fetus would function as a receiving antenna for the signal. Because both the brain of the sender and receiver would have similar anatomical structures provided by human DNA, the received signal (a neuronal pattern) would awaken a similar response or resonate with the broadcast signal. The strength of the signal and accuracy of the transfer of information would depend on the anatomical compatibility of the two brains.

To understand the thought content and meaning would *not* require the understanding of language. There may be a genetic predisposition for "understanding" if the brain were "wired" for this capability. On the basis of my own experience, I claim that there exists an understanding of the spoken thought after birth and likely even before. This understanding is in real time and does not happen, as some may argue, later after learning the language.

In the third part we will discuss the prominent role that consciousness plays in our communication.

Knocking on the Wall

In this poem, we find the preborn in a considerably more advanced stage of development in which it is aware of its large size and the tightness of its enclosure (womb): **I have grown big. I am proud of my size* [and] *all I can do**

It is also conscious of its expanded mental capabilities: **I have confidence, can think ahead and direct my future course**

The preborn has a challenge: **How do I find a way to get in touch with Mati and tell her about my need to begin to communicate with her?** It has to find a way to indicate to her that the time has come to begin a physical communication with her.

The thought of not knowing sweeps over me, elicits a strange new feeling how to act We all know that feeling of hesitation and uncertainty when we face a new task or have to play a new role in our life. We have a good example of this in the first sentence of the foreword to *this very book;* in the words of Dr. Graham Farrant, "The unique opportunity to write a foreword to the collection of poems ushered a familiar feeling of tentativeness as I conceived thoughts and ideas..."

I can think now, get ideas and try them out. I will find the way The preborn is referring to its new-found faculty of thinking. For us it is a chance to witness the beginning of the process of the development of the mind.

For several days I puzzle where and how I approach Mati First, the preborn has to find a place in the womb to initiate the communication. To find it, it uses the method we know as trial and error.

I lean left but cannot press close enough to hear her The preborn is looking for a place where it would be close to Mati to "hear" her. It already knows from experience Mati's reaction to its general movements in the womb. This time it also needs to "hear" Mati's response to its specific signals (knocking) to establish communication with the muscles engaged in the birth process.

In the first attempt, the preborn—to whom we will from now on refer more frequently as *fetus*—leaned to the left side but could not hear Mati because it was unable to press close enough to the wall of the womb.

In the second attempt, it pressed higher on the other side only to find that she was **not on that side**. We would assume that the fetus was moving its head.

In the third attempt, it turned down its head and rolled its body into an upside-down position and found that **Being upside down seems right. I am close to the wall.** This offers an insight into the prenatal child's preparation for its birth, which is normally in a head-first position. In this position, the fetus felt close to the wall.

*In the afternoon... I make my move; with my right elbow, I knock slowly three times on the wall, listen and wait... Mati has not heard me. Again I knock, again no response... I knock four times... no reaction yet... Mati chats with her friends, I grow anxious. If I cannot reach her I am doomed, my life will end** Thus far, the fetus's attempts to elicit a reaction from Mati have failed. In its last attempt, it increased the number of knocks. This would show that repetition (more knocks) is a way to emphasize a request or demand, and appears to be part of our instinctive nature.

As its number of unsuccessful attempts increased, the fetus grew anxious and fearful. It realized that if it did not succeed in establishing a communication with Mati, its life, as it knew it, would end.

We have seen a very similar situation of despair and fear of life ending, when the fetus as an embryo was trying to implant (see the poem *The First Journey*). That experience might have influenced the current feeling of doom by the fetus. In any case, it shows that prenatal life has its challenges and difficult tasks, which the prenatal child has to perform to survive.

Another day, at four* [p.m.], *again I try, knock several times and pause. Mati hears me! She moves inside to let me know. I burst with joy. She tells others how I am trying to get her attention The success of establishing a working cooperation with Mati brought the fetus great relief and joy. It happened after a long wait of one day and a more emphatic action of knocking. Mati at last got the message and "moved inside" to let it know. Feeling the pride of an expecting mother, she shared this event with others telling them that her baby was trying to get her attention.

We can learn from this episode that it is the child that initiates the preparation for its birth by awakening the mother's internal organs to respond to the knocking on the wall of the uterus. The mother reacts by moving the muscles and other internal tissue structures, which are engaged in the birth process. The purpose of this training of the internal anatomy of the expectant mother is to allow the baby a natural and, as much as possible, a pain-free passage during its birth.

Since the cooperation between the fetus and mother in preparation for birth is one of the key events in the reproductive process, we might expect it to be part of our ongoing life experience. This appears to be so. For instance, the custom of knocking on a door before entry, expecting someone to come and open the door, bears a striking similarity with knocking on the wall of the womb by the fetus. From the Bible we have the words ascribed to Jesus Christ: "Seek and you will find, knock and it will be opened" (Matthew 7:7).

From the Norse mythology we have a symbol of god Odin, who is hanging upside down, tied by his feet to a branch of a tree. The legend tells about Odin gaining a gift of speech and writing while in that position. We can compare this to the upside-down position of a prenatal child "tied" by its umbilical cord to the tree of life (placenta). At this time, the fetus starts its communication with the mother by knocking on the wall of the womb. Also at this time, as was stated in the analysis of the poem *Thoughts*, the fetus is absorbing thoughts and listening to spoken words outside. We would interpret the knocking, the processing of thoughts and listening to speech sounds as the precursors of speech and writing.

The method of trial and error that the preborn used to establish the communication with Mati is a natural way of overcoming obstacles or solving problems in adult life, when the solutions are unknown to us at the start. The method is also used in scientific research and statistical methods. Successful entrepreneurial people are especially aware of it. That is why we often hear their advice: "If at first you don't succeed, try, try again." In the case of a fetus, the successful outcome would be known instinctively. We can also say that the method of trial and error is one of the ways life maintains its cohesion in a constantly changing environment.

Force of Change

We have met and described many examples of the prenatal child's awareness of energy as an action of force. We have experienced, in our prenatal life, the manifestation of life force and the force of movement, in particular. In this significant poem, we are learning about yet another force: the *force of change.*

A strange new energy pervades my body, pulls me out of here The fetus becomes aware of a new and strange energy welling up in its body that has a psychological effect of "pulling" it toward the outside. We are familiar with this kind of feeling in our life. For example, we may get excited about an impending trip; athletes are in the full grip of such a force waiting for the starting gun to sound to start the race.

Mati walks along a sunlit road... rests beside a tree on a sunny bank, gazes down the road ahead... my future unfolds... Soon I'll leave this place for another, further along my journey's path. A woman in advanced pregnancy may take a walk to be alone and think about the delivery of the baby "down the road." The future is also in the consciousness of the unborn child, who regards its future as a spatial change or translocation. Space changes, not only due to relocation but also because of the inner rearrangement of matter. Those changes imply the use of energy. We have here an example of the interplay of the four elements of life and the physical universe as we know them from classical physics: space, time, energy and matter. The first two, because of their contiguity—**Time and change always go together**—are also referred to as "spacetime." The joint effect of these four elements is described by Einstein's Theory of Relativity. The preborn does not know anything about the theory but is aware of those four players and their action in its experience of life.

The fetus reflects upon its current place in the womb, which it calls a good home, and is sad to have to leave it:

So much here I will miss: the tree, abundance, friendships... But I cannot resist the force of change urging me when the time comes The sad feeling of having to leave our home is well known to us. It is caused by having to disconnect from what was part of our physical world, both externally and internally.

The fetus misses most the friendship, generosity and sustenance of the tree of life (placenta) but is resolute in its compliance with the force of change when its time comes. We could be equally right by talking about the life force as the force of change.

Let us revisit the statement by the preborn: **Time and change always go together** We could reflect here on the meaning of time. The fetus perceives it as something that accompanies change, relates to its rhythm as something that does not exist by itself. By this definition, time would not exist if everything stood absolutely still. Some people approach this state when meditating. Since we can imagine it as a possibility, can we say that something in life does not change? Stays the same? Cannot disappear?

The force of change... flows into everything. I feel it in my cells, everywhere outside, nothing stays the same. Moving energy spins inside every particle. The fetus is engaged in sensing the force of change and its presence and manifestation, not only in its cells but also outside in inanimate objects. It sees it even as the energy spinning inside each particle. It would appear that the fetus can sense the energy within such small particles of matter as molecules and perhaps atoms.

Each being outside also knows this force and the sadness it leaves behind We are all familiar with the feeling that accompanies changes in our lives that we regard as unpleasant or unwelcome. We would prefer to keep things as they are. The difficulty with acceptance of change as an inevitable process in life and the world we live in arises from our feeling of having to separate ourselves or give up something that we perceive to be a part of us. In this case, the force required to separate ourselves leaves behind in our psyche a reactionary force that goes on unexpressed. This violates the law of Life's Order and stimulates us to seek new connections of a similar nature to compensate for the lost ones. Life always seeks balance and wholeness.

Preparing to Leave

In this insightful poem, the fetus becomes aware of a steadily growing energy that brings about its search for **the door to enter the world of light and space** The search goes on at night during its sleep and may thus appear as a recurrent dream.

Only a few days left before I move out... I must prepare. The fetus knows quite definitely that there are only a few days left before its birth. It feels a need to prepare for this event, which it feels will require an enormous force that **will grow, explode, propel me out... I feel its tension build, can hardly hold it back.** It knows that this huge, almost unbearable, force will be necessary to accomplish the task ahead. We should notice that it is not effort that will be required; rather, the force alone will carry out the task. The fetus will let the force do it. This is a very important consideration that we discussed in the analysis of the poem *Force of Change.*

At night, during sleep, I make the first move, enter an empty room, feel around and find a door. It is shut The unborn child makes its first approach to find the "door," which we interpret as the exit from the womb. It finds it shut.

Next day, I practice stretching my neck, feel the propelling force During the day, the fetus practices the exercise of strengthening its neck by moving its head through the loop, aware of the ever-increasing propelling force: **At night, I enter another empty room with a closed door that points ahead.** The child repeats its search for the exit door. Here we may be interested in what is meant by the "empty room." It is not the space of the womb that is implied here. I believe that the fetus is living an archetype of being located in a house with many rooms, with only one of them that has an exit outside. A similar archetype is invoked in the method of trial and error discussed earlier.

The night after, I find yet another empty room and closed door. Another night, another room, another door I cannot open. The search goes on. For the first time, however, we notice that the fetus refers to the door that it "cannot open," whereas previously it was just trying to locate the door.

How many rooms, how many doors must I try to find the way out? The fetus grows impatient in its search. We have come across this kind of feeling before, when the embryo was trying to implant, and again during its effort to establish a working communication with Mati. However, those were conscious actions as part of its growth and development. In the present case, we have an episode playing out that consists of a series of dreams coming from the realm of the unconscious. Although dreaming is normally considered a subconscious activity of the soul, its role in life should not be underestimated.

After experiencing a steadily growing energy that causes an enormous tension in its body, rising to the point of a breaking force, and makes it speed up its search, the fetus, at last, finds the right door: *I know that it is the one to lead me out. In the morning I will be born!* The fetus is finally rewarded for all the effort it put in to the search for the exit and its physical preparations for birth. It has found the exit from the womb and declared, triumphantly, that the next day it will be born. We have here a marvelous example of the life force that advanced and energized the development of a human being in the womb and now prepares it for entry into a new stage of life.

Into Light and Space

In this last poem, the birthing child describes the process of its birth:

This is the day I will open the door, move out into the world where light and space abound. In the dawning of the day it announced as the day of its birth, the child about to be born states its decision to open the door and exit from the womb into the outer world that abounds in light and unlimited space. The child is confident of carrying out the task ahead. First, it becomes aware of people outside who are beginning to wake up, then it gathers strength for action and begins its first move to announce its readiness to Mati: *Arms crossed and folded tight against my chest, shoulders curved in, I tense my body, stretch my neck and with my head press against the door.* The child describes the body posture it takes in preparation for birth. After a short rest, it pushes harder and repeats the action, still without a response from Mati. Again it rests.

On the third attempt *with all their might, my legs thrust me forward to hit the door. It stays shut, but I sense a response. Mati seems to know what I am up to but is not ready yet. I am! My spirit soars. Like a king, I want to command, direct everything.*

We notice the child's body posture and action in starting the birth process. Using its legs as a spring, it thrusts its body, head first, against the wall of the uterus, signalling Mati that it is ready to exit. It does it with a feeling of confidence and power, which it likens to that of a king commanding his subjects. Its confidence and sense of power are remarkable:

The outside stirs into motion, but not fast enough for me. I want to go now! The child is determined to exit now and finds the preparations outside too slow. We have met its impatience before and may conclude that it is most probably due to its genetic makeup.

With energy renewed, I lunge forward, bang my head on the door. It does not budge. Again and again my head pounds the door till I am spent. I have to stop and rest.... Refreshed, determined, I ram the door again and again in vain... I cannot struggle on for long The birthing child continues pounding its head against the wall of the uterus, each time pausing for a rest. Doubt creeps into its mind. It begins to sense that it cannot continue this struggle for long.

We would interpret the thrusts of the baby's head and body against the wall of the uterus and the inner muscle responses of the woman giving birth as contractions. We mentioned the origin of these muscle responses during the analysis of the poem *Knocking on the Wall*. The frequency of contractions signals the proximity of delivery.

I hear voices from outside: Mati's and a woman's who came to help. The woman tells Mati to relax and rest The child notices the arrival of a woman, presumably a midwife, to assist and help Mati with the delivery. Seeing Mati anxious and stressed, she advises her to relax and take a rest.

She* [Mati] *asks for Him, wants Him here... He is hunting a stork. No! She wants Him home... find Him, bring Him back Mati wants to know the whereabouts of her husband, whom she wants to be present during the birth. From this we can conclude that she regards the birth to be a very important family event that requires the presence of both parents. Usually, men may not be aware (by their nature or cultural background) of the importance of their presence at the birth of their children.

As the woman soothes Mati, my anger at them grows... This is no time to rest, I must get out!... I beat my head senseless... the stress is killing me. "Let me go! Let me go!" One last time, I push. It's no use, Mati will not understand. I cannot get out. I am doomed... energy spent, stuck in this place of horror, I can do nothing but die... I accept my fate

We see a frantic, desperate effort described by the child as it struggles to get out of the womb. It blames Mati and the midwife for not allowing it to get out of the "place of horror." This struggle of the child exiting the womb, which may not always be so traumatic, has been a subject of study and interest in science, arts, mythology and other forms of expression in an attempt to understand human life. There seems to be a consensus in the scientific community about the seriousness of the birth trauma affecting the life of an individual. In our analysis, we can look at it also from a more positive view and regard it as an example of an extreme form of life struggle for survival. After all, life presents us constantly with challenges that we have to overcome. To have an earlier experience of this kind can be both damaging and beneficial. In the words of Nietzsche: "That which does not kill us makes us stronger."

The birthing child exhausted its energy to continue its struggle and decided that there was nothing else it could do but die. It accepted the defeat—the inability to have its way—and its fate, obeying the law of the life force. We can deduce from this event and the similar situations that we discussed before in the poems dealing with implantation (*The First Journey*), life dependence on Mati and establishing communication with Mati (*Knocking on the Wall*) that the prenatal child is aware of death as part of its life. It feels that the life force contains both life and death. These are very significant findings and will be given more detailed attention in the third part of the book.

I succumb to the end-of-life wish... let go of my body. With only my soul consciousness I stagger onto a wide plain, find a river, lie down on its bank to die. Fog rolls over me. I feel an unending space To fully understand what the child describes would require an understanding of the world in which the prenatal child lives. We will deal with that topic later. For now, let us call it the hidden world. The hidden world is not separate from the external visible world we enter after birth. These worlds are interfaced and constantly interact with each other. The division is made only for the purpose of an easier understanding of the child's birth episode describing its separation from life.

The child gives in and accepts its "fate" to "die," since it could not continue the struggle to exit the womb. We would not call it a suicide attempt, such as we know in the visible world. Accepting death as part of its life, the child shifted from *conscious inside its body* existence to *out-of-body* existence. It resembles, what today we would think of as falling asleep, which we know as a part of our daily life. However, the circumstances and the description the child gives are not what we normally experience going to sleep. In our case, the child *surrendered* to the force of life, which includes death. In sleep we surrender to the need of the body to get a deep rest, expecting to wake up. The child's decision to "die" necessitated a shift of consciousness from the way it knew as life to a state without that life. It describes how its self/soul consciously exited the body and moved outside onto a plain, eventually coming to a river, dropping on its bank to "die." If we regard consciousness as a faculty of the self/soul, then that which exited was the child's self/soul.

Whatever the interpretation we may attach to the above journey, one thing appears certain: our conscious self/soul can detach from the body when the need arises. This state has been often reported by people who have had a near-death experience.

The "death" experience of the fetus gives us an insight into the way consciousness functions in life. We have assumed that the out-of-body journey of the conscious self/soul took place outdoors. The reason for that was the description of the scenery that corresponded very closely to the appearance of the outdoor landscape at that time. The "plain" was a meadow and the "river" a creek swelled to overflowing by the runoff of melting snow close to the end of February. The question arises: Did the self/soul's journey take place in the actual outdoor space or was it a "movement" of its consciousness in its fetal "knowledge" of the landscape? The reader may recall a similar kind of "travel" by the newly formed first cell (zygote) in its search for identity during conception (*The First Journey*) or the journey of embryo to its elementary origin in the poem *Hungry Birds*. Also, the child might have fallen into sleep and been dreaming. If we consider consciousness to be a point or a small cloud of light energy, we could find the answer to the above question by asking: What if the child's consciousness could have been in the two places (outdoors *and* in the body) at the same time?—(In the third part of the book, we will define consciousness as a quantum thing, which, according to the quantum mechanics theory, could indeed be in two places at the same time.)

What? Is someone calling me? I stir, I am not dead yet... I must go back where I left and try again. That "someone" calling the baby could have been Mati or the midwife or both, deciding that it was time for the baby to come out. Their waking consciousness communicated with the dormant consciousness of the baby to wake it up. It is similar to the episode of waking up the sleeping heart of the embryo by the mother's heart in the poem *Flame and Friendship*. Responding to the call, the conscious soul returns to its body. The child's body feels a renewed strength, and the child decides to continue the birth process.

I find the door [and] thrust forward. A change! An opening around my head! Harder, harder I push... the gap grows... out slides my head. Now my arms, still crossed, reach the opening, elbows first. I push out to my waist. Sharp pain! I stop. The woman tries to help—[her] hands around my neck, she twists it right and left. I want to yell "Let go of my neck! It hurts! The child describes in detail the motion (head first) of its body through the birth canal coming out to its waist, where a very sharp abdominal pain stops its progress. The midwife, who is trying to help, takes hold of its head and tries to pull the baby out by twisting it. This brings on a pain in the neck that the baby is unable to voice. It wanted to scream at the midwife to stop doing it.

Back to the abdominal pain: **Each time I try to push myself out, the pain knifes... I cannot cross it! I squeeze my abdomen, still I cannot bear the pain, I am caught... I must get out! Pushing with legs, again I try but can't get past the pain... the woman grabs my arms and pulls... the pain wrenches, knifes my abdomen. I strain to stop it in my head... (finally) I succeed to block the pain in my head.** This is a highly instructive passage that illustrates what can go wrong during the birth process. The baby's abdominal pain was probably caused by a stiff umbilical cord that pressed against the tender and sensitive area where it opens into the abdomen. The stiffness could have been caused by the delay in delivery and the baby's loss of aware consciousness during its out-of-body travel. The pain exceeded the threshold of its pain tolerance, which eventually forced the child to block it in its head. It is a confirmation of a scientific belief that the human body has a built-in physiological capability to disconnect from an unbearable pain in a conscious way.

Past the painful point I slide. I am out! Joy springs up in me and everyone. I have made it, arrived into the world The baby entered the world of light and space feeling a great joy. Its long journey into the world ended. It became a newborn child.

Gasping for air I open the throat, wheeze in the first big gulp of air The newborn child describes the difficulty of opening its throat to start breathing, a memory which all of us probably could relate to.

A small regret enters my head to return to where I came from, but ecstasy turns me forward. I am born! The newborn child describes a feeling of wanting to return to the womb, a feeling that we all have when we leave a place that meant a lot to us, where we spent a long time, formed lasting relationships and sank our roots, a place we would call home. However, the baby's feeling of regret was overcome by a stronger feeling of ecstasy at having been born.

Part 3

Return

call that one back who
gave a newborn wisdom
beyond anyone's learning...

—*Rumi* (translated by Coleman Barks)

1
Introduction

Each passage of our life contains events that connect us to the previous ones and prepare us for the ones ahead. All has its order, meaning, degree of importance and individual value to our existence. Our life, like a river, has its flow of continuity and completeness as a single entity. It would not be sufficient to describe a river if we did not talk about its origin, upper and middle course, its low channel and estuary. Even that would not be the whole story. A river, like a human life, has a hidden beginning.

A raindrop falls,
disappears.
Lost in the ground?

An earthworm:
"I see others joining in,
seeping through soil,
pressing through drift,
growing..."

Now a trickle,
now a streamlet
hugging a rock,
always cleansing,
purifying.

Now a cool,
life-giving flow,
ready to burst

Out of the ground
it springs!

Over the centuries, sages have advised us to know ourselves, and for good reason: To know—to be conscious of—one's whole life, including the prenatal period, is psychologically unifying. People who have experienced near-death situations often report that their whole life played out before their eyes. They also state that their lives subsequently became more meaningful. We know from experience that consciousness is independent of time and space. It is possible, therefore, to embrace the whole life as if it existed in this very moment. In this case, we are not aware of the individual episodes or segments; we perceive life as a whole, one unit, something like an abstract or a sketch by an accomplished artist. We are all aware of that kind of feeling when we live through an intensive life situation and then return to it later in memory.

To feel the whole of one's life at once is not a fantasy; it is a reality, a moment of truth. The opposite—when life consists of fragments—is not a healthy state, sometimes leading to a mental disorder. The problem is fragmented identity.

I have titled this third part of the book "Return," since in it I will go back to the first part, the prenatal life story, to extract from it the prenatal child's essential nature and seek its connection to our postnatal life. Based on this knowledge, at the end, I will contemplate a way in which one might prepare for the last journey—the exit from life.

Some may question whether meaningful and general conclusions can be drawn from one individual's subjective experience. This is a valid point of view in our adult worldly existence, but it does not apply to the prenatal period. Prenatal life unfolds, as we have read, in a different, very cohesive and organized way and in a precise manner, which remains on the whole a mystery. We will explore the way and essence of this realm. Its characteristics include unified laws and stable processes. In prenatal life, we all follow the same basic course of development, directed by the DNA molecule. We all have to go through the same developmental stages such as conception, implantation, building our bodies, experiencing the order of life, starting our heart, building an image of the outer world, discovering the flow of the life force and the force of movement, getting to know the tree of life and our bond with Mother Earth, starting and developing a communication with our human mother, preparing for birth and executing the birth itself.

While each prenatal being experiences these stages in an individual way, the experiences are similar. We can talk about a collective experience in which the experience of one being is not essentially different from that of another, and each one can provide us with an accurate view of prenatal life. How is this different from postnatal life? In postnatal life, our individual experiences are influenced by many differing circumstances that shape our individual perception and consciousness of who we are. While we still may have many similar experiences, the amount of diversification reduces and conceals similarity.

During the prenatal period, we are not influenced by the outer world to the degree we are after birth. In prenatal life, we exist more in the role of observers, passively receiving—yet consciously participating—in the process of growth. We are experiencing a truth that is not falsified, and that alone makes each experience pure and trustworthy.

In trying to understand prenatal life, we are entering the invisible realm of existence, the beginning of life. We are discovering and becoming familiar with our roots. When a seed germinates, it first sends a root into the soil below before it pushes its head above it. Human life follows the same order of nature.

Those who believe prenatal life has a deeper meaning that reaches beyond its physical and physiological aspect will be moved to seek its knowledge within themselves and, in so doing, enrich and fulfill their life and gain understanding of it. Those who do not believe in prenatal life and its paramount and fundamental value to our postnatal existence—for whatever reason—can regard the following discussions and explanations as theoretical and seek their proof themselves.

2
Beginning of Conscious Life

To know something fully, we must include its beginning. This holds true for our individual lives as well as life on Earth as a whole, indeed the whole cosmos. It may not be a beginning in an absolute sense, but we could say that our current life began when we became conscious of existing as an individual living entity and can recall that moment. The same must be true for the beginning of life on this planet. The above definition of life presumes the existence/presence of the self and soul.

We can imagine the beginning of life taking place as an interaction between energy, supplied by the sun, and matter harbouring energy, supplied by the earth, in a chemically favorable environment of a liquid medium. This gave rise to chemical formation of organic molecules and their aggregates that grew progressively more complex until one of them added the last "atom" and became aware of being *complete*. That moment was highly significant. We will define the state of awareness of being complete by *I exist*, which implies the awareness of form and the presence of a *self*. If it could have spoken, the molecular compound, to which we will refer as *proto-life (pre-life)* might have said, "I am complete, you [other aspiring proto-life] can be like me." The words *whole, complete, completeness* are fundamental developmental stages of the evolution of a form, dormant or alive. They are the stepping stones in its progression.

What gave the molecular aggregate the "feeling" of being complete? Its growth stopped. Later, we would be able to say that the wave function of its growth was collapsed by consciousness to reveal form (particle).

The collapse was caused by the omnipresent consciousness of the creative force.

The awareness of form can be regarded as the awareness of matter. The awareness of form was the first step in the evolution of life. It makes sense that the first step was the creation of a form out of matter by the creative spirit. The resulting form was not, however, conscious of the process of creation and remained in a state of dormant consciousness. Does it follow that working with matter in an unconscious way is a state of dormancy or sleep?

In the scientific community, the awareness of the self has been thought of as an *emergent* property in the evolution of a biological system. I believe that to understand the self, we need to know the process that led to its origin. An aggregate of organic molecules grew until it reached completion. It became complete when the omnipresent consciousness (energy) collapsed its growth. How did the consciousness "know" when to collapse it? This is a difficult question to answer. If we consider the growth of the molecular aggregate to be a quantum process, we may think of its completeness as a state of maximum probability to survive. All of the other preceding states were less stable and short lasting. Collapsing the wave function (growth) revealed the "particle"—the self. The emergence of self thus signifies the completeness of a form.

The more elusive *soul* is usually considered as something that arrives rather than emerges. If the self emerges, where does it come from? Since we feel its presence instinctively, does it come from our subconscious or unconscious? Does that not imply that our soul also comes from somewhere? The self and soul play a central role in the manifestation of life in a lifeform. The individual self and soul have been regarded in spiritual circles as the offshoots of the universal Self and Soul.

Henceforth, the terms *self* and *soul* will be used independently, depending upon the particular context in question. We will use the *self* when referring to our being that leads and oversees our life (ideally our highest or essential self) and the *soul* as that which animates us, enjoys and suffers through our life experiences. I regard self to be my *masculine* aspect—mind and reason—and soul my *feminine* aspect, the heart. This locality, like gender association, is really not necessary, as both of them act in tandem. We can think of the self and soul as an awareness of oneself that resides in the head and in the heart. The self is action oriented, whereas the soul experiences life as it unfolds. We will return to discuss these "properties" of life later.

Physically, the proto-life (a molecular structure) had the potential to become alive. We have characterized it as having dormant consciousness similar to that of a seed. This first stage was a necessary step preceding the awakening to life. Life cannot start before the conditions for its start (both internal and external) exist and the full physiological *action potential* to start is reached. Stated as a rule, nothing in nature can happen before it *can* happen. We will later mention the relation of this statement to the teachings of the Tao.

At this point, it is helpful for the reader to recall the episode of starting the heart described in the poem *Flame and Friendship*. At the beginning, the "sleeping" heart was conscious of its existence but not yet alive. We recall that the embryo's consciousness connected with the mother's heart and "saw" it as a radiant source of life's vital energy. The embryo's sleeping heart (a lifeform with its dormant consciousness) was thus exposed to stimulation by the energy of the mother's heart. Similarly, the proto-life with its dormant consciousness was stimulated by the energy of the sun. Both the proto-life and the embryo's heart had to reach the full (action) potential to become alive, signified by active *waking* consciousness. For a while, the sleeping heart had to grow some more to reach the required potential to create the spark of proper strength. We know from experience that every important step in our life requires a state of preparedness and readiness.

The sun kept shining and "inviting" the proto-life to become alive. So one solar day, a proto-life succeeded in raising its potential to a full (action) level, absorbed a quantum of the sun's energy (analogous to the electric impulse to the heart) and awakened to life—the heartbeat. Its self became conscious of the light (energy of the sun) within. The first lifeform was born. Sunlight became its life energy, and the awareness of life energy (light) its consciousness.

The thirteenth-century Persian poet Rumi describes in one of his poems a traveller whom he "saw" between daybreak and awakening as the "light of consciousness." Rumi is right: the best time to be aware of waking consciousness is the time when we wake up in the morning.

We may be interested to know where the awareness of consciousness (sun's energy) was located within the first newly born lifeform. Most probably, its locus was at the physical centre of its body. This locus eventually became the heart and consciousness the light of its spark that makes the heart beat.

During its sleep-like state, the dormant lifeform hears a voice: "You can wake up from your sleep and be like me, have life." Following the inspiring invitation ("a wake-up call"), the dormant form raises its potential (prayed?), absorbs a quantum of light (from the sun) and becomes alive, with a soul contained in the light. This first soul knows nothing more than *I am.* Its first identity is *I am alive and live here.*

In the beginning, the life entity was probably short-lived; later on, more durable and longer living.

The evolution of life moves in small steps, more or less continuously, each step resulting in a new lifeform, more or less different from the last.

There is a continuity and contiguity between all the stages of evolution. Although we may think of each living form as a separate entity, the same life energy unites them all. We can say, generally, that life is independent of form.

As a river has a continuous flow, it too may alter its path and volume but remain a whole.

Initially, the tendency of each lifeform was—and still is today—to keep the evolutionary stage it has reached. This leads to species preservation by reproduction. However, the goal of preserving the status quo is not possible in the long run because of the changing environment. So the evolution, which is both a biological as well as a creative process, has to go on.

It is not only the changing environment that influences change. Life itself constantly seeks better adaptation to the given conditions by using its intelligence together with other faculties, primarily consciousness and creative spirit. It strives for its betterment, which supports the idea of the creative aspect of evolution, discussed next.

Thou...my life hast lighted...
light, steady, ineffable, vouchsafed
Beyond all signs, descriptions, languages...
With a ray...

—*Walt Whitman, Prayer of Columbus*

3

Role of Consciousness and Creative Spirit in Evolution

It seems appropriate at this time to propose a theory of evolution that unites the elements of the classical theories of Lamarck and Darwin, the science of genetics and the role of subtle faculties, such as the mind, consciousness and creative spirit.

Life on earth moves within a changing environment. Organisms use their consciousness, intelligence and creative ability to adapt to changes to maintain and better their lives by making adjustments to the current design encoded in their DNA.

Having in mind primarily human beings, we could imagine such a process to work in the following manner: Using its consciousness, a human organism has the ability to "view" its DNA and impart an intended change (adjustment) to its current structure, if it deems that beneficial to its life. All it has to do is to be conscious while it carries out life's daily tasks. By using its intelligence, the organism can visualize a new "improved" way of being and doing. By trial and error, it can find a way to better its performance. If this calls for a change to its makeup, the organism can use its creative spirit to make these changes permanent in its DNA.

At a young age, the organism has the strongest flow of life energy and a correspondingly high level of consciousness. This heightened awareness and desire to express life as well as it can provides an individual with the best opportunity to make changes to its "design." A change may be related to its physical makeup or an adjustment to other functions and faculties. By focussing its consciousness (energy) on the image of its intent (a mental process) and with the awareness of the DNA and its structure, its intention is encoded in the genetic memory. I am unable to describe the physical process behind the conscious recognition of DNA. Intuitively, it may have to do with energy "resonance" between the two, which will be discussed later.

The best choice for making a permanent genetic change would be in the reproductive cells. The egg cells were formed at the beginning of the life of the female, so the choice would be the sperm cells that are "freshly" created. This would make sense from the point of view that, among humans, it is the male that would be the one to initiate a change in survival strategy because of the nature of his work and male principle. It also makes sense that huge numbers of sperms are created. This ensures that a small number of the most "capable" will be able to receive and pass on the instruction of genetic adjustment (change in the DNA). These energized "messenger" sperms will have the greatest chance to reach the egg during conception.

We can look at the DNA as a blueprint pertaining primarily to the physical design of an organism. Because it has evolved over eons, we can also regard it as the evolutionary memory of the form. Since consciousness creates memory, it is also able to awaken it. When we realize that, at some point in the distant past, the DNA or its precursor had to have had an origin, it seems reasonable to assume that it must have been in some way either created or followed an *a priori* design. The creative view of evolution allows for this possibility. This view also indicates that the human organism, because of its higher intelligence, creative spirit and, probably, strongest consciousness, possesses a faculty for the fastest evolutionary changes among the organisms of similar complexity.

The Darwinian postulate of natural selection is nature's way of confirming whether the organism's change to its design has proven beneficial. If the organism's choice did not appear beneficial to its life under the new set of conditions, a corrective change will naturally follow. Thus, the driving mechanism behind evolution is the change of the environment and an effort by the organism to adapt and better itself using its intelligent mind, consciousness and creative spirit.

Since the human creative spirit can be seen in all walks of life, it stands to reason that it would also be used by the organism in its most important ambition, which is to maintain and better its life.

There is a widespread belief that we go through all the evolutionary steps or stages leading to *homo sapiens* during our prenatal life. This makes sense, since all of us started from a cell, although it would be a formidable task to recall all the past states of consciousness along the evolutionary path.

4

All Lifeforms Are Conscious of Being Alive

The elementary lifeform became conscious of the sun's light within itself. The first identity that its conscious self assumed was: "I am the light (of the sun)." The first "living sun" was born. All living forms that derive their energy from the sun and use it for survival and growth also radiate the consciousness (energy) of the sun. This prompts a question: "If the sun gave life to a form on the earth, is the sun alive?" We will keep examining the evidence.

The Persian poet Hafez (1320–1389) believed that the sun conceived man to give birth to itself as reality and truth.

When the lifeform became an absorber and manager of the sun's energy and conscious of it within itself, its dormant awareness *I exist* was elevated to a new identity of *I am alive, I am life* or, simply, *I am.*

Let us look more closely at what we mean by *I am.* This initial and basic consciousness (light perceived as the awareness of life energy) is our connection with all life. The consciousness *I am* is pure consciousness without identity.

The consequence of this universal truth is that—through *I am*—we have, theoretically, a conscious access to every expression of life on Earth, past or present. This amounts to having a potential to know everything about life apart from form. However, it is not easy to be consciously aware of being only light—*I am.*

Ever since the beginning of life on Earth, this sun-provided, life-awakening and sustaining energy remains the essential property of every living form. Every living form, therefore, must possess the consciousness of being alive, in other words, "know" that it has life energy. The consciousness of being alive has been passed from lifeform to lifeform through countless generations of evolution. It is the inherent property of all living forms.

René Descartes' well-known statement, "I think, therefore I am [*Cogito, ergo sum*]" will be replaced in our theory by "I am conscious, therefore I am [*Conscius sum, ergo sum*]."

Examining Descartes' statement more closely, we find it describes only one of the possible states of being. During thinking, consciousness is with our thoughts by its definition as the awareness of energy (thoughts consume energy). Therefore, while thinking, *we are* indeed. Descartes is right. However, thinking is only one of innumerable conscious states of being. Others include, for example: I am in pain, I am running, I love you, and so on are other states of being. What is common to all of our states of being is consciousness. Descartes' idea is only one of the states of being.

To be fair to Descartes, thinking is our dominant state, especially in current times, generally referred to as the work of the mind. The human mind has its origin in the need to survive although survival today may far exceed the basic requirements of food and shelter. Mind plays a very important role in our life. Its frequent use is responding to the call of the heart to examine the properties of an object in which the heart became interested. However, its most common activity is analyzing, evaluating, comparing and uncovering relationships among the bits of information laid down as memory in the brain and body, which enables our highest self to make decisions and find solutions in directing life.

Once the mind became aware of being energy, the elementary life set out on an evolutionary journey to find a way to store and manage it. Eventually, it succeeded in becoming a biological engine running on solar energy. That is what all living forms on Earth are.

During the process of evolution toward more complex organisms, the sun's energy has undergone a variety of transformations and transfers. The various forms of life on Earth obtain and use solar energy in many different ways for their survival. For us, the most important fact to remember is that life energy comes from the one original source—the sun and, in a negligible amount, the rest of the universe and the earth itself. It is the energy of which all living forms are conscious as the *inner light*. We started our life as light beings. Consciousness can thus be linked with the state of enlightenment.

The sun, as the creator and sustainer of life on Earth, keeps on giving and asks nothing in return. It "delights" in the light it gives. It would follow that, if the sun is the source of life, it must itself be life. Among the living organisms, the plants are the closest to the original sun-sustained lifeforms. They absorb sun's energy directly and they show it to us. Let us recall a passage from the poem *Life Force*: **fields of daisies quiver, bloom into light, reach for the sun, effuse life.**

Light is also our link with the universe. People who have experienced a close encounter with death often speak about "seeing" or moving toward light.

Since the sun is the creator and sustainer of life on Earth, it is also a healer of any ailment or sickness caused by a lack of its energy in our body. We have said that, through evolution, the energy of the sun has been transformed many times, and numerous times transferred before it could be available to the various parts and organs in our body. Obviously, the shortest and healthiest way for our body to obtain the sun's energy is by eating fresh plants. Plants offer themselves and wish to become part of us. Animals run away from us; they do not want to become part of another animal form.

Availability of plant life enabled the appearance and evolution of the herbivorous animals, and their matter, in turn, the omnivorous and carnivorous kind.

> When, on a bright clear morning,
> as you take the first step
> toward the task of the day,
> your soul lights up:
> thank the Source
> for the light of life
> —*consciousness.*

Some plants or herbs are known to help an ailing organ by making it more receptive to life-sustaining energy. We can say that for every ailment there is a *healing ray* and a *healing substance.* While we as humans cannot use the incident sun energy directly as plants do, sun exposure still has a beneficial effect on our health both physically and psychologically. It reminds us of the inner light, our consciousness. We all feel better on a sunny day. The saying "On a clear day you can see forever" speaks of the connection between sunlight and consciousness.

The sun can be a healer but, used in excess, also a hazard to health. It is up to us to find a healthy relationship with the sun and its tolerance level by "listening" to our body.

4.1
Sun and Earth – A Love Story

In the beginning of the creation of our solar family, there was a cloud of stardust, something like a cloud of water vapor in the sky. Through a sudden impact of energy, the cloud started to condense, dust and gas particles joining, squeezing, building pressure, spinning, gathering energy and heat until they began to glow. Sun was born.

None of the other parts of the cloud made it to become a glowing sun. One of them, a smaller one, gave rise to the planet Earth. The particles of that small part also compressed and heated up but did not have enough matter and energy to develop a nuclear glow like Sun and cooled off.

Sun and Earth are both aware of each other. They were parts of the same cloud. They lived within each other. This special kind of bond has endured, and even though they appear to be separate now, they maintain their union by orbit.

All living forms owe their existence to the loving bond between Sun and Earth. Sun supplies the energy, and Earth the material substance. Thus, all lifeforms have light and matter bodies. Being the progeny of Sun and Earth, living forms are also children of the universe.

Note: Although we refer to Earth as the source of material substance, based on scientific evidence, we will keep in mind that it is, physically, encapsulated light.

4.2
Role of the Sun

There was a time in our early life when we became aware of the sun for the first time. If this first meeting happened when we were alone and of open mind and heart, we might have had an opportunity to feel the sun's essence and learn about it in our life. Try to recall that meeting. This author recalls his first meeting with the sun as a few-weeks-old infant.

The sun has been recognized, celebrated and worshiped by many cultures throughout history. Sun mythology dates to the time of the earliest civilizations. It played a prominent role in the old Egyptian, Mayan and other civilizations. The nations that had one of the closest relationships with the sun were the Aztecs and Incas.

The Aztecs lived in constant close contact with their sun god. They engaged in human sacrifices to maintain it. They realized correctly that their beating hearts received the energy from the sun, and were known to hold the freshly extracted hearts of the sacrificial humans for the sun god to "see." Unfortunately, their practice of human sacrifices was motivated probably by fear of losing the sun as it disappeared every night in the sky.

The Incas had a wider view of the sun as a living being. They considered themselves to be its children. To get closer to their "father," they built temples in high places to celebrate their oneness with their sun god Inti.

In our current civilization, we seem to take the sun for granted, not recognizing the light and life energy that it provides. We consider it to be an inanimate object in the cosmos. What we ignore becomes part of our ignorance. Since we owe our life and consciousness to the sun, it is difficult to think of the sun as not being alive. Have we alienated ourselves so much from nature that we do not recognize truth and reality anymore?

5

Nature of Consciousness

In this chapter, we will discuss the nature and role of consciousness, present its empirical evidence based on prenatal life, discuss its quantum nature, its role in building and using our brain, and the formation of its memory.

5.1
Aware and Unaware Consciousness

We have put forward a theory in chapter 2 that life consciousness is light (electro-magnetic radiation) as well as the awareness of this light in all its energy transformed states. It all began when a proto-life absorbed and retained a quantum of sunlight and became conscious of it and alive. Light became the first lifeform's life energy and the awareness of that energy its consciousness. It makes sense that, when we accept something and make it part of us, we would have to be aware of it. Otherwise, our self would reject and eliminate it. Further, since light became the source of life's energy, the lifeform had to find a way to manage it.

It may help in the understanding of consciousness to know how consciousness, as the awareness of life energy, functions in our life. For example, suppose that we are walking to work in the morning. Every step we take requires energy. Our consciousness, as the awareness of energy, would thus, ideally, follow every step of the way. If we are aware only of the energy (light) of walking and nothing else (movement of legs, thoughts, etc.)— not easy to do—we might have a feeling that our energy (light) is shining on the way as a flashlight in the dark. This may be difficult to experience in adult life but is relatively easy in childhood. Therefore, we may remember it as a childhood memory.

The consciousness that we experience, in the above example, is the *aware* consciousness. If, on the other hand, we do not experience the energy of walking, consciousness will still be there—in the physical performance of walking—as the *unaware* consciousness, while the *aware* consciousness might be busy with some other energy-consuming process, such as thinking. The strength of our energy would determine the strength of our consciousness and, consequently, its memory. This author had such an experience in childhood.

We must also be clear about what or who is *aware* (the subject of awareness). It was then (at the beginning) and still is now the self and soul of the lifeform. Its awareness of light energy was the first and fundamental consciousness of life. It follows that life consciousness is an inherent property of life. All life is aware of being alive.

We will use the term *consciousness* to mean the *aware* consciousness that is part of the awake self and soul. Later, we will have a need to distinguish between the *aware* (self-aware) and *unaware* (self-unaware) consciousness.

5.2 Universal Connection Using Consciousness

Science tells us that light (electromagnetic radiation) is a universal force. So is, therefore, our consciousness. Consciousness thus establishes a connection between life on the earth and everywhere in the universe. Consciousness is omnipresent. Can we say that the universe is also conscious? By our definition, the universe is conscious because of the ever-present, electro-magnetic force, but its consciousness would be the unaware kind unless it had a self. In that case—like a lifeform on earth—the universe would also be self-aware and have *aware* consciousness.

Some people, especially those spiritually awakened, would subscribe to the idea of the self-aware universe. Otherwise, where does our *self* come from? If the universe were not aware of being alive, its consciousness would be latent and un-manifested. My personal position is that the universe is alive and self-aware.

Being children of the universe should make us feel at home with the vast unknown.

> Smelling the rose
> I learn the only truth:
> when life becomes light,
> everything is lost
> and nothing ever ends.
> —*anonyma*

5·3
Empirical Evidence of Consciousness

To gather empirical evidence about life consciousness, we need to look at times and in places when we had a pure experience of life, as it naturally unfolded. Such periods of pure, primal experiences of life are rare in adult life. They are frequent in childhood and commonplace in prenatal life. The following examples illustrate the activity of life consciousness in the prenatal child. The selected examples and passages from the *Poem* that illustrate consciousness are restated here for convenience.

Example 1. Touching Stars

Recalling the poem *Touching Stars*, the embryo, after implanting, burrows a hole into the uterus, which connects it with a tunnel (umbilical cord) and sets out to explore it. Eventually, it finds a chamber

> **where glistening particles swim in the dark like stars at night...*
> *I lure them back with me. Now inside me, I touch one,*
> *it fills me with light. I touch another and another*
> *and resonate with light which*

leads me far into the universe,
stars I came from...
I am delighted to be with them again!

Alas, a star fades, loses the light it gave me
Another grows dim. All shed their light they gave me.
*My space darkens, I need more stars to keep alive**

Interpretation: In this poem, the embryo, traveling through the umbilical cord, discovers glistening particles. Its consciousness, responding to their energy charge, "sees" them as "lit up." The self of the embryo, which carries universal memory, recognizes that their light comes from the stars (in our case the sun). It finds also that it needs this energy to keep alive. This confirms consciousness as the awareness of energy that comes from the sun (a star) and is needed to sustain life. It also confirms the statement put forward in chapter 4 that we are indeed living *suns.*

Example 2. The First Heartbeat

In this example, we will examine the nature and role of consciousness in starting the heart action described in the poem *Flame and Friendship.*

**Above me a source beams light toward me*
It wants to say, "You can be like me."
I hesitate... now ready, I gather all my strength,
flame engulfs me, I leap... join the radiant friend
spark-jump, spark-jump in rhythmic harmony.
*Now I hold my own flame**

The above experience by the embryo of starting its heart resembles the story put forward about the evolution of life from the dormant existence *I exist* to an active life existence *I am alive.*

As the proto-life was stimulated by the sun, the sleeping heart was stimulated by the energy of its mother's heart. Both the proto-life and the sleeping heart had to reach the required full (action) potential to absorb the appropriate quantum of energy to become alive.

The heart holds a unique position among the body's organs. It generates its own electrical spark (sun's energy) and thus acts independently, unlike other organs that receive energy via the nervous system. Sun energy is the life energy, consciousness the awareness of the life energy, and heart the acting force in the body. Together they form the basic dynamic physical system.

***Example* 3.** Light and Eyes

In a paper submitted at the ISPPM Congress (1992) on the theory of 3D vision, I described the importance of the role of consciousness in stimulating and maintaining the connection between the two eyes during their prenatal development. Below is an excerpt from my prenatal memory of that event (rearranged) from the poem *Light.*

> **In my head I have found a place that lights up when I visit it.*
> *The feeling delights me. I linger, enjoying its brilliance...*
> *Now there are two places, a short distance apart, that light up*
> *to greet me...*
> *I know (that) light and open space await me outside*
> *Everything (there) glows with bright light**

The most important finding is the unborn child's discovery of, first one, later two places in the head that lit-up when visited by its consciousness. Since these tissues (places) become the retinas of the eyes, which are sensitive to light, we can draw the conclusion that consciousness is light (energy).

***Example* 4.** Tree, Earth and I

In this poem, the unborn child describes its friendship and communication with the placenta (tree of life). It *sees* (is conscious of) it *lit-up.*

> **Above me a luminous tree... alight with life...*
> *shares everything with me.*
> *When I wake up to start a new day, the tree*
> *lighting up, greets me with joy...*
> *The tree at my side, I command my life,*
> *send Mati my love**

The preborn describes its close friendship with the tree of life that brings it nutrients charged with life-sustaining energy of light. It is aware of the energy-charged particles of food and *sees* them and the whole tree as being "lit up".

Example 5. Attacks in Anger

In this example, the prenatal child tells about its experience of its mother's anger, which causes "angry" chemistry in its body and a need to fight it.

> **The attackers alight, linked in chains,*
> *pulsate forward and stream toward me...*
> *I begin to shake, my body is on fire,*
> *enraged**

The attackers were probably molecules of hormones, such as adrenalin, released into the blood of its angry mother, and through her into the body of the fetus that saw them blazing with high level of energy, causing its body to shake violently. The fetus had to defeat and neutralize them with its own chemistry.

The five examples above illustrate our hypothesis that the physical nature of consciousness is light and the awareness of life energy. However, there are scores of other examples described in the *Poem* in which the experience of light and energy is not explicit or apparent. We will address that in example 6.

We stated that the initial awareness of the energy of the sun is the basic consciousness defined by *I am,* and that the myriads of states of consciousness and identities that a living form has experienced throughout evolution were derived from it. Life is a process in which the self, imbued with intelligence and creative spirit, and endowed with consciousness, leads the unfolding growth and evolution of the organism. Since growth of the organism requires energy, the conscious self with its awareness of energy has been present at every step in the evolutionary process. The following example illustrates that point.

Example 6. Egg Finds Purpose of its Journey

In this episode from the author's prenatal life that describes the ovulation and conception (refer to the poem *The First Journey*), the egg wants to know from where the *call* comes that urges it to keep moving. It looks at its centre and discerns a design: **a white, sacred human form. I understand the sign and the purpose of my journey. It is: to deliver the sacred form on time **

The self of the egg followed its inner call to keep moving and discovered its DNA. It saw it as a sacred human form and found in it the purpose of its journey. Our explanation would be that the egg's consciousness contacted and interacted with the energy of the DNA. The self with its consciousness was present during the formation of the DNA, an energy-requiring process, and all of its subsequent evolutionary stages. Therefore, the egg's conscious self was able to recognize what the DNA represented.

To recognize something, we have had to become conscious of it in a prior time. This indicates that consciousness leaves memory. It is the memory of the organism's experience of life as a flow and action of energy. It is stored in the cells and their molecular structures. An example of a molecular structure that stores memory is the DNA.

Consciousness works in the same way in the prenatal as in the apparent world of the postnatal life. Therefore, we could say that the egg simply recalled its past state of consciousness. This raises a few questions: how does consciousness establish contact with the DNA molecule? How does it recognize what the DNA represents? Why is it a **sacred human form**? The author is not qualified to answer these questions scientifically but can offer intuitive ideas.

The DNA molecule, a part of a living cell, carries an electric charge. Consciousness is light (energy). Through its interaction with the DNA, the energy level of the DNA was raised until it began to "resonate" with the past state of consciousness of the DNA of the egg's self. The resonance enabled the self to recall this past state of consciousness. It "rang a bell" of recognition, similar to two friends meeting after a period of separation. We may recall the resonance with stars felt by the embryo when it contacted the first energy particles described in example 1.

5.4
Consciousness and Quantum Experience of Light

We described the origin of consciousness as the awareness of absorbed sunlight, the energy that made a proto-life alive—quantum leap at the beginning of life on Earth. It established consciousness as life's first and basic experience. We have learned also that it was light (electrical spark of required strength) to the heart that made it spring to action. Could we say that the signal to the heart is the consciousness of the heart? The Aztecs thought so by conducting human sacrifices and offering the extracted hearts to their sun god. We would say that the spark that activates the heart is the energy derived from sunlight. We can be even bolder and suggest that consciousness is present at the beginning of every energy-requiring life action ever since that time. Thus, we could conclude that consciousness is the root of life.

Although we may not be able to supply a scientific proof of how the sun's energy that gave rise to our consciousness became the electrical spark to the heart, we can see a similarity between the two of them. In each case, they changed something that was not alive into something alive. The apparent difference between sunlight and the spark that moves our heart is the result of a long evolutionary chain of events of energy transfer and transformation. We can, therefore, view the electrical signal to the heart as transduced (transformed) sunlight. We talk about the "sunny disposition" of someone who shows vitality and energy of the heart combined with joie de vivre.

An Associated Press article (8.5.2016) tells the story of two Pakistani brothers (aged 9 and 13) known as *solar kids*. They are normal, active children during the day but lapse into a vegetative-like state after sunset, unable to move or talk. Doctors have conducted extensive research to identify the cause of their strange behavior without success. Their father says: "My sons get energy from the sun." He is right.

Our interpretation would link the boys' behavior to a very early evolutionary life stage, in which the lifeform relied on the presence of the sun during the daytime for its energy and waking consciousness, and went into a state of dormancy after sunset. The reawakening of such a deep historical life state of consciousness could have been aided by their current parents being first cousins. In such a case, the boys' common evolutionary path would be reinforced.

The quantum theory in physics has demonstrated the dual nature of light as *wave* and *particle*. According to our theory, consciousness is energy (originally sunlight) and the awareness of energy, therefore, a quantum thing. Since energy is part of our living body, we must be aware of it and be able to manage it. This is not a common view among consciousness researchers. Some of them put it aside as either a hard problem or ignore it as unimportant.

What then is this feeling of energy of which we are aware and call consciousness? We know that we can direct consciousness to an ailing organ within our body and give it energy and become aware of it. Consciousness, therefore, acts as an agent of maintaining and balancing body's energy. There is an expression: "If something is ailing, surround it with light." This sensation of light can be felt as a glow of light. If the sun is shining, we can direct the light of the sun to the problem area internally. Another way to bring healing energy to our body, especially in springtime, is to take a walk outdoors along the edge of a forest on a sunny day—my experience. A forest is a large assembly of lifeforms that together generate powerful life energy.

Since we are unable to observe and measure consciousness—we can only be aware of it and feel it—calling consciousness a quantum thing may seem problematic. At the beginning of life on Earth, when consciousness arose with the awareness of sunlight energy, we could have said confidently that the self-aware consciousness *was* a quantum thing. Since that ancient time, consciousness has evolved together with life until today we are aware of only some energy-requiring processes within our body. Its presence is not needed everywhere, since many processes are conducted by self-directing and autonomous systems, something like an automatic pilot. Today, consciousness accompanies mainly our thinking, communication and physical and creative work.

An example of the absence of aware consciousness, based on my own experience, was driving home from work without being aware how I did it when I arrived. Obviously, an "automatic pilot" inside me did the driving. I do not recommend this form of driving to a novice, especially in a big, crowded city, but I wonder whether this experience, which many others had also, led to the development of the self-driving car.

We have described consciousness as a faculty of the self that acts as a force directed by the self. In the movie *Star Wars*, it is referred to as *The Force*. As such, consciousness must have a physical nature. Electromagnetic radiation (light) is one of the four fundamental universal forces. It is omnipresent. Consciousness, as a derivative of sunlight must, therefore, also be omnipresent. Many believe that God, too, is everywhere. Are both God and consciousness light? It may not be so strange to think of the Creator as our inner light or that God communicates with us using light.

Since consciousness is the awareness of energy, its role in life cannot be overstated. We would have difficulty regarding consciousness as something that would be subject to uncertainty of a quantum thing. We regard it as something definite, the ultimate reality, the root of our experience as a creative process.

The answer to our question as to whether consciousness is a quantum thing must be yes! We can sense light and feel its wave aspect. We would call that (sensory) experience the unaware consciousness. When we collapse it and become aware of it, we see its particle aspect, photons, in our aware consciousness. Collapsing the wave function of light makes the unaware consciousness *self-aware* and becomes part of the self. The unaware consciousness and aware consciousness are the two complementary aspects of the quantum nature of light. Consciousness is indeed a quantum event.

Many philosophers view the *self* as an emergent property in the evolution of form. Here we are interested in knowing what the self is and how it came to be. Let us examine the process leading to its emergence. We need to begin at the time when we first experienced the feeling of self. The earliest experience of the self for me was at the beginning of life on Earth when an aggregate of organic molecules—a precursor to lifeform—reached a stage of being complete. We gave that biological form the name *proto-life*. In quantum theory, we would regard the growth of the molecular aggregate as the wave and the emergence of the self as the completed form, the particle. The collapse of the wave function was caused by the omnipresent consciousness. Does this mean that the omnipresent consciousness somehow *knew* when an evolving form became complete? We need further reflection. Every process of creation by consciousness, including that of the proto-life, is an inherent property of the evolution of life. Through the process of creation, the self is constantly redefined (reinforced) by the particle aspect of the life journeys we undertake during daily living. This also results in the split between the subject and object duality.

Let us pursue this topic further by asking: What does an observer bring to the experiment? The human brain and mind can be regarded as an apparatus to observe and perceive the behavior of a quantum thing such as light. The two aspects of a quantum thing, wave and particle, are contained in a ray of light that stimulates our brain. Our mind is not able, however, to perceive the two aspects of light simultaneously, since they are located in different parts of the brain. For example, we can experience the wave nature of light as a *vibration*, a feeling of *lightness*, in the right brain hemisphere and as an accumulation of particles of energy (photons) in the left. To perceive and analyze them, our mind needs to observe them separately.

The perception of the wave nature of light is part of our usual daytime experience, but the perception of its particle form (photon) requires darkness, night time or closed eyes. A way to experience the particle nature of light is as follows: With the eyes closed and imagining light, we may begin to see first a few large white spots in our mind's eye. These large spots will in time be replaced by many smaller white spots bunched together. Next, these will give way to a larger number of tiny white dots and so on, until the whole space is filled with almost an infinite number of very tiny white particles bunched together (photons), giving the impression of a continuous light space.

Our brain receives both complementary aspects of light (wave and particle) at the same time, but for us to be aware of them, we need to observe them one at a time. The aware consciousness cannot perceive both aspects of light at the same time. Could we say that the dual nature of light is a *mind construct based on separate awareness of its wave and particle aspect?*

One of the tenets of quantum theory is nonlocality, characterized by two correlated quantum things always behaving the same way, even if they are so far apart that their behavior cannot be attributed to the same force acting upon them. Classical physics cannot explain such a behavior without postulating the influence of some *local (hidden) variables.* Einstein with some of his colleagues tried unsuccessfully to prove that quantum theory was inconsistent in its claim of nonlocality.

I agree with Einstein in his insistence on locally present influences that affect the behavior of a quantum thing. I suggest that the force acting on the correlated quantum partner is the omnipresent consciousness. This calls for further exploration.

Our basic consciousness *I am* (life energy awareness without identity) is by our definition omnipresent, at least in the realm of the living. Therefore, changing a property of one of the quantum things of a correlated pair causes its correlated partner to change the same way because of the influence of the omnipresent consciousness *I am* of the two observers.

The best way to experience life energy as consciousness is to become aware of it as we wake up in the morning—when consciousness awakens from sleep. Another way to experience consciousness is as the awareness of the light (spark) of the heart. The light intensity of the spark is governed by our vitality and sunny disposition. The sun plays such a strong role in our lives that we form a permanent image of it in the frontal cortex between the eyes. We can turn to this image on cloudy days. In winter, the light image will dim and disappear, only to reappear and be renewed in the spring. I believe that this image gives rise to our consciousness, referred to as the third eye.

Within our body, the sun energy that we receive in food is many times transduced (transformed) into different forms of energy. In Latin, the word 'transducere' means to lead across or pass. The light of the sun *passed* through the proto-life to make it alive. It was led further through evolution to the heart, to make it also alive. However, we would say, more commonly, that sunlight was transformed into an electrical signal that caused the heart to start beating, in a similar way as a light bulb lights up or a muscle moves as a response to electrical current conducted to it.

Summary: While there is still ground left unturned to form a clear view of the nuances of consciousness that accompanies the myriads of energy-driven processes in our body—most of them hidden from our aware perception—we can rest assured that we were originally consciously aware of them, before they were placed under a self-regulating system (e.g. feedback mechanism) and became part of the unconscious realm. It is, therefore, theoretically possible to awaken those states of aware consciousness with the knowledge we gained from them.

5.5 Directing Consciousness

Consciousness is a faculty of the essential or highest self and is directed by it. However, it may happen that, at times, consciousness will fall under the will of a *lesser* self, such as the ego or an emotional state induced by the mind, even a deceptive form of illusion and fantasy. Living in unhealthy circumstances and with many forms of dependencies, including addictions (even the "innocent" kind), is often the cause of swaying our consciousness into situations that inhibit the flow of spirit. Addictive tendencies remain one of life's biggest problems. They are a problem when they become substitutes for an unresolved trauma or other forms of separation of our true self/soul from the force that propels our life. In many of those cases, consciousness is trapped by the mind, which may not always serve our best interest. Through a watchful eye and focus on our essential self, we can take it out of troubled waters. This is achieved by relocation (shift) or transformation of consciousness. Thus, for a healthy life, consciousness must be directed by the essential or highest self.

An intuitive thought about life design

The Creator designs and directs life using the light of consciousness. If we accept consciousness as (1) light (physically) and (2) the awareness of light (psychically), and understand light (electromagnetic radiation) as a universal force, it is not difficult—given light's countless ways of interacting—to consider consciousness (light) in the hands of the Creator as the tool of creation.

It is important to mention the requirement that consciousness and intelligence need a certain dwell time to make sense of what we put our attention to. If we do not allow this dwell time, for example, by flashing images of a message on a TV screen in a too-rapid sequence, our perception is unable to handle it. The result is often just a blur or meaningless noise. Noise clogs up the brain just as cholesterol plaque clogs up the arteries, or sticky matter our kitchen sink drain, or weeds inhibit the flow of water in a small creek.

The necessary dwell time is particularly important for older people and others whose perception may be slower than that of the makers of the commercial. Even the young, whose perception works at a high level, do not fully benefit from a rapid presentation of events. Unable to make full sense of the collage, perception becomes, at best, shallow. We become surface feeders. As the saying goes: One may dig many shallow wells and not find water or one deep well and find it. There is yet another possible harm to the mind: The mind may become dispersive, unable to focus properly as time goes on. We can all imagine what that does to our ability to learn.

5.6 Consciousness and Memory

Consciousness leaves a memory track. Memory is laid down as we go through the experiences of life. Because consciousness is part of the essential self and soul, so is memory. To recall an experience, we follow its memory track in the brain and body cells as described by the prenatal child in the poem *Order of Life.* Since we cannot experience something without having been conscious of it in a prior time, we link consciousness with conscious memory. Awakening the memory of an object or event requires illuminating it by the energy of consciousness.

In addition to a brain memory, organisms also possess cell memory. This memory, laid down in the cells, is generated mainly by physical growth. In simple organisms, there is only one kind of memory, the cell memory, the same as at the beginning of life. The mechanism of cell memory is not well known although we are certain that it exists. An example of laying down a cell memory is portrayed in connection with the first cell division described in *The First Journey*: **Now there are two rooms* [*cells*] *in my house, the closer one and a new one...* [*where*] *I will store my new life experience.**

Since consciousness had been with us from the beginning of life, our memory also reaches to that time. With the development of the brain, we have acquired a powerful tool for storing memory, but even before that, our consciousness left memory tracks in the cells.

We are all familiar with a loss of memory with advancing age. It is my belief that the main contributing factor of this commonly experienced condition is weakening of consciousness which is a result of weakening of physical energy, concentration and focus. We know from experience that strong consciousness results in strong memory. Our brain has a much greater capacity for memory storage than we ever use. Thus, the main reason for the weak, "geriatric" memory is weakening concentration and focus, accompanied by weakening energy and consciousness. To strengthen memory, we can strengthen focus and concentration. Physically, this requires more energy, which in turn increases consciousness.

Some people have experienced a sudden loss of memory brought on by a brain injury. They can recover some of the memory of their life experiences deposited in the cells. Cell memory is holistic, not as detailed and logical and easily retrieved as the brain memory, but it is always authentic.

Memory could be actual and short-lived, long-lived or archival, or permanent when encoded in the DNA. Strictly speaking, even the DNA memory is not permanent as it is subject to creative and biological changes. It is deemed permanent only at the time of reproduction.

5.7
Different Way of Viewing Memory

There is another way of looking at the process by which the human organism handles its life's experiential content. This model is based on the concept of regions (in the brain, body and outside of it) that psychics call bodies, such as physical, emotional, mental, light and spiritual bodies, to mention a few. These bodies, other than the physical one, are invisible. They can be thought of as layers or regions within the brain and body, even outside the physical body. They grow along with the physical body and change their shapes and content. They are generated and are *accessible only by consciousness*, and are present in their totality at all times.

We nourish these bodies in the same way we feed our physical body as we go through experiencing life. If our experience is physical, such as eating, we are feeding and maintaining growth of our physical body. Some of the food is retained, the rest eliminated. When we are using our mind, we are feeding and promoting mainly the growth of our mental body. Some thoughts are kept, some eliminated at the end of each thought journey. Similarly, when we are experiencing an emotion, we are feeding our emotional (astral) body; the light body is generated by our energy and the light of consciousness. We can compare it to the gravitational force of a body acting on the water in a river.

These bodies (layers) are interconnected. They change and grow by adding new information and also by atrophy of parts that are no longer useful, a result of inattention and ignoring. Their important feature is that all of their contents are accessible each moment by consciousness. We live in them all the time. This implies that we can live only in the present—have no past and future (a state of divine existence?).

The foregoing way of looking at the nature and structure of human experience carries a great deal of intuitive truth. The feature that is most appealing is that the whole life plays out constantly in the now—the most desired state. There is no past weighing us down, no future, just the present. We are one organism, one coherent whole. The key role in it is played by consciousness directed by the essential or highest self and soul.

6
Origin of the Unconscious

During its early stages, the consciousness of the fetus was present at every step of its development. However, as the fetus became biologically more complex, its consciousness was unable to be part of all its energy-consuming growth. Thus a lot of its growth, physiological processes and functions were put under the control of self-regulatory, autonomous systems and run automatically without the assistance of conscious awareness. Although consciousness in these cases is not actively present, the unconscious growth still contains it in a form as *unaware consciousness* discussed chapter 5.1.

We can describe the unconscious growth as containing unconscious or dark energy and unconscious or dark matter. One of the functions of the unconscious growth is to hold our body together, but it does more than that. It contains life information, which becomes part of the unconscious, a large realm of our psyche. This life knowledge can still be reached by our basic life consciousness *I am*. This is the *modus operandi* of the fetus, which the adult may not access as readily. They can do so, for example, during sleep and dreams, certain states of coma, a state of deep meditation accompanied by empty mind, or through intuition and instinct.

It may be interesting to note that the dark (vacuum) energy and dark matter are considered to be the major sources of available energy in the universe, as is the case in the body. This does not suggest a correspondence between it and the human unconscious although the similarity is very tempting.

7

Role of Consciousness in Prenatal Life

A prenatal child lacks an active sensory apparatus. It has no need for one. Consciousness is its principal faculty in experiencing life. It acts like the *third eye* in a metaphysical sense. Although it does not have awakened senses, the unborn child has their prescriptions in its DNA, which it can access with its basic consciousness *I am*. Later, it also has at its disposal the developing sensory organs. A few examples in the *Poem* indicate that it might be able to use its consciousness together with its intelligence as a cognitive tool in understanding and interpreting its genetic code.

Our conscious life as we know it begins, according to the *Poem*, at ovulation when the egg becomes aware of itself as an energized entity and drops into the **world below**. Before that, the egg has existed as a part of the mother's body in a dormant, waiting state of consciousness, similar to the proto-life or a seed before germination.

In the early stages of its development, the unborn relies on its cellular consciousness and memory. Its consciousness plays a crucial role, especially around the time of conception. At that time, the incipient fetus has the basic consciousness *I am*. This basic consciousness enables it to open freely to other energized bodies. We have seen many examples of it in the *Poem*. The most fascinating is the ovulating egg's ability to *see* its DNA as a *sacred human form*, discussed in example 6, chapter 5.3. Due to the quantum nature of consciousness, the egg is able to collapse the wave function generated by the DNA and see the particle—the human form.

Consciousness of the prenatal child works on the same principle in other, less obvious cases than those mentioned above. It requires a finely tuned consciousness to "see" small particles of matter such as molecules or to detect fine elementary energies that we have come across in, for example, the poem *Hungry Birds*.

8

Maintaining Life's Wholeness

Many people feel lost in their lives. They do not know where they came from, where they are going and, as a result, may become afraid of the unknown. They do not know the purpose of their life. Yet we are told by spiritual teachers that all such knowledge lies within us. What has happened? We have forgotten that knowledge. It became a part of our subconscious. You may wonder: "How could we forget our life or a part of it?" The main reason behind forgetting is ignoring segments of our life by seeing them as unimportant.

Ignoring leads to ignorance. We all have forgotten a part or parts of our life journey, especially the early life, including the prenatal period and early childhood. Such statements as: "You cannot remember life before birth"; "I can only remember when I was three"; "A little child does not have a developed memory and knowledge of life" lead us to disregard the importance of early life and contribute to its dismissal as a valid and essential part of the whole.

Another example of ignorance is counting our age from the date of birth. Discounting the intrauterine life is the reason that we feel lost in adult life. This situation is similar to walking into a forest and forgetting the way we came in, then walking around, trying to find a way out, growing tense and afraid, often getting lost even more. If we do not remember where and how we entered our current life, if we do not pay enough attention to remember our journey, we are also at a loss to know where we are going. It is worth repeating: the *key* to memory is aware consciousness.

Generally, the early part of our life contains the basic way of life. By ignoring and forgetting it, we also find it difficult to see the direction or goal of our life. The forest can represent just about any situation in life in which we lose direction and become confused or at a loss as to what to do next.

It would appear that we all have sinned by not adhering conscientiously to the advice of maintaining wholeness. Forgetting small, unimportant life occurrences would not endanger it. Sometimes, however, it happens that we are forced to suppress the memory of an unbearable event or situation to safeguard our physical and mental health. This is a natural survival mechanism. Such actions create blocks and obstacles and require energy to keep them that way. They rob us of the energy that we require to maintain them whenever something in our current life reminds us of, or is similar to, the suppressed event. In time, when the trauma is forgotten, these blocks hold fear. Fear cripples our actions and imprisons our soul. There is no specific rule for dealing with suppressed traumas, except to remember that we created them, thus we know the way to bring them up into light and deal with them now, when we have more ability and tools at our disposal. By doing so, we find the truth and can restore wholeness.

Small discontinuities are not as serious as forgetting large parts of life. The process of memory renewal presents a great opportunity to get to know ourselves at a deeper level, thus restoring our life to its fuller expression.

A word of consolation: not all is lost in forgetting early life. Its memory exists in the subconscious realm and can be, with some effort, recalled. For those who do not want to do that—for whatever reason—they still can draw on some prenatal knowledge indirectly. This is possible through the connection between all events and life experiences and their organization. Experiences of a similar nature form natural links and bonds. It is one of the properties of integration and growth. Thus later events of a similar nature are linked to the earlier ones, and although an earlier event lies in the subconscious, it still influences the present to a degree through the tie between the conscious and subconscious realms. For example, we can consider conception and birth. It would be difficult to accept that they would not influence us throughout life.

9
Conception

Conception is not only the beginning of our current life; as a gate to prenatal life, it determines our gender and identity and, according to the poem *The First Journey*, our basic biological role in life. Furthermore, it leads us to understand the original forces at the beginning of not only our current life but also the start of life on the earth, all based on conscious experience of daily living.

9.1
The Role of Spirit

According to the *Poem*, our consciousness and memory of our current life extends at least to the life of the reproductive cells of our parents. Our current life as an independent and self-directed individual begins when the male and female sexual cells unite; their roles as cells are completed, while their individual identities disappear. The combination of the chromosomes from the two cells gives rise to the first self-determining cell (zygote) of a new human being. (See the poem *The First Journey* and its discussion in the part 2 of this book.) During the process, the cells' memories of their journeys and gender characteristics (spirits) are preserved. So are their individual cellular selves with the basic consciousness *I am*.

The egg surrendered its identity to the sperm first: **Consciousness leaves my body... I lose my identity** This was a very significant move by the egg. Embracing the sperm with its consciousness, the egg connected with its energy, surrendered its identity and emptied itself psychologically, thus creating a condition to receive the sperm.

The sperm then completed its journey by merging with the egg, its identity also dissolving in the process: **Dissolved, suspended in fog, my role met, who am I?**

The act of cell unification must be appreciated fully and, therefore, merits further explanation. We can recognize several steps. In the first step, the egg created the condition to receive the sperm and, in the second, the sperm *gave* itself to the egg. Thus, we could view the merging of the cells as an act of giving and receiving. The subtle truth of this process is stated as a principle of life in the Tao:

> If you want to give something,
> you must first allow it to be received.
>
> —*Chapter 36. Tao Te Ching*

The loss of identities of the sexual cells is commonly felt as their *death*. It represents an end of their life as reproductive cells, but it is not a physical death.

At this stage, the amorphous union of the two cells still contains two living entities, each possessing an identity-less self, the spirit of its respective gender and memories, laid down by consciousness, of their journeys as cells. We should keep in mind that consciousness, being light, is not divisible, and as energy and memory (energy vested in growth), it cannot vanish.

In the third step of conception, the cell union, as defined above, set out to seek its identity. It found it in an *archetype*.

The archetype features a pair of young people (in spirit form) who choose to live together. They decide that the male spirit will lead and incarnate (acquire body) and the female, complementary spirit, will accompany it as his inner spirit mate. The life's purpose of the incarnated male would be to share his life with his inner female spirit and to live for her.

The cell union thus established its identity. Where and how did a cell union find the archetype? It could have found it (1) in the subconscious realm of the parents or (2) in the transcendent realm of mankind's collective consciousness, which may be in the same place as the former.

The above explanation of the process of conception is rather analytical and may appear complex and too abstract in its attempt to describe the psychological nature of conception.

We used the word *spirit*. We need to elaborate on its meaning. The common usage of this word includes strength, heart, essence, vital force (chi) and soul. While none of them seems to be fully true by itself, taken as a whole, they come close to it. The proliferation of terms describing spirit and its meaning indicates the elusiveness of its definition. Most of the definitions refer to the manifestations of spirit within a human being rather than its origin and nature, in a similar way as symptoms are manifestations of an illness.

Can we narrow down the question about the nature of spirit? As has been our custom throughout this writing, we need to go to its origin, which requires starting at the beginning of the creative process that leads to the formation of a lifeform.

Starting in the realm of elementary existence, we can imagine elementary units of energy acting on particles of matter to create more complex forms. We could look at it as a random process. However, to be consistent, we will regard it as an indication of the existence of an à priori design. Since we consider the formation of a lifeform a creative process, we can regard the divine creative *spirit* as the *will* of the Creator.

We will define the divine spirit to be the creative, universal energy that enables life to express its creative potential. When this energy imbues a human body, it submits to the will of the self/soul. It becomes the human spirit.

The divine spirit becomes the property or faculty of the self/soul. Simply stated, spirit is the human creative energy that conforms to the physical form and submits, ideally, to the will of the essential (highest) self. Since it is a neutral energy, it may also fall under the influence and control of a lesser self, such as ego, emotion, addiction, mind, etc.

When an object receives spirit, it becomes an *agent* of the spirit and may undergo a change as the spirit *moves* it. For example, when a person feels love and is filled with spirit, they become an agent of love and will have an urge to spread it everywhere, all the time. Rumi describes the spirit as a dancer whose light becomes art—in his case his poetry.

In a similar manner, the human reproductive cells receive the spirit through their parents and thereby become the agents in creating a new life. We will use the term *spirit* with this meaning in mind and will refer generally to its expression in man and woman as the masculine and feminine spirit, respectively.

In the poem *Hungry Birds*, the embryo visits an elementary (essential) world, where it finds elementary forces assembling (creating?) the initial substances of all living forms. These elementary forces (we will refer to them also as *elementals*), according to the embryo, are alive and follow exact physical and biological laws. We can imagine them to be tiny segments of variable levels of energy that wriggle and dance in space, *looking* for particles of matter to energize in a quantum way. When a particle of matter is energized, it seeks a *home*, which becomes the starting material substance for that particular species according to a design.

The preceding brief theory is intuitive science—not a fantasy. Its main points are (1) there is a basic design (*home*) for a lifeform of a species that is unique to that species and (2) the building of a lifeform is carried out by a process of variable energy (spirit) transfer between these elementary units of energy and matter and the subsequent migration of the charged particles to their *home*, a place of their prior existence or design. We can think of a particle as a small child separated from its mother, who suddenly sees her and runs (like charged particle) to her. This would indicate that consciousness plays a key role in this process. Therein might also be a lesson of quantum physics. The same idea of an energized particle looking for a home (mother) is expressed in poetic form by Walt Whitman:

> It is the central urge in every atom,
> to return to its divine source and origin, however distant,
> latent the same in subject and object, without one exception.
>
> —*Walt Whitman, Persian Lesson*

As consciousness is the *seeing* faculty, spirit is the *creative* faculty within a human form. Spirit works through the body and thus influences the mind. As part of the essential self, it is felt as inspiration. Both consciousness and spirit are part of the life force (originally the energy of the sun) and of the universe. We will define *life force* as the life-sustaining energy. Both consciousness and spirit will be regarded as electromagnetic radiation of different frequencies. They are both fundamental universal forces.

Consciousness and spirit could be regarded as our resources. They are both neutral and are available to everyone and everything at all times. We can also regard them together as one energy. Everyone can use this energy to better their life as they wish.

Spirit is very much in action during the building of our body in the prenatal period. Without its action, we could not develop that perfectly, in such a complex way, in such a short time. Life before birth can, therefore, be regarded as a spiritual existence. Rumi says, "We want the kiss of spirit on our body throughout our whole lives."

A prevailing scientific view posits that the building of our physical body is under the direction of the genetic code contained in the DNA. This certainly holds true when it comes to the physical form of the body and its parts. However, a question remains, namely: Who or what formed the DNA in the first place? There is little doubt in my mind that consciousness, spirit and intelligence played a key role in the creation of the original DNA (or its predecessor) and continue to do so throughout the evolutionary process. We are all familiar with the magnificent works of human spirit. Why would spirit and intelligence not be used in the most important creation of all: our physical and mental life?

To know how far the almighty genome reaches in influencing our physical life, let us consider a few examples. Genes are responsible for growing our legs, but we have to learn to walk; genes carry out the design of our hands, but we have to learn to use them to play piano; they are responsible for the design of our eyes, but we have to learn to use them to develop their full potential for seeing; genes create our heart, but we have to produce the spark to get it started; genes design the brain and so on. On the whole, the genome is mainly a collection of prescriptions for design of the form and organs of the body and its parts so that we do not have to start from scratch each time we begin as a new life in the womb. However, the jury is still out as to how, and to what degree, the genome influences our life on the one hand, and the self with all its faculties plus the environment, on the other.

We can regard our current genetic code as being the result of evolutionary forces over aeons of time. Our DNA is shaped by environmental forces—both external and internal—as well as by creative intelligence of spirit. The internal psychic state associated with our soul plays a huge role in our life as we all know from experience. For healthy living, we need all of our faculties to be functional; we have to have all our wits about us.

During a short time after birth, babies have an opportunity to *view* their chromosomes. Their consciousness may detect a defect that they may attempt to repair. Genetic engineering would not be possible if human beings did not have the ability to change their genetic code themselves.

9.2 Feminine and Masculine Spirit

The presence of the spirit of the opposite gender in man and woman has a wide acceptance in eastern philosophy. In the West, C.G. Jung called them *animus* (in the male)) and *anima* (in the female). They are also called male and female principles. They represent the *essence* of the past states of consciousness of each gender. We have discussed their presence in the reproductive cells at conception. Historically, the same idea can be found in the yin-yang symbol (Figure 4.), which is one of the most powerful of mankind's symbols.

According to the Taoist philosophy, everything contains within itself some measure of the opposite (the small circle in each of the yin and yang fields). The symbol represents a spirit union of man and woman. Each of the gender spirits—male and female principles—contains a measure (small circles) of the opposite gender spirit or principle. We can also regard each gender individual as an androgynous spiritual being. No human being is completely either male or female in spirit. Spirit does not differentiate between sexes on the basis of its action—mind does. We can be aware of that. The whole yin-yang symbol represents a *union* of two androgynous beings in spirit form.

Figure 4. Yin-yang

To comprehend the yin-yang symbol fully, we need to understand that it does not depict a static state. Rather, it should be interpreted as a *dynamic* relationship, a changing balance between two spiritually androgynous beings as life goes on.

In the language of quantum mechanics, each androgynous being represents interplay of two quantum entities—in our case spirits. Spirit, according to our definition, is energy, part of the life force (originally light of the sun). As a result of the interplay within an androgynous being, the two spirits become correlated, starting with conception. They form a spiritual union. This union holds true, no matter how widely those two spirits (gender principles) become separated.

Suppose that each of them inhabits a body. Because of their quantum nature, if we know, for instance, the position of one of the spirits, we also know, automatically, the position of the other spirit. Therefore, each body harboring correlated spirits knows the position of the body harboring the other correlated spirit. This promotes the meeting of these two bodies. If they do meet, their spirits begin to act as if existing in *one body*—a state of an ideal yin-yang union. The two individuals possessing these bodies will stay together like animals that mate for life.

The above scenario is difficult for the mind to understand. What can help is the realization that this form of union is still common among hermaphrodites. It may be that the so-called *soul mates* still remember somewhere that they were hermaphroditic in the past. Soul mates, simply put, have stronger and wider consciousness of each other.

When these opposites, such as a man and woman, are unified in a balanced way—which is individual and unique to every pair—the relationship will express a state of harmony or maximum probability in a quantum way. An example of an *ideal* quantum state (the most probable outcome) is the first human cell that results in conception: the zygote.

Meeting and uniting of the female and male cells at conception thus represents a balanced state, a state of the Tao. Let us recall the passage in the poem *The First Journey* that describes the union formed by the egg and sperm. The sperm: **I reach the centre, begin to spread, extend, permeate the liquid substance. My role met, who am I, what's next?**

The sperm describes how it reached the balanced state between itself and the much larger egg. First it had to equalize its size with it, then dissolve in it. Herein also lies the way of the Tao whose power we all experienced at conception.

To summarize: *To realize the state of the Tao, we must first become aware that we are not bigger or smaller than our counterpart (equalize size) and then dissolve in it. This is also the path of the Tao.*

Corollary: *Conception describes the role of man in nature.*

Because of incarnation of only one of the gender entities (female or male), the adult human being is unbalanced and is forever challenged to seek the right balance. Every person has the potential to become more balanced by acknowledging the existence and awareness of his/her inner opposite-gender-spirit mate and practice this union with its gender opposite on the outside.

A conscious union between man and woman—physical and spiritual—engenders vital information between them and nurtures the psychological wellbeing of both. Since we all have experienced the state of perfect unity at conception, we have in us the knowledge of that state. It is also an ideal we strive for in adult life.

A skeptic may ask: Why do we aspire to reach the state of the Tao, enlightenment, perfect order, harmony and other similar high standards in our life? The answer is: those states represent the best way to live. Life itself provides the proof.

9.3 Conception: Gate into the World

Conception has a fundamental influence on our psychology. The uniting of the two cells leaves a strong imprint in us to unite with everything around us. We see the evidence of that in infants who put everything into their mouths and young children, who try to touch everything. It is much less common among adults because of the fear stemming from social taboos. While accepted among animals, human physical closeness in public runs a risk of social misunderstanding.

We were created from life's unity and have an innate tendency to seek it in whatever we relate to. We seek compromise in solving problems involving opposing sides at work and in social situations. We build our inner image of the world on the principle of unity. We seek a harmonious relationship with everything, naturally. We feel good when we do that. It can be shown that this approach is also the path of least resistance, and is the easiest and most successful way to live.

Strictly speaking, unity is not the same as union although they can both manifest in one grouping. In a union, the individual identities in a grouping persist. In a unity, individual differences disappear. We can regard the first human cell after conception as having physical unity and at the same time having a spiritual union.

Finally, conception is a model for love that creates the right environment, not only for maintaining the species, but also as a principle of all creative work. The best examples of creative work are a result based on love between the artist and the object of his creation. We have said that the union/unity of the cells at conception requires the surrender of their individual identities. This is a necessary condition for the creation of a vacuum to be filled by the new identity.

9.4
Man–Woman Relationship

The relationship and union between man and woman is one of the greatest—perhaps *the* greatest—of divine creations brought into mankind's existence. Conception shows a way this relationship was designed to function. We have discussed the archetype in which two human beings of opposite gender, both in their spiritual bodies, decide to live together. Guided by that archetype, the incarnated male spirit (in our case) kept his promise during the prenatal life and continued to be conscious of it for a time after birth.

To make the above idea complete, we have to assume that a similar archetype would also be found when the feminine spirit incarnates. We would assume that she, too, would promise her inner male spirit (animus) her version of a desired life together, based on an archetype or ideal.

A true, ideal love begins at conception.

The original promise of the male/female spirit to its female/male counterpart plays a key role when, in adult life, a man becomes interested in a woman, and vice versa. At that time, man's feminine spirit (anima) will be reawakened. The degree of aliveness of his feminine spirit, felt as emotional energy (love) by the male, will determine the strength of his attraction.

Since the carrier of the feminine spirit is the egg, it may lead us to think that man might be attracted in life to a woman who embodies qualities most closely associated with his mother. We need to address that.

Spirit requires a form in which to manifest, in our case the egg. The egg is a living form that contains the feminine spirit. Being part of a woman's body from the very beginning of her life, the egg would be exposed to actions of her spirit, but since it is in a dormant state up to ovulation, it will not partake in them, consciously. Thus the spirit of the egg will be the inherent woman (gender) spirit that imbued the original form of a woman, modulated by her evolutionary history. This feminine spirit, also called feminine principle, is recognized by the incarnating male spirit and endorsed by him with the promise to share his life with her.

We learned that the male fetus carried out his promise consciously during the prenatal life and, for a time, after birth. In summary: The adult male is attracted and guided to a woman by the feminine spirit (anima) it harbours. This is depicted well in the yin–yang symbol, discussed earlier.

Similarly, a woman might be looking to meet a man according to her innate male spirit, given to her at conception.

> ***Spirit Gender and Physical Gender***
> While the presence of the Y-chromosome in the sperm determines the *physical* gender of the being, the *spirit* gender is determined by an agreement—in our case supplied by an archetype—by the spirits desiring to live together. So, it may happen that the adult physical form of a being is male, determined by the Y-chromosome, but the spirit gender is female, determined by the spirit agreement. When such an individual reaches maturity, the spirit gender may claim its priority (superiority) over the physical gender, leading to a conflict whose resolution may be sex change or same-sex marriage. We have many examples of this in society. This suggests that the spirit gender generally has a priority and justification over the physical.

Conception thus establishes the presence of the spirits of the opposite genders within each human being and forms the psychological basis for attraction between them. A man will, therefore, seek a woman in the outer world who most closely *fits* his feminine spirit (anima) and *only to his anima he will be forever faithful.* Although I cannot speak about how a woman will be guided in finding her life mate, I presume that a similar process would play out within her as well.

As the attraction between a pair of lovers grows, there comes a time when they begin to feel a desire to stay together and unite sexually. Let's describe the actors more closely. We have here two different individuals, each harboring the *spirit* of the opposite gender and each possessing a grown-up body that is imbued with the male and female spirit.

If we could accept that the *pure gender spirit* is not modulated by growth into adulthood, we would have only two spirits whose interaction would follow the yin-yang symbol.

Let us start with the man. Usually, at night before the day of the desired sexual union, the man with a conscious spiritual awareness, will have a dream—or a strong sensation in a daydream—that his body is being invaded by another body. What is happening is that his inner feminine spirit is *integrating* the body of his beloved. We could say also that his inner feminine spirit is "acquiring" a body. This is possible, since his feminine spirit (soul) is a pure spirit without a body.

This step leading toward a union is very significant. We will call it *spiritual embodiment*. Spiritually, the man thus prepares his sexual cells (sperms) to set out and seek the union with the egg.

We would assume that a similar spiritual event will take place, as a day or night dream, in his beloved, if she is spiritually awakened. She will also have a strong feeling before the advent of the physical union that another body is about to invade her. It means that her inner male spirit (animus) desires to acquire a physical body of her beloved. Her male spirit is going through a spiritual embodiment. She, too, will transmit this information to her awakened (ovulating) egg cell: "accept the union with the body of the sperm." This may remind us of the teachings of the Tao: Nothing can be given unless it is first received.

Figure 5 ***Soul Mates*** **by Maxine Noel**

If everything proceeds ideally, the sexual cells of the two partners will be filled with the spirit to seek their union following the sexual act. Spiritually awakened people thus enjoy a deep experience of sexual union and reap its rich health benefits. This is also the only way the true (divine) love may be expressed. All other forms of sexual conduct are pleasure-oriented and do not offer deep and lasting life benefits.

Spiritual embodiment and the following union are felt by spiritually awakened couples as something natural, almost magical. They are both aware that they belong to each other, that they are experiencing the will of God. This is an ideal state—a manifestation of divine love—in which to *conceive* a child. In those individuals who are not spiritually aware, the event of spiritual embodiment will pass unnoticed, subconsciously.

When a man plans to enter into marriage with a woman—depending on his degree of success in matching his anima with his bride—he may face difficulty in fully reconciling his feminine spirit (anima) with the spirit of his future wife. No wonder, he is already *married* to his feminine spirit! The man with spirit consciousness will be attracted by a woman who most closely approaches his ideal. If we regard the inner spirits as souls, he would have found a soul mate. This is the ideal way (ideal love) the creation process intended the union to be. A beautiful illustration of soul mates, with their spirits shown beside them, is given in the painting by Maxine Noel, *Figure 5*.

More often, however, a man will come only close to such a perfect union. Also, the selection of his life partner will be influenced to a significant degree by practical considerations that make people want to live together. We may add that he will have no such problem with the physical union, since his feminine spirit would have already accepted his chosen partner's body through the spiritual embodiment discussed above —consciously or unconsciously.

9.5 Religious View of Conception

It may be interesting to note how two major religions present their beliefs about the role of spirit concerning the conception of their deities and spiritual leaders.

The Catholic Church speaks about Saint Mary, mother of Jesus, of having experienced an immaculate conception during which she was filled with the Holy Spirit. In religious teachings, the spiritual aspect of life takes precedence over the physical, which is ignored. The idea of spiritual embodiment in which the spirit is the divine creative spirit (The Holy Ghost) thus offers an explanation. Also, in biblical times, the physical aspect of conception, as we know it today, was not fully understood.

In a similar way, Queen Māyā, mother of Gautama Buddha, spoke about a dream preceding the conception of the Buddha in which she was visited by a white elephant. In his last incarnation, the Buddha is believed to have entered his mother's womb in the form of a white elephant.

Both the births of Jesus Christ and the Buddha were accompanied by unusual natural phenomena. Nature celebrated their arrival. Nature was aware of their life missions on Earth.

9.6 Conception Summary

Conception is the most fundamental, formative event of our life. It not only holds the secret knowledge of the beginning of our current life, but it also presents the key to our understanding of the apparent duality of life. It is the entry into our current life and may also contain clues to its exit. During conception, the creative spirit (energy) has its finest manifestation, resulting in the creation of new life.

Conception presents a model for love. We can recall its three stages: (1) meeting of the cells and their decision to stay together, moving together with rising attraction and closeness (2) spiritual and physical uniting and loss of individual cell identities and (3) finding the new identity and the way to continue the union. We can apply conception as a model for adult love relationships leading to a marriage.

The physical and spiritual union of the third stage of conception is, ideally, a sacred act whose consequences and benefits to the psyche are profound. It is, therefore, sacrilegious to trivialize it and—in any way and for whatever purpose—to exploit it. Those who exploit the human sexuality and use it for commercial purposes, and those who become seduced or victimized by it, unfortunately also miss its huge benefits to their lives.

Foremost, conception serves as a constant reminder that the natural state of life is unity, not only in our personal life but in all life.

Conception teaches us that the loss of identity (psychological death) of both sexual cells is a necessary step for the pure consciousness *I am* to appear and find a new identity through an archetype. At that point, spirit manifests itself and becomes active as the true agent of creation, giving rise to a new life.

Finally, conception leaves a lasting imprint on us to seek a harmonious relationship with fellow humans and the world. Its creative spirit fosters human accomplishment and progress.

If more people come forward with their memory of conception, we could be in a better position to understand more fully this important act that is the true beginning of our life. Perhaps then, too, we could start counting our age from conception.

10

Energy–Matter Interaction

There are many descriptions by the prenatal child in the *Poem* that deal with its ability to recognize energy as the active force in its life and matter as the building substance of its body. But before we examine the energy–matter relationship that results in growth, let us consider the original situation when energy and matter were one. This *oneness* is described mathematically by Einstein's well-known formula. We could say that matter is amassed energy (light) or light trapped in elementary particles of matter. We could also describe the energy–matter relationship as an eternal bond held together by mutual oneness.

An intuitive thought: Could we say that energy awakens matter to remember itself as energy? All earthly lifeforms have energy and matter bodies. Their energy is the light of the sun in its various transformed states. Following the above thinking, could we say that, when a particle absorbs light, it moves to its previous state... its previous home... and all the way to its source, which is light? This would suggest that light created matter to conserve itself and hold the universe together.

Examples of energy consciousness and awareness were already discussed in greater detail in chapter 5. In the poem *The First Journey*, the egg became tired and thirsty during its travel. It was fed by friendly hosts when it landed in a bay. We would assume that the nourishment was received by osmosis from the nursing cells gathered at that place. These might have been the cells that went ahead during the ovulation.

In the poem *Touching Stars*, the embryo, after implanting, discovered light particles that transferred energy to it and filled it with the joy of life. We also noted that these charged particles followed the embryo's consciousness on its return to its home, a place in the womb. This supports the theory according to which a charged particle is attracted to and seeks to connect with the lifeform of a particular design that is known to it as its home. Recalling also the *elementals* in the poem *Hungry Birds*, we could say that our bodies accumulate matter and energy following the laws of quantum energy transfer and unification.

In the poem *Upward Bound*, the developing embryo describes the way of building its body. It observes the particles of matter moving in a stream and selects the ones it likes. We are dealing here with the kind of matter from which we construct our bodies. The embryo selects matter on the basis of whether it *likes* it or not. This suggests a self-recognition. The law of attraction—like attracts like—applies, even if we are not fully conscious of what it is that is like us. It is the same law mentioned above in connection with a charged particle seeking its home or source. The ultimate goal of a particle seeking a place where it belongs, results in a tendency to unite. If this reminds us of conception all over again, we are on the right track. We could generalize and say that *life is a continuous reliving of conception.*

This holds for the physical process of building our body as well for all the other ways of experiencing life. We will call this the *law of attraction and unification.*

We have already put forward a theory that the process of building our body at the elementary particle level consists of finding the right match, according to the law of attraction and unification. We can speak about the whole process as the *quantum law of unification*. This law guarantees that our bodies are constructed and maintained in a manner that follows true physical, biological and spiritual values. We can be grateful for that. Physics seeks the unifying force; and life strives to maintain its unity.

In the poem *Life Force*, the unborn child describes an enormous flow of life energy generated in its body as a result of intensive growth. The sun's energy transformed into an electrochemical energy by the mitochondria stimulates the cells to rapid division. This generates a strong life (energy) force that expands and renews the body and moves it forward along the journey of life. The inertia of that life force is sensed by the embryo as a predictor of its future. The self of the embryo and its consciousness are under pressure to keep up with the rapid growth.

10.1 The Process of Growth

The foregoing discussion of the physical design and evolution of a living form—even with the beauty and attractiveness of the law of unification—is incomplete and may never work alone because it leaves out the role of the self and soul in the process. As we have learned, the conscious self plays a key role in the life creation process, right from the beginning. Growth is adding a new part to what already exists—the self or soul. It is not sufficient to create a living form, or any stage of it, based solely on the *automatic* application of physical laws. We have learned in the poem *Upward Bound* that the self is engaged in the process of selecting matter and energy at every stage of its body formation and identifies itself with it using the basic consciousness *I am*. Similarly, the creation is of interest to the soul, which delights itself (grows) in the creative and learning process.

To maintain its physical unity, the embryo had to periodically reassure each part of its body that it belonged: **Now I must stop, go back where I started and tell my base it remains a part of me** It is my belief that, without the acknowledgment and acceptance of each step of the growth by identifying with it, i.e., adding to the self, living form could not maintain its unity and survive.

If we look at the creation of life in its totality, we could say that nature gave us the gift of a live body. It placed this living gift into our care after birth. We have received this gift with joy and gratitude, and identified ourselves with it. This awakened in us the feeling of love and oneness. As a result, we not only cherish this gift of life but also want to look after it by giving it the best care we can. Since all life had the same beginning, our living body is *connected* inseparably with all life. That awareness moves us to support and care for all lifeforms on the planet. Experiencing life leads to a realization that living is both a taking as well as a giving process.

Being in a state of oneness with all life—a rare feeling we have when we are deeply relaxed and conscious of what we truly are—enables us to look inside the relationships among different living forms and their evolution. Plants are the earliest and most numerous lifeforms on the earth. Being at the base of the evolutionary ladder, they aspire to become animal and human life. They do so by offering themselves as food. In the process of eating plants, animals become like plants and plants like animals at the elementary level. Some animals eat other animals and fall in love with them. Unlike a plant, an animal—being already animal—does not aspire to become another animal and resists being eaten. However, in the end, the prey succumbs (gives itself) to the predator. What remains of the prey in the body of the predator? Obviously, it loses its waking consciousness of being an autonomous living form. In the end, at the elementary level, it finds a new home in the body of the predator. At this point, we may recall the words in the poem *The Tree, Earth and I *Anything I take and make my own binds me forever to its source.**

The presence of the prey in its body causes the predator to hunt that prey for the rest of its life. The predator becomes dependent on the prey for its survival. Hunting often requires great physical effort. That makes us wonder: Who is better off, the hunter or the hunted? The predator imprisons the prey and in the process becomes imprisoned by it. When the predator dies, the soul of the prey—if it is still around—is freed.

10.2
Energy and Healing

When a lifeform encounters a lack of life energy in one of its parts or organs, it grows weak and may become ill. We feel it as pain. It is possible to heal that part by supplying its missing energy in two ways: (1) using consciousness to raise its energy as described in chapter 5.4 and (2) by lifting the whole body into the plane of life's force-field.

The first method is the one commonly used by acupuncture, acupressure, etc., in which the energy flow is re-established around the ailing part mechanically by a healer, ideally with the patient's conscious awareness. The second method is done by the ailing person alone by becoming aware of their force field. The latter method is clearly more difficult, requiring a high level of conscious awareness. If we consider the body's life energy to be a quantum thing, then we are directing healing in (1) to its particle aspect and in (2) its wave aspect.

11
Image of the Outside World

Early in its life, the prenatal child begins to form an image of the outside world. It constructs it from the physical activity of its mother; as she moves and works outside with her hands and tools in the garden or field or just walks. Work requires energy. It is her energy that the prenatal child is *tuned* to with its keen consciousness. It constructs the image of the outside piece by piece, as its mother engages in different tasks. The pieces fit together seamlessly, forming a new whole every time a new piece is added to the previous whole. We can compare this composite image forming to a countryside seen from a moving train or plane. However, the *image* that the unborn sees is nothing like the image our adult eyes produce. Its image is constructed by the light (energy) of consciousness. It exists only in consciousness as a light (energy) body (chapter 5.7).

It may be of interest to reflect on the above prenatal experience as another example of the function of fetal consciousness. Physical activity is an energy-consuming process. Consciousness is the awareness of energy. As in the episode of starting its heart, in which the preborn tuned to the energy of its mother's heart, so also in this case it becomes aware of the energy accompanying her physical movements. At the same time, it is also aware of the energy generated by her visual process. Putting all of this together, the unborn child becomes aware of the outside world in transparent "shades" of light. The shades in this case are the differences in light brightness and frequency.

In forming the impression of the outside space, the preborn describes a relationship among the four basic physical variables: energy, mass, space and time. Energy and mass originate with the mother; space and time are a consequence of a conscious experience (energy interaction) of the first two by the prenatal child. We could say that space is generated by energy and mass in a time sequence, and that space and time are inseparable. We may have here an empirical (prenatal) proof of Einstein's theory of relativity (matter and energy tell space/time how to curve). If we go in our imagination all the way to the beginning of the universe, we could say that the universe began as a source of infinitely large radiant energy that became its *life* and latent consciousness, the rest being a history of its evolution.

By combining the flow of the mother's energy, her physical activity as well as her sensory perception, the child is aware of the outside world as a formless spatial form. Is it an oxymoron? We can look at the formation of space in another way. The poem *My Inner World* states that the pieces **fit together seamlessly**. It appears that the preborn, using its faculty of consciousness, builds an invisible spatial body. We defined the concept of a *body* in chapter 5.6. The inner image of the outside world can thus be thought of as an ethereal part of the physical body that contains information about space. Many people (including the writer) report having had an experience of looking for a place without knowing how to find it. Then, almost magically, they stood before it.

After birth, the image of the outside world is formed by our eyes during waking consciousness, but the process of making a composite remains the same as during the prenatal time. The inner image (when our eyes are closed) of the outside becomes an ethereal body surrounding our physical body. Because the essence of the body is the awareness of space, we will refer to it as the *spatial body*. The spatial body contains not only the space awareness generated at the current location but also all the previous images at other times and different locations. The most important property of the spatial body is that any part of it can be instantly accessed by consciousness. Since consciousness can exist only in the present, the spatial body also exists in its entirety in the present.

The spatial body contains the images of all the places, near and far, where we lived or visited during our life. Central in this structure is one's home and birthplace. Building of the spatial body continues throughout life. Each person has their individual spatial body. The spatial body is the inner world we live in. It is a place where we feel at home.

Another important aspect of the spatial body is the motivation leading to its creation. Let us recall the lines from the poem *My Inner World: *As I unite with the world, I feel again the union with my inner mate when we united.**

The prenatal child reflects on the feeling of the cells merging at conception and finds it to be the same as forming the image of the outside world. At conception, the feeling was of the two life cells merging and the union of their spirits. The feeling now is that of the union between the outer and inner realms. Seeking and maintaining union/unity appears to be the inherent property of life. Loss of life's unity can be life threatening and deserves further discussion.

12
Unity of Life

Uniting with all things in its life and assimilating them as part of itself is felt by the prenatal child as the natural way of living. However, life's unity cannot be taken for granted in our postnatal life in which it is constantly subject of disruption or breakage and often requires an enormous effort to mend it.

In the process of growing, unity is fundamental to its purpose and meaning, as is its threat or breakage. This may not be immediately apparent, but the way to recognize and maintain it is easy. Often, the truth of unity is hidden by layers of disunity that we generate in life.

Let us begin by considering, for example, the union/unity between mother and her baby. When a baby is put down by its mother, it may experience a loss of the unity and begin to cry. The mother might try to alleviate its fear by reassuring it that the physical separation is only temporary and that she will be back soon. In time, the child will understand that. However, if the separation is frequent and not well managed, the baby may also begin to experience fear of losing its mother, felt as a loss of its internal life's unity.

12.1
Separation and Regaining of Life's Unity

Continuity of life is constantly challenged by man-made and environmental changes. A living form has to cope with these changes. When a very important need in its growth (governed by developmental design), especially during very early life, is not being met, the child will start asking repeatedly for what it needs. If its repeated pleas and needs are not met and satisfied, the child will eventually stop asking by suppressing its needs, such as the feeling of hunger or thirst, the need to be recognized, the need of close contact with its mother, etc. It may say to itself, "I cannot have what I need." This creates a threat to life's continuity. Suppression of hunger may later result in making insulin ineffective and lead to diabetes. It is a defense. The child has to preserve its integrity and survival. Although the need would outwardly disappear after repressing it, its content will continue on the inside. Eventually, the child may suppress the need that brings on the pain altogether, and with it that part of the self that felt the need. This, of course, does not eliminate it; it puts it to sleep, and out of the way.

When the child grows up, the content of the original need will likely be unavailable to its conscious awareness as an adult. It will remain as an unidentified feeling of emptiness or a need resulting in the longing to satisfy it. The individual will try to satisfy its unconscious need with whatever will bring relief, a standard maneuver to keep it under control. However, none of the substitutes will satisfy the original need of the child. Instead, it may lead to dreaming and reaching for unknown, even unreachable goals. The result will be a feeling of ongoing frustration. We may be reminded of the Greek myth of Sisyphus forever rolling a stone uphill only to have it roll back down from the summit. It may lead some individuals to turn to alcohol, drugs and other forms of addiction, in order to ease the persistent distress of longing. Others may be caught up in accumulating money, fame or power without ever feeling they have enough.

Is there a way to deal with such an unhealthy state? The realization that desires are at the root of our suffering, while true, is not enough by itself to cure the condition. It is similar to trying to deal with an illness by eliminating its symptoms. A sounder approach to reach peace is to use one's power of conscious awareness and fully awaken the original need of the child. If that is achieved—it is not easy—the adult will be able see the true cause and nature of their suffering and may accept it as part of their past. In doing so, the adult might lessen the pain and get off the merry-go-round of dreaming. Using willpower, the person may be able to control the desire, but they will still not be able to satisfy the past need. The person has to find what their life as a child was like before its unity with the world was severed. Finding what we have lost will stop the search. This sounds simple, but is not easy to realize.

The purpose of searching is finding. To become completely healthy requires finding the lost health. That implies re-establishing the unity or oneness with life and the world we live in.

Before we examine possible ways to repair a broken or damaged internal unity and separation from the world, let us review what has been established up to this point. By awakening the memory of the childhood trauma, the person has a clear view of the unsatisfied need, but they also begin to realize that knowing about it does not erase it. It persists. At this point, the person may fall into thinking that all the effort to awaken the early memory was for naught. That would not be correct. The gain of seeing the original need in its full light—including the circumstances that led to it—is that it gives the adult an opportunity to deal with it using their current ability, means and knowledge (as compared to those of the child). Also, the awakening of the inner child leads to a feeling of rejuvenation and increased vitality. All this is achievable and is the usual aim of conventional psychotherapy.

However, what has not been achieved is that the adult person still has not reached the root cause of their problem, which was the separation from life and the world. The feelings of residual frustration and longing might persist, especially if the suppression involved a vital function such as hunger or thirst, the sucking instinct, crying, anger, etc. To recover full health, all these feelings, bodily sensations and functions must be revitalized.

This last phase consists of healing the whole organism. This step can only be carried out by the person themself. It requires a complete integration of the child's life into the current life.

The person here deals with their individual life in the intimacy with the divine self of the child that issues from the Creator of life. Full unity with life marks complete health. The highest unity is the unity with the source of life. That is the true and ideal expression of life in a human being. It is a sacred state and the path to it is a spiritual one.

The main feature of this final phase of healing is finding the lost state of health within the inner self. It is a difficult task and may take a lifetime to achieve. The reward, however, is huge. Finding the true (divine) life within oneself is our life's highest achievement.

How would one recognize the right path toward life's unity? To start with, the person would feel progressively healthier, more relaxed and freer. They would feel peaceful and confident, and perceive the world as a right place to be. They would have found true love.

The above is not a fantasy, it is the reality. When one surrenders one's ego to that state of being, life itself (not one's will) will become one's guide. The person will become aware of opportunities and invisible guidance and follow it and maintain that state. The divine design of life contains intelligence to sustain it and repair any damage incurred along the way.

Longing will disappear. It will be replaced by the joy of being alive. The inner child will be well again. The person, now enjoying full physical and mental health, will pursue readily achievable goals that are beneficial not only to them but to life in general. Logically, if life gives to us, and we are part of it, we will also give—not because we should; we will do it naturally. Thus, the original content that brought on the unsatisfied feeling will be distilled into new, worthwhile ventures that bear fruit through the grace of God, generosity of nature and compassion of human nurturance.

Problems in childhood are caused by the inability of the child to understand circumstances and parental ignorance. It is important, therefore, that we as parents and teachers do not teach and give our children explanations about life that they are unable to understand. Rather, we should help them to discover life they can feel themselves.

Generally, we can say that a loss of life's unity is a frequent occurrence. It would be difficult to find a person who has not experienced it. This may lead us to think that separation, resulting from breaking of life's unity, is an inevitable life condition on this planet and is the consequence of duality of nature. An example of natural duality is life and death. We can think of the yin-yang symbol. We all know that life contains a seed of death based on our observation and experience. Similarly, death must contain a seed of life, which is not normally part of our experience while we are still alive.

It is interesting to learn how the prenatal child copes with the threats to its life. We have good examples of those in the struggle of the embryo to implant; the effort of the fetus to establish communication with its mother before birth and the life/death struggle to be born. In all of these cases, the prenatal child realizes that its current state of life is threatened and may be terminated. The child fights for its survival but is prepared to accept the end of its life as a possible outcome. It does not want to die but is not afraid to lose its current life either. This is well illustrated in the last poem *Into Light and Space,* which describes birth during which the baby's conscious self (soul) separated from the body.

While some separations occur naturally such as those caused by diseases, sudden changes due to disasters of various kinds, death, etc., many more are caused by man himself. Because they transgress the law of life's unity, they must be regarded as ignorance of real life or deviations from its true reality, or both. It would take an enormous amount of work to compile a comprehensive list of examples of violations of life's unity caused by man himself. It would take even more effort to describe the process of trying to recover this loss.

Loss of and disrespect for life's unity is particularly harmful if it affects a large number of people, or even the whole society. Disunity in a society weakens it. It may lead to its breakdown into factions caused by differences due to religion, race, economic conditions, etc. Hostilities may escalate and lead to the killing of people. The worst kind of violation of unity and integrity of life occurs in war in which innocent people die, or when masses of people are exterminated in a genocidal or sectarian struggle.

13
Role of Man in Nature

The question of man's role in nature has been with us for a long time. It has gained importance since the industrial revolution, which intensified the exploitation of nature. The rapid increase in world population has been another factor. According to the poem *Hungry Birds*, man's role in nature is determined at the very beginning, at the time when a human being is given the first particle of matter.

According to the poem *Hungry Birds*, that beginning took place in the invisible realm of elementary particles as discussed earlier (chapters 9.0 and 9.1). In this poem, the first matter was given to the prenatal child by elementary life forces that work in that essential world. These elementary forces select matter for all lifeforms according to their standing and role in nature. Man is given the highest standing and the best matter. With it he carries a responsibility to lead all lower lifeforms, in a benevolent manner, toward betterment of life.

The above statement implies the existence of an à *priori* design for each major category of lifeform. This idea was advanced earlier when we discussed the unifying force and unity of all life. The elementary forces that are alive (have energy) and work in the elementary world are tiny charges of energy that activate particles of matter (encapsulated energy) to life. We could theorize further that each lifeform is assigned a frequency or a small range of frequencies of light that would act as the building energy for that lifeform. Because of the quantum principle, only a certain kind of matter, appropriate to the lifeform, would be selected.

We could say that there is a ray and a particle of matter for the beginning of every lifeform.

The poem *Hungry Birds* describes the matter given to a human being as rare and precious, the best these elementary forces could find. With that matter, the human being receives a gift of high virtue, which is to carry the hopes and aspirations of the lower life for betterment of their existence. Thus man is given the role of a benevolent leader of all lower life. By 'lower' we mean life that has not yet evolved to the human level, not life that is less important.

The carrier of that precious matter is likely the sperm cell, since its formation is more current and is also more *spirited* than the egg cell at the time of conception.

The idea that matter can influence the standing or pecking order among the members of a group of animals, such as a pack of wolves, is known. The leader of the pack receives the privilege of eating first, presumably consuming the best parts of the kill. Among people, important and valued guests are treated to the best meal by their hosts. Bees feed a selected worker royal jelly to make it a queen.

Man, whose life is deeply rooted in nature, was created to act as its benevolent leader, protector and caregiver to all life ranked lower. His role and responsibility may seem to be a difficult task to fulfill, but it is, in reality, the way of the least effort. Any other role that does not fulfill this commandment of creation is more difficult and may not lead to the betterment of life. It concerns not only individuals but also societies, even nations.

A natural and responsible political system is one which supports the preservation and development of life in that society. If we value certain rights and freedoms for ourselves, we would naturally grant the same rights to others. An aggressive and highly competitive approach in dealing with people, nations and their land is a pathological behavior.

14
Life's Order and Truth

Of all the knowledge we gained in prenatal life, the most significant is the experience and knowledge of the Order of Life. We are all familiar with organization and order of things in our daily life. We know that order makes it easier to carry out our daily tasks. However, the Order of Life we will discuss here goes much deeper than that. It reaches to the very roots and purpose of life, which is growth. It is, therefore, imperative for us to understand the prenatal Order of Life fully.

> Order is heaven's first law.
>
> *—Alexander Pope, An Essay on Man*

In the poem *Order of Life,* we read that our life has an order based on the concept of life as a journey. Some life journeys are short, others long. One lasts a lifetime. Each journey has a beginning and an end.

A journey is generated anytime we engage in and consciously follow an action, whether it is physical, mental, emotional or any other form of experience. In the poem *Order of Life* and others, we learned that a journey is everything that we are consciously engaged in, every road that we travel, every experience we live through, every thought we reflect on or emotion we feel, every memory recording, simply everything that unfolds within us as a linear, conscious, energy-requiring happening.

Every action we pursue and consciously follow will at some point terminate, come to an end. When it is finished—and only when it is finished—we are able to see the result. If we like it, we accept it as part of the self and file it in a proper place in provided memory. It will be added to our overall experience, similar to the growth of a tree adding growth at the perimeter of its trunk and crown. Every such new experience, therefore, will influence and contribute to our life from that time on.

What exactly is the result of a finished journey, the harvest at its end? Some may think that it is the object or goal of the journey, for example, a finished job or any of the myriad things we do, but that is true only on the surface. The full truth of a journey, from which we are able to ultimately benefit, like in a tree, is growth. Only conscious growth, be it physical, mental or spiritual, can add to our experience and wisdom. We can say that the expression of life is growth.

During growth, we generate our personal truth, discussed below. Therefore, starting and finishing every journey, reaping and reflecting on the fruit of the experience and adding it to our overall growth is our way of fulfilling Life's Order. Maintaining the Order of Life brings the greatest psychological reward to our soul; the experience of life's (perfect) order is the best feeling we can have.

Nothing that we do can surpass the benefit to our life or match it in quality than experiencing its perfect order that we learned in prenatal life. Recall the words of the unborn child **This awareness [of life's order] is the best state of being I know. I want to retain it forever.**

It is a state that can be described by statements such as: "Everything in my life is happening as it should" or "Life can't get any better." The feeling of Life's Order is supreme, better than any ecstatic feeling we can have. It surpasses the feeling of love, taste, beauty, energy, success, etc. It contains all of the feelings we would have by living an ideal life. It represents the highest state of love—love of the Creator.

Finally, a subtle reminder: to follow Life's Order implies living consciously in the present.

14.1
Life's Truth

It may be easy to accept the idea that our life is a journey along which we are carried by the life force. What is not obvious is that every life journey is an indispensable way of gaining our personal *truth*. Without the journey generating life experience, we cannot know our personal truth. Yes, we can often hear statements of others about their truth, but unless their truth becomes our own experience also, it is no more than a piece of advice or information. However, if a statement implying truth *rings a bell*, then we ought to give it attention. It makes sense on an intuitive basis.

There is a common sense saying: "You have to walk the walk before you can talk the talk." It rules out any other way of gaining personal truth. Even the best advice we hear must be tried out by us before it can become our truth.

What is our life like if we live in truth? The one who lives in truth—not in the moral, religious or socially accepted truth about life but in the pure truth of their being—leads the best life. A prenatal child lives in the natural world and truth. For some time, small children are also natural and live in truth. *Truth is the essence of being natural.*

To behave in a natural way means that we are not trying to be something or someone we are not (an unnatural state).

In our lives, we are constantly under pressure to play certain roles to conform. This does not always work. Sooner or later, we will find that playing a role is a form of self-deception. It is a personal lie, and as the saying goes, a lie has short legs.

Even if we differ in experience and the length of life journey, if we all practice Life's Order, we will live in truth. Such life is also a spiritual existence as written in one of the most profound statements in the Bible in the words of Jesus Christ (John 14:6): "I am the way, the truth and the life." Our interpretation of this truly compelling and powerful statement is: Jesus Christ remembered who he was and where he came from. He trusted his life journey (way) as a means of expressing it in his life and never deviated from it (remained true to himself and His father).

The prenatal being in our story expresses it this way: **My life's journey stays the same... to follow the way, wherever I go, whatever I do, whatever I feel, whichever way I learn. Journey is my way to grow, to know who I am... beyond this state, knowing all that I am, there is nothing more I could be... I wish the world outside to have the order I have.**

If we liken the prenatal period to a divine existence, both Christ's and the prenatal child's statements have the same meaning.

It needs to be emphasized that a journey must be truly finished, that is, felt by us as completed. We must know that we crossed the finish line. In quantum language, it would be described as the collapse of the wave function (journey) by the self (consciousness) resulting in finding the particle (goal). A journey and its goal would be considered complementary aspects of a quantum system. When a journey reaches an end but not its goal, it is not completed. In that case, our effort has not yielded fruit. Our journey has been suspended. It will remain in our mind (the wave function has not collapsed). If this happens repeatedly, it results in a cluttered or scattered mind. In such a state, it is difficult to carry out a new action or follow a new idea in an unhindered way.

You might have heard of so-called *multitasking*, an ability to carry out two or more tasks at the same time. This is like following several roads at once. Since our full focus and consciousness can only be given to one thing at a time, we are forced to juggle the tasks by switching among them. This requires more effort and is stressful. Our performance suffers from a lack of a full, undivided attention to each task with a concomitant weakening of consciousness (dwelling time). While the juggling act goes on, we do not have the benefit of each individual sequential termination of a task. The solutions become tangled in the mind, which can lead to increased stress levels and be ultimately unproductive. In my view, multitasking as a way of increasing productivity is a bad idea. It goes against nature because it generates an unnatural degree of stress.

We live in our truth when we behave and act in our natural way without trying to be something we are not. We are under constant pressure in life to play certain roles, say the right things deemed by us to be necessary for our well-being and survival. To be something we are not is a personal lie. It is a burden we do not have to carry.

We all feel good when we finish a job or any other undertaking, bring it to an end, and accept it as being the final form of our work and effort. If we only reach an end but do not accept it as the end and final form, our journey is not finished. It is only terminated, and we are not able to reap the full benefit of our experience. In that case, Life's Order is not met and our truth (goal) is not realized. We are left with unfinished business. Only when we accept the result of our journey as truly final, and file it in the place where it will live as our newly gained knowledge, will our life experience be increased by it and contribute from that time on to our capability. This is the way our personal truth is realized, and the way our experience and wisdom grow with age.

Even though we differ in our life experiences, we all live in truth if we fulfill Life's Order. To live in truth is simple, efficient and economical. In truth, we are only that which we are, being aware that we cannot be anything else. It is a life lived entirely in the present. Boring? On the contrary, it is free of stress. A confident life utilizes energy optimally. The one who lives in truth—not moral, religious or conventional, but in the pure truth of their being—leads the best life. The prenatal child lives in a natural state and truth. For some time after birth, all children are natural and live in truth.

A question arises as to how to apply Life's Order as adults when the life's tempo greatly increases and the number of activities expands. It is not easy and often seems impossible to maintain Life's Order. We are forced to travel along several paths at once (self-imposed multitasking). This, of course, is not possible. We have to interrupt the natural flow of our journeys. To remedy the situation, we can start eliminating unhelpful activities and prioritize other pursuits. Discipline and awareness of the highest self are necessary.

What effect does technological development have on Life's Order? Today the rate of technological development is reaching the intensity of a runaway horse. This has a profound effect on the way we experience life. There is not enough time to observe the way, to notice the surroundings, to go deeper with our consciousness and feelings. We are becoming more and more robot-like. This has a serious negative effect: loss of life intelligence. Life is presented to us as data rather than as experience. In my view, this is an evolutionary digression, if not regression. Like everything else, evolution does not always move forward. It can move sideways, backwards and, in the worst case, result in the extinction of a species.

What can we do about it? The simplest way is to stop buying unnecessary gadgets, especially those in the areas of personal communication and entertainment. It may cause only a small negative ripple in the employment market that will be more than offset by redirecting growth to where it benefits life most. As an experiment, let us try it for one year and examine the results scientifically.

Let us recall Marshall McLuhan's statement: "We shape our tools and then our tools shape us." Prolonged exposure to television watching has been shown to have a negative effect on the mental development of a child. In my own university teaching experience, I noticed some of my graduate students becoming more fascinated by colours during digital processing of images rather than the factual information they contained.

We can use neuroscience to study experimentally the effect of smart phones and similar devices on our brains and the mind's cognitive function, compared with direct exposure to the real object. Communication devices present virtual reality, commonly in images. Past images require the mind's imagination to describe an object, producing imaginary reality that is a sterile and incomplete view of life. Direct experience in the present moment, on the other hand, offers an opportunity to communicate with life and nonlife as it is unfolding before our senses. It offers the highest form of learning opportunity based on maximum cognition. The cognitive function describing an image is greatly diminished and leads to low-grade, insufficient knowledge. The long-term result is the loss of knowledge and experience of life.

Returning to Life's Order, a helpful way to regain it is by observing its manifestation in nature. An even more effective way is to undertake a trip on foot to a distant place or a pilgrimage to a place of some religious or historical significance. A long trip on foot that is physically and psychologically demanding, during which the pilgrim has to rely on their own resources and is focussed on reaching the point of destination and has time to look deeply into the psyche, is especially beneficial and rewarding. In the end, the pilgrim finds that the goal of their journey was not a physical place but rather a place within their inner self, their self/soul knowing.

One of the best examples of the journey in prenatal life is given in the poem *The First Journey*, which describes the travel of the egg cell. The egg discovers the purpose of its journey, which was to deliver the sacred human form (physically the DNA) on time. The egg succeeded in finishing and completing its journey by merging with the sperm.

A common failure to maintain Life's Order can also be faulty psychology. Let us consider a society that demands of its people a high degree of performance driven by excessive competition, one that rewards primarily material success or offers people too many options that lead to indecision, as well as weakened commitment and dedication. All such activities require an output of life's energy and can generate stress. Many individual journeys are undertaken, but many are also left unfinished, resulting in slowing down of the individual's development and, consequently, the civilization's progress. The other extreme, in which society does not offer its people enough opportunities and incentives to foster a fulfilling life, leads to similarly slow personal growth and diminished progress of civilization. In both cases Life's Order does not function properly.

We have two examples of unfinished journeys explicitly dealt with in the *Poem*. The poem *Order of Life* deals with unfinished work assigned to a farmhand by the mother of the fetus. Her unfinished order (assigned work was not done) was felt by the fetus as not following Life's Order.

Another example is found in the poem *Unmet Love* in which the fetus takes on itself a duty to complete the unfulfilled love between an employee and its mother. As before, the fetus, emotionally drawn into the case, felt that Life's Order of the man was not fulfilled and was left for it to complete when it grows up.

Life is an ordered journey of the conscious self/soul propelled by life energy (containing spirit and consciousness) that causes growth and brings the discovery of personal truth. It is felt by the self as the highest state of being, a pure spiritual state, imbued with God's love.

A question arises: If life is an ordered process, can life sciences, physics and mathematics describe it? It should be possible. The theory of quantum mechanics describes, in a physical and mathematical way, the behaviour of elementary particles such as atoms, electrons, photons, etc. The theory has been proven to be also applicable to macroscopic objects. We will show that it can be used to understand the journey of life discussed next.

14.2 Life's Journey as Quantum Object

The theory of quantum mechanics describes in a physical and mathematical way the behavior of elementary particles such as atoms, electrons, photons, etc. Although it has been proven experimentally using primarily elementary particles, it has been shown to be applicable also to macroscopic objects and—more importantly to us—it can also be used to understand the journey of life.

The building blocks of the quantum world are called *quantum objects* or *things*. A quantum object is not an ordinary object we are used to. For example, we can never "see" a quantum object as a whole. We can see only one of its two aspects, *wave* or *particle*, at a time. The other, called the complementary aspect, is shrouded in uncertainty.

Let us apply this theory to a life journey as we have defined and discussed it above. While we are journeying, the end of our journey remains hidden. It becomes visible only when we stop the journey, reaching its end. If we call a journey a wave and its complementary aspect a particle, revealed by collapsing the wave function by consciousness, we can see the correspondence between a journey and a quantum object. We can say confidently that *life journey is a quantum object or event.*

Interestingly, considering life journey to be a quantum event, establishes correspondence between science and life, and—as we will show later— religion.

15

Power of the Heart

How vital is the heart to our life? I believe that we are not fully aware of this magnificent organ and are not fully utilizing its potential. We are familiar mostly with the physical side of the heart, but its role in life is much broader. In this chapter, we will explore the heart's important functions revealed to us in the poem *Flame and Friendship*. We will begin with a story for children told by Heart about its mission in the life of people.

Heart: "Let me first tell you whence I came, what I do, and what my mission is. I am made of two parts: one comes from the sun and the other from the earth.

I will begin by telling you about my first part, how I became the light of the sun. I worked and tried for a long time before I succeeded. When I finally did, I flared up like a flame. For a short moment I was consumed by the fierce light and fire. Then it subsided. In time, I got used to the light in me and fell in love with it.

Before I was born I thought that the light in my heart came from my mother's heart, which fascinated me with its energy and radiance.

After birth, as a tiny baby, I met the sun for the first time. I wanted to get close to it. Two monks heard my wish and took me to it. We journeyed close to the sun until we reached an observation platform. Beyond that no one can go closer. The sun received me and said it was glad to see me and invited me to come again, anytime. Then the sun told me to go back and remind people on the earth that it can heal them. It was then that I remembered our previous meeting, eons of time ago, when life started on the earth.

My second part is solid, made up mainly of the substance of the earth. It brings me the joy of being active physically, but my main work is to bring life nourishment to every cell. I take great satisfaction doing that.

Now I wish to talk about my mission, the gifts I bring to people. The gifts are not material. Those perish. The gifts I bring are invisible and everlasting. They grow more precious with time.

My first gift is what people call friendship. Although they cannot see it, people can feel friendship in their hearts. They enjoy the feeling. It makes them want to stay together. Some of them want to get even closer. Those ones try to keep that very special feeling deep in their hearts, hidden from others. They look at it as a precious thing and guard it. Feeling friendship is also very healing. It is the finest light that can penetrate every cell in the body and heal it.

When people lose the feeling of friendship and closeness they feel separate and distant. Feeling separate is not a good feeling. It brings on longing. Longing seems necessary to find a way to find and appreciate friendship again.

My second gift to people is the power and courage to do things and overcome obstacles and difficulties. I am using this power all the time. It is the light that makes darkness disappear. It gives people the ability to face uncertainty without fear of the unknown that sometimes stands in their way. When they use the light of the heart, darkness takes flight. They grow stronger. They also feel more powerful afterwards, and others recognize it and may try it themselves. However, I do not spend all my time chasing darkness. I like to spend most time—using my brightest light—to enjoy myself, to play, sing and dance, to laugh with happy people, to feel beauty and love, to share my light with others.

Now that you know all about me, may we be friends?"

Reading the above story will make us feel that the heart acts like an independent being, like a confident child, wise beyond anyone's learning and anxious to show it. If we feel like that, we are close to the truth of the heart. But let us try and find our truth about it ourselves through experience.

Research in neuroscience has identified chemical compounds that are produced in the brain when we feel friendship and love. Such chemicals as serotonin, dopamine and oxytocin have been found during such psychological states and physiological stages of reproduction. We would suggest that the *love* chemistry is a consequence of feeling friendship and love, which came first. The production of these chemicals is simply an effort by the organism to maintain that state. An attempt to supply these chemicals externally without the full understanding of the body's chemistry may lead to undesirable side effects and could be a pathway to addiction. We all have the capacity to produce all we want simply by loving.

Starting one's heart signifies the beginning of the prenatal child's physical activity. It also directs the child to focus on birth. The poem *Flame and Friendship* informs us that our heart action begins when the sleeping heart of the preborn becomes inspired and stimulated by the mother's heart. If the mother's heart plays the role of a stimulator during the initiation of the prenatal child's heart into action, the health and vitality of her heart will influence this process in a way similar to a teacher awakening a student's curiosity and interest in learning. We recall that the energy of the heart's spark comes from the sun. We can thus expect that a *sunny* disposition of the mother's heart will *rub off* on the temperament and health of the child's heart.

In the heart, we find a good example—even a classical one— of the interaction between energy (spark) and matter (muscle), which is the basis for all creation. It may remind us of a car engine whose development might have been subconsciously inspired by the beating heart.

We have learned that the first "action" of the awakened unborn child's heart was an embrace and dance around the mother's heart. We indicated that this event signaled the origin of dance as we know it.

Body hears music,
Heart turns to light and soul moves
In a dance divine.

While the movement of the body, usually as a response to music, is physical and spiritual, dance with a partner to a rhythmic sound has a dimension of friendship with another heart and represents more closely the prenatal event. Heart as a dancer is best symbolized in the statue of the Dancing Shiva, one of the gods in Hindu mythology (Figure 2). This symbol also shows other aspects of the heart discussed below.

15.1
Heart as a Starting Place of Action

Both the above story and the description of starting its heart by the preborn in the poem contain explanations and discussion of the origin of the two main psycho-spiritual aspects of the heart (1) friendship and love and (2) strength and courage. These two fundamental properties of the heart suggest that we ought to approach every task and start every action from the heart

Starting all actions by first engaging the heart makes a lot of sense because it establishes a personal connection (friendship) with the object or person of our interest. We can recall that the first physical action the prenatal child took was to move—to gain more space in the womb—using its heart.

Not engaging our heart more in life keeps us from fully utilizing this great human resource. The culprit is usually the mind. It appears that all the emphasis on developing the mind of the child at school is a one-sided approach to education, which often fails in not being able to spark and hold a child's interest in the subject, preventing it from developing its full life potential. We must be aware that the mind is a powerful tool indeed, but it becomes the greatest and most productive tool when it works together with the heart.

Let us consider an example. Suppose that we meet a new and strange object (the object can be anything that we become aware of) and do not have a robot to analyze its properties like in the science fiction movies. If we engage our mind only, we can gain only general information. However, if we first accept the object in our heart, then invite the mind to analyze its properties, we not only encourage the mind (which has no courage) to do its best, but we also lead it to discover subtle properties that we otherwise may miss. This is especially true when we deal with living objects such as people. People like to feel accepted and secure before they are willing to yield information about themselves as do animals and even plants. We utilize the friendship aspect of the heart.

Let us now consider an example that illustrates the courage aspect of the heart. Suppose that we have a night dream wherein we are trying to catch a train to a distant destination but are not ready. There is only a short time left to gather things that are in different places, in different buildings. We enter the buildings to look for them but cannot find a way out. The frenzy of activity to get ready is a terrible feeling. Suitcases still unpacked, we miss the train.

Since this or a similar kind of dream is quite common, we can deal with it in a general way. Why did we miss the train? Obviously, we needed more time to get ready and greater ability to manage our things. What often keeps us from being ready is procrastination. That could be brought on by fear of failure in completing certain tasks, thus postponing them and creating an accumulation of incomplete journeys. This bears directly on not engaging the courage aspects of the heart to deal with the tasks as they come up. If the dream is a recurring one, we are not using the heart's power to deal with situations in our life.

There is a wise saying: "When reason and heart are in conflict, heart always wins." This is easy to see when we consider what the heart brings to the table, namely love and courage. The ancient Persian poet Hafez writes that our fear comes from being out of tune with love (found in the heart).

It is important to be aware that (1) a problem that is being solved in the heart requires time and (2) the decision arrives in its own time. At the time the decision comes, reason and heart embrace and form a union that will be felt as the power of conviction.

The discussion would not be complete if we did not consider some of the aberrant states of behavior that may develop when the role of the heart is left out. A friendship that resides purely in our mind is a pretense. Friendship and love are spiritual commodities that cannot be bought, negotiated or traded. Neither can they be judged.

Similarly, power generated by ego and residing only in our mind can reach dangerous proportions. Usually based on fear and/or greed, it can lead to wars and the destruction of life and property. War is an aggressive act and, by definition, excludes friendship and love, no matter how its purpose is justified. Only war as a defense against an attacking force is justified, never as a pre-emptive act. We can place in the same category sanctions that are applied against nations to force them to submit to the will of other nations that want to control them. Sanctions punish ordinary people and have little to do with actions of the government. Using innocent people as a means to exert pressure on their leadership in order to change its course of action is not only ineffective, it is immoral, a form of abuse and enslavement.

> Weapons are tools of fear;
> a decent man will avoid them
> except in direst necessity
> and, if compelled, will use them
> only with the utmost restraint.
> His enemies are not demons
> but human beings like himself.
> How could he rejoice in victory
> and delight in the slaughter of men?
>
> —*Tao Te Ching* 31

15.2
Heart as Starting Place of Love

Starting our heart in prenatal life shows the interplay of both action and love. The stimulation of the sleeping heart by the mother's heart was an act of love (divine love), which came first. That love empowered the incipient heart of the fetus. It is emulated in the passing of the light from Mount Olympus to the country staging the Olympic Games, which were conceived as heart games. Athletes agree with that.

We conclude: love is à *priori*, power à *posteriori.*

Love between people starts in a similar way. Attraction (message from the heart) is broadcast by a man to a woman (for example) via his heart light signal along the field of his consciousness. We could interpret the message as: "I want to share with you (give you) the light of my heart." If she accepts this gift, she will also send her heart light in her field of consciousness to the male. This is how a true love relationship begins. It may not stay that way, being subject to many other forces in life.

16
Light and Sound

Light and sound are the most common forms of energy experienced by human beings. Humans have well-developed sensory organs for both.

16.1
Sound

In the poem *Sounds and Sights of Him*, we learn that music has a power to bring people together and creates harmony when they have lost it. We also know from experience that harsh and loud sounds are accompanied by unpleasant feelings.

It is much less known that sound as a vibration can help us to orient in space and locate objects in it. From the description in the poem, it is not clear how the prenatal child recognizes sound vibrations. However, the description suggests that the unborn child has an ability to synthesize waves of various frequencies, reaching it in different time intervals from different directions to form a 3D image of space. This would be similar to space orientation by bats whose mechanism of space perception is based on the synthesis of echoes of self-produced radar frequencies. The prenatal child in our story tried to synthesize sound waves produced by the violin.

In the poem *Sounds and Sights of Him,* the violin music produced by its father is received by the fetus as a pleasant sound. This is reinforced by the pleasant feeling about the music by its mother, transmitted chemically to it. We know from prenatal studies that classical music inspired by nature has a pleasant and calming effect on the prenatal child. Flute music by mountain people living in close contact with nature, as well as pure nature sounds, such as bird songs have a similar calming effect.

We may be interested to know what makes us like certain sounds, certain kinds of music. Earlier, we established the truth that we like what is like us. This implies that there is something in us that *likes* certain frequencies of sound. That something in us resonates with the sound vibration in question. Oneness and the law of unity apply. Resonance is unity of sound between two vibrating objects. What would strike a resonance within our body? The organs, tissues, even individual cells and their components. The more these anatomical *structures* in us resonate, the more we like the sound. This creates a feeling of well-being similar to being with someone we like.

How do loud sounds during our younger years affect us when we are old? This may be important to look at in regard to age-related hearing loss.

As we age, the sensitivity and acuity of our senses diminish. Are there any contributing factors that affect this process? Those of us who still remember how our senses functioned when we were very young would agree that it took very low levels of stimulation to satisfy them. Our senses were fresh and had a high degree of acuity. Gradually, they lost this fine sensitivity and became duller. This happened because of repeated overstimulation that we, in time, became accustomed to. A good example is overeating. There is a sensor in our body near the stomach that will come "*online*" to inform us that we have reached the point of satiation. After a prolonged time of ignoring it, this sensor grows weaker and may even waste away. Continuing to ignore this sensor may also lead to addiction. Most people do not know that there also exists a sensor in our body that informs us about the composition of food we eat. This sensor is the first to atrophy if we ignore or override it. The result of eating unhealthy foods contributes to diseases, even cancer.

Technology and its users are to blame for excessive loudness of music played in popular music venues, theatres, dance halls, etc. It assumes wrongly that if a little sound is good, then more sound is better. Loudness often becomes a substitute for lack of melody. The upshot is that continued exposure to loud noise becomes "normal," and we may gradually lose sensitivity to low and normal levels of sound. The damaging effect on hearing is apparent, especially in old age.

Some relaxation and meditation exercises make use of the ancient sounds of "OM" and "HU." These sounds chanted by participants in unison and continuous way for a period of time are believed to stimulate the pituitary and the pineal glands. These glands play important roles in proper functioning of the endocrine system by regulating metabolic and physiological processes.

16.2 Light and Consciousness

In the poem *Light*, we learned about the *meeting* between the consciousness of the prenatal child and the original cellular tissue from which the retinas of the eyes developed. The tissue reacted by lighting up. These meetings negotiated by the consciousness of the unborn child continued after the eyes separated, through to its birth. In a paper given at the International Society of Prenatal Psychology and Medicine (ISPPM) Congress in Krakow (2001), the author showed how this stimulation helped maintain the mutual belonging and the original unity of the eyes and how, after birth, it resulted in their co-operation and formed the basis for the development of 3D vision.

(An intuitive thought about the origin of 3D vision: 3D vision developed as a desire of the organism to "touch" things at a distance.)

Let us look at the original oneness and its implications for growth more closely. Every organism has a tendency to re-establish its state of unity when something causes it to be broken. The eyes *remembered* their common origin, as identical twins remember being part of the same egg. Although they were later separated (broke their union), the eyes found each other and continued the memory of their original oneness by converging and focussing on the same point. We suggested in the story about the evolution of our solar system that there was an inherent relationship, a mutual belonging, between the sun and the earth that caused them to stay together. Astronomy and physics may have a scientific explanation of how this came about. Here we are concerned with a living organism that is much more sophisticated and subject to forces of creation still unknown to physics.

Would the law of unity and natural belonging work in the case of an inanimate object subjected to a disruptive force that would break it to pieces? I remember as a young child the excavation and relocation of some soil by my father to create a better approach to our farmyard. At that time, I still had a feeling of things, like the soil, "belonging" where they are and *not liking* relocation. This holds true for dust particles, maybe even molecules. At that level of smallness, the unifying force is very much smaller than the disruptive force, but even then, the particles would move to unify with others in time. It may not be the original unity, but it is a unity nonetheless. On a very large scale, an example might be the creation of the solar system.

The above ideas may not conform to current understanding in classical science. They ought to be taken as intuitive. The situation is different in the case of the original light sensitive tissue in which the cells formed a unity. After the tissue was split and the two halves parted, the *mutual belonging* force remained.

16.3 Hungry for Light

The interaction between the conscious self and the response of the eyes to it as light in the life of a prenatal child helps us also to understand what consciousness is and how it functions. It offers an empirical proof of the proposed theory that consciousness is light energy, originally received from the sun. The outdoor sun stimulates the retinas of our eyes in the same way consciousness in the prenatal period stimulated their histological tissues. This established a connection between consciousness and energy. Moreover, it brought evidence that consciousness and sunlight are one and the same energy. Since there are other suns (stars) in the cosmos, human consciousness also has a cosmic origin. Some spiritual teachings refer to it as cosmic consciousness.

> I praise the sun, stars and moon at night
> for the light that puts to flight
> my inner darkness and
> lets my soul see
> eternity.

17
Life Force

According to the poem *Life Force*, the energy that the human organism requires to sustain its life and development is highly evident during intensive growth, the result of an accelerated cell division. When the cells multiply rapidly and the body of the fetus is gaining size and mass, the life force generated by the original sun radiation moves it forward as if it were carried by a moving stream. Recalling the words of the poem **My body swells with energy, leaping, bounding vibrant. An enormous force thrusts me forward in space and time, clears a winding path into future.**

We have here four physical elements at play: energy, mass, space and time. The preborn describes its energy and body (mass) as clearing a winding path (space) into future (time). This would agree with the relativity theory that predicts how a body shall be moving in space-time. In our case, the body of the preborn is growing, adding mass. Although it is not moving anywhere visible to our eye (it remains in the womb), its movement in space-time is due to growth, an outward (inflationary) movement. The perception of moving along a path could also be a feeling stemming from this inflationary pressure (big bang theory?).

The poem also indicates from where this enormous energy comes: **Daisies quiver, bloom into light, reach for the sun, effuse life...**

The life energy, acting as life force, comes from the sun. It is up to us, in adult life, to be conscious of the life force and try to find the best way of putting the sun's energy into our bodies by means of nutrition.

Often, we hear about situations which *take away* our strength (life energy) and also about ways to increase it. Nothing can take away or create our energy. Energy can be only transferred. However, the flow and distribution of energy in the body can be slowed down or impeded by emotional, mental or physical blockages.

Some of the most serious among *energy-wasting* situations are unresolved past traumas discussed in chapter 8. Here we have to tread carefully. Freeing up the energy trapped in the past, especially in early childhood, may involve confronting our ego, which is normally very reluctant to give up its reign when backed by a strong, perceived early life need that still persists. The ego may resort to an evasive maneuver that may lead to neurosis, illusory dreams or addictions, all of them examples of energy wasting. Those unhealthy conditions further mask and complicate the resolution of the initial trauma. However, the brave souls who will tackle and eliminate these aberrant behaviors are rewarded by a discovery of deep, spiritual levels of their true, strong and vibrant self.

18
Tree of Life

The reader may want to review the poem *The Tree, Earth and I* and its analysis. That prenatal experience deals with the relationship between the fetus and the earth and also plays a similar role in adult life.

In prenatal life, the relationship is mediated by an organ especially created for that purpose—placenta. We will call it *tree of life*. By means of this tree-like structure, matter of the earth, which contains the energy of the sun, is transferred into the body of the developing child. It is one of the most significant life processes during which nourishing substances that originate in the body of the living earth find, after further revitalization in the body of the human mother, their *home* in the body of the child.

> *The roles of the earth and sun as the makers and keepers of all life should be the fundamental philosophical thought behind all the environmental debates and protection measures we are engaged in as a society.*

We learned that elementary particles of matter that the fetus received and gave a home to in its body tell a story about their journeys since they left their home in the earth, looking for a new one in the body of the developing child. According to our theory of consciousness, the energy contained in that matter is consciousness.

Through the assimilation of the earth's matter, the preborn is also bound to it. This bond created by everything that we accept and make our own cannot be broken without the *pain of separation*. That is why we do not want to die and leave our body with all that it contains.

Nature chose and empowered woman with the divine task of procreating the human race. It equipped her with special organs for that purpose and ensured that a new, completely individual and autonomous being could develop naturally and as much as possible, independently. Fetal growth and development is governed by hidden, more profound natural laws than we are able to comprehend. Its development should, therefore, be safeguarded as much as possible.

The tree of life (placenta) plays a very important role in the physical and psychological life of the fetus. It is its source of nourishment, bliss, friendship, knowledge and joy. With its assistance and influence, its organs are formed that take over this role after birth. Every one of us carries in our subconscious an image of the tree of life.

Figure 6 *Tree of Life* by Gustav Klimt

Figure 6 is a painting of the *Tree of Life* by Gustav Klimt. It fits very well our description of the prenatal tree (placenta). In the curvilinear and spiraling branches, we see particles of matter. They grow larger as they come closer to the trunk of the tree and ground (body) in agreement with the poem. The fact that the fetus perceives them larger as they come closer shows that its consciousness is aware of the *size* of an object and space. The size may, in this case, be related more closely to the intensity of consciousness (energy) rather than physical size.

There are three tree-like images of placental cotyledons (little "bonsai" trees) and a picture of an Egyptian bird, a symbol of wisdom and knowledge. We could conclude that the painter had imagined an image of a placenta from his prenatal life quite well.

18.1 Tree of Life After Birth?

Is there a tree of life after birth, and if so, where could we find its locus? We could begin by looking in the place at the navel where the umbilical cord entered our body in prenatal life. According to yogic teachings, the place just below the navel is the seat of the second chakra, which is associated with sensuality, sexuality and creativity. None of the symbols associated with this chakra seems to bear an image of a tree directly, except for the last one. The estuary of the umbilical cord may not be the place to look for a *postnatal tree of life.*

Still, what could we imagine by the term tree of life in adult life? Taking as an example the prenatal period, it would have to be something that nourishes us both physically and psychologically. Some may think of a family tree, but more realistically, we would have to find and create such a tree by ourselves. It is one of the main tasks of life.

Can we imagine a way in which a tree of life is generated in our postnatal life? In chapter 29 we will discuss the meaning of prenatal life as a learning period of life's principles that we put into practice in postnatal life. Our prenatal child regarded the tree (placenta) as a source of nourishment, joy, friendship and knowledge. Thus, we would strive to find—this time by our effort and work—the same in postnatal life.

> Our current life connects us
> to the origin of life on Earth.
> After birth, we are instinctively led to become
> one with Nature. This inherent need

seeking fulfillment is led by the self
with our senses and body's nourishing
and growing needs. Our digestive tract and
metabolism supply matter and energy.
In the process it unlocks consciousness
trapped in matter that contains
knowledge of life imbedded in Nature.
Thus we become Nature which
fills us with joy and love and makes
our life a continuous celebration.

The tree of life after birth becomes our creative work. It becomes our life's purpose. This shows that work is a means necessary for a happy life. Not having an opportunity to work, being unemployed, is an unnatural state and a debilitating feeling.

18.2 Tree as a Symbol of Spiritual Life

I feel it important to the overall theme of life described in this book to express my own close relationship that I have with trees. In my view, a tree personifies in the simplest and most direct way the relationship between the sun and earth, which is one of a mutual bond and spirit love. This kind of love is characterized by giving and receiving, and its outcome is the creation of living forms.

To my way of thinking, trees are the most successful lifeforms on earth. They are the longest living lifeforms, have an enormous strength and endurance, and play a most important and useful role. All of us learned about them in school and by observing them in nature. They take the energy given by the sun and substance from the earth to create growth in an optimal way. They show us a way to live naturally.

19

How Not to Get Lost in Life

Before it started its journey, the egg received advice on how to find its way in the world it wanted to enter and not get lost in it (see the poem *The First Journey*). The analysis of this poem revealed a mystery as to where this advice came from (see discussion of that poem in part 2 of the book). The suggestions put forward ranged from God to the brain/mind of the earthly father. With its consciousness *I am*, the ovulating egg became aware of the father's brain/mind when he was in close proximity and talking to his wife. The self of the egg perceived him as someone who knew the order of the world. The egg united with his brain/mind through the *I am* consciousness. The advice on how not to get lost in the world was revealed to it. This is the author's most believable version of the invisible *Source* perceived by the egg. It would indicate a possibility of a communication between two selves: (1) the father and (2) the ovulating egg via consciousness. It resembles also the communication between the mother's heart and the sleeping heart of the embryo described in the poem *Flame and Friendship* and discussed in part 2 of the book.

While the above explanation is the one preferred by the author, we would also say, according to the discussion in chapter 14, that the advice is part of Life's Order, an inherent property of the life force. In the end—if you believe that God created humans in his own image—it really does not matter whether the advice came from the heavenly or the earthly father. The divine nature of the advice is apparent.

The advice of how not to get lost in life itself is simple: to consciously follow and remember the way, including its beginning. Everyone knows from experience the truth of this general rule. We have all erred by ignoring major parts of our life journey, such as the prenatal life and early childhood. Society led us to pay little or no attention to them by labelling them unimportant, advising us to "grow up." Even if we have forgotten important segments of our life, all is not lost. The memory tracks of our experiences exist in our subconscious and can be recalled and made conscious again. However, the road to recovery of early life memories is not easy and is not for everyone. Those who do not wish to try it can be assured that all is not lost. They can still draw on the knowledge of that time indirectly. This is possible because of life's connectedness. Later events in life are connected to and influenced by the earlier ones, all the way back to prenatal life, the beginning of the current life, of life on the planet and beyond. In this way, important experiences from the past penetrate into the present from the subconscious without us being aware of it. As examples, we can think of conception and birth. Those events are so paramount that we cannot imagine them not to accompany us or influence us throughout the whole life.

20

Life's Mission and Our Star Origin

Like the egg cell that discovered the purpose of its journey **to deliver the sacred human form on time**, every one of us seeks the awareness of the purpose of our life or would like to know their life mission. Often people regard their life's purpose to be their life's work or some significant accomplishment, distinguished professional excellence, service to mankind or just plain survival.

Life's mission is something that reaches beyond the realm of the individual. Its design is transcendental, and its beneficiary is not only the life of the individual but life as a whole. It is hidden in the deepest parts of our being. People who have a mission in life also have a feeling that they were sent or chosen by some higher power to carry it out. A life mission gives our life a firm goal, a feeling of confidence and an impetus that takes on a deeper meaning because it is not directed toward a selfish end. Selfishness is perishable, but life is eternal. The mission of the egg was straightforward and required only a subtle action of consciousness. The overall purpose was biological—preservation of life and species—which benefits life as a whole.

Generally, the awareness of life mission is not common. Many questions about it may arise in the mind: Why should we have a life mission? Where does it come from? Is there only one mission? It is difficult to answer such questions. The author's personal view is that it relates to our individual unfolding, the maturation of our soul. It may be the continuation of the thought evolution of our ancestors, a process of evolution of civilization in which we play a part, etc.

The point at which the self becomes aware of its life mission comes at the *proper time* when the conditions are ripe and the organism is ready. The whole mission may not be revealed at once, only that particular stage needed to advance it toward its next stage and completion.

The author considers his life a mission to make people aware of their prenatal life, its meaning and importance to the postnatal life, the origin and nature of consciousness and the origin of life on Earth. He reveals the steps in his mission at the end of the book.

We ought to distinguish life mission from a wish although they may both manifest outwardly in the same way. A wish is normally connected with a desire or ambition and is directed by ego, whereas a mission springs out of the depth of our being, is directed by spirit, and transcends the individual.

While the awareness of life's mission generally occurs naturally like growth, it is also possible to seek it actively. An example comes from the life of North American native peoples that I observed in Canada. It is a custom for a young native man, upon attaining the age of maturity, to seek his life mission by means of a ritual. He will retire to a secluded place in nature (to him a place of power) where he spends several days and nights. Through fasting, sweating and night vigilance, he cleanses his body and quiets his mind. In this manner, he reaches a state in which he can see more clearly who he truly is and is open to hear a voice expressing his life's purpose or mission.

20.1
Our Star Connection

Matter and energy connect us with the universe. We have stated that the original form of consciousness was the awareness of the radiant energy of the sun. Early in prenatal life, we had an opportunity to observe and experience the elementary energy-matter interactions and processes. The self of the embryo, in its first interaction with particles of matter carrying encapsulated solar energy, discovered its origin and oneness with the light of the stars. The interaction reminded the embryo about its *home* among them.

Sensitive people feel their bond with the universe when, on a clear night, they gaze at the stars in the sky. Some believe that they have their own star from which they came. Others may seek their life mate among them. This widespread common experience is another indication that we are universal beings.

Although we depend almost fully on the sun for our survival, another question arises: "Is there a way other stars could influence our psyche?" There might be a way, if we assumed that stars have aware consciousness like our sun-star. We could regard them as universal beings that know about each other via consciousness. We said earlier that the awareness of sun's light became our consciousness. It might work the same way among the stars. Through the sun, we are thus connected to other stars.

21

Power to Move

In this chapter, we will examine the process behind physical movement. Since the basic movements of the limbs began in prenatal life, we have had an opportunity to get to know the fundamental processes that comprise movement and become aware of the primal body movements and exercises. The poem speaks about a centre of the *power-to-move*. It may refer to a major nerve centre in our body known as the solar plexus. In yoga, it corresponds to the third chakra, which is considered to be the psychic centre of energy and a source of power. Ultimately, the power to move starts with consciousness.

We discussed the source of power and courage in connection with the heart where we emphasized the role of the spark (electrical impulse = consciousness of the heart). The electrical impulse (flame) is the source of the function and strength of the heart muscle. This also applies to the movement of all muscles and functions of all organs. All of them require electrical energy impulses distributed by the nerves. A great concentration of these nerves in solar plexus is why we feel it to be the locus of strength and power. Going deeper, we take the source to be the life force we are conscious of.

For the maintenance of good physical health, we need energy and proper functioning of all nerves that result in optimal activity of all muscles and organ functions. We can strengthen our muscles by exercises and support the functioning of organs by a healthy diet.

We have stated in the analysis of the poem *Power to Move* (part 2 of the book) that the execution of a physical movement consists of (1) an intention regarding which part of the body (e.g., a limb) to move, conveyed by consciousness and (2) engaging the source of the power of movement to execute that movement in the intended way. After we have practiced the movement many times, the power to move is placed on *autopilot*, so that we do not have to be consciously aware of it.

Aware consciousness of energy was crucial to the proper execution of the movement in prenatal life. If we do not have enough energy or put excessive energy into a movement, led by mind, and in both cases being unaware of the states of energy, we are putting the process in danger of stress that can result in pain and injury. Repeated exercise that results in pain will, in time, damage the physical components engaged in the exercise. This will show later in life when our stressful force diminishes.

One of the best ways of getting in touch or awakening the physical force is trying to pull something apart with both hands and arms. When one exerts the maximum force (felt as the force of separation), it may bring on the feeling of trying to be born and pushing through the birth canal. We will describe this later.

21.1
Strengthening Neck Muscles

We are led to think about body intelligence when we read the poem *Through the Arm Noose* and its analysis, which describes an exercise that a prenatal child performs to strengthen its neck. Why would it want to strengthen its neck? The child somehow anticipates that it will need a strong neck for a physical task that awaits it in the future. A person knowledgeable about birth would be quick to suggest that the task in question is connected with birth when the child must use its head and neck to initiate and execute its passage through the birth canal.

The way the child goes about its neck exercises is another example of innate intelligence and ingenuity. The child creates a loop by clasping the elbows with its hands raised in front of its face and then tries to thread its head through the loop. This simulates the forceful movement of the head through the birth canal using the neck muscles. After birth, a similar movement is needed when a baby tries to lift its head while crawling or lifting its head in the crib or carriage to see its mother. Proper functioning of the cervical vertebrae and strength of the neck muscles are important when we consider just the work our necks have to do to keep our heavy heads upright.

21.2
Touch

The sense of touch in a prenatal child appears to exist from its very beginning, and although it is implied in many examples in the *Poem*, we are not sure how it functions. For example, at conception, the two cells are described as touching before merging. In *Touching Stars* the implanted embryo describes *touching* the energized particles of food. All we can say is that some form of contact was made, negotiated by consciousness and energy that left a memory.

In the later stages of development, during which the fetus makes contact as a result of a deliberate physical motion, we can speak of real touching that we know in postnatal life. The most obvious case is the fetus's establishment of communication with its mother by knocking on the wall of the womb.

There are also many examples of the fetus exercising its body through movement. By means of ultrasound imaging, scientists have accumulated many records about that.

A person with prenatal memory is able to mimic these movements in adult life, which is one of the best proofs of the authenticity of recalling prenatal memories.

22
Anger, Bliss and Place of Silence

A prenatal child does not show many emotions originating in its own life, but it reacts to the emotional states of its mother via chemical pathways. On the whole, it accepts life and the world as it unfolds naturally. It has no likes or dislikes because it does not choose things and is not confronted with options that we have to deal with in postnatal life.

Among the emotions passed to it from its mother, the fetus finds anger to be the most difficult to deal with, as described in the poem *Attacks of Anger*. Its mother's anger secreted **angry molecules** that the fetus describes as **lit-up attackers, moving in chains** toward it. Its consciousness was intensified by their high-energy charge, causing them to be highlighted against the background. Such hormonal secretions, as we know in adult life, alert and prepare our body for fight, flight or freeze. The fetus could not fight physically and had no place to run. Its only means of defense was to conquer the attackers chemically. It succeeded in doing so but not without enduring severe shaking and fever while its body fought and tried to neutralize the poison. In the end, it found that the attackers changed into guards that would defend it against future attacks. We might also look at this process in a positive way as training the child to face its own anger in postnatal life.

In the episode *Unmet Love*, the fetus is a recipient of loving feelings between its mother and a male employee. The amiable chemistry resulted in an emotional attachment between the fetus and the man that had potentially unpleasant consequences.

There are many examples of enjoyable feelings described by the fetus in its life story. These have to do mainly with feeling good about its life energy—*joie de vivre.*

22.1
Bliss

In the poem *Wellbeing,* the unborn child reflects on its life in the womb and describes its feelings as comfortable, being suspended in the radiant warmth of the amniotic fluid. The use of the word *radiant* is telling us that the fetus is conscious of the thermal radiation of the liquid rather than of its temperature. It describes its life as beautiful, meeting all its needs and bringing it peace and well-being. Many people may think that such a state is the way things are in the womb. Unfortunately, it is not all like that.

22.2
Place of Silence

Exploring the feelings of the prenatal child further, we find an episode (*Place of Silence*) in which the fetus discovers a place in its head where it can go to *hide* from an excessive noise outside the womb. The disturbing feeling or sensation that we get from exposure to an excessive level of sound is quite familiar to us. To be able to retreat to such a place of silence, described by the fetus, would be a very useful skill to have: Find a place in the head – the memory of the histological tissue from which the eyes developed before they differentiated. Why would this stop the sound? Because, at that time, the ears were not developed either.

Whether it would be possible to revive this useful prenatal skill is debatable. Those who believe in awakening their prenatal memory would have an advantage.

23
Thoughts

Thoughts are constant companions in our life dating back to the latter stage of our prenatal life, as the poem *Thoughts* indicates. They play an important role in our lives, especially those that come to us from outside.

Let us begin by examining the physical nature of thoughts. The fetus describes thoughts as moving **ribbons of light**. Light refers to their electrical charge and light origin. A question: If thoughts are ribbons of light in the head and can move in space, are they alive? We will answer that question later. You may think of the answer by considering the way consciousness works as explained in chapter 5.3, example 5.

In the brain, we can think of thoughts as live electrical circuits made up of chains of neurons that are lit up by our consciousness (energy). At this time, we may recall example 3 *Light and Eyes* in chapter 5.3.

Thoughts are food for our mental life. As food particles feed our physical body, thoughts feed our mental body. As food particles need our invitation to find a home in our body, thoughts also need our acceptance to live in us. As the fetus says, thoughts are beggars, **Take me, accept me, keep me alive (in your life)** This would indicate that thoughts are indeed alive. As consumers of large amounts of our life energy, thoughts play a huge role.

However, not all thoughts and ideas may be beneficial to our life, depending on their properties, especially their content and intent. It is necessary, therefore, to examine each thought before we give it life within us. We do this by consulting our highest self, as well as the liveliest centre(s) in our physical self. The seat of our highest self is located in the upper region of the brain, the neocortex. It is indeed remarkable that there is a place in our head where the ability to know, evaluate and discriminate is located. The main role in it is played by reason. This ability, closest to our personal *I*, is obviously very important for the unfolding of our potential. It is accompanied by a feeling of lightness and clarity.

Note: We have encountered the feeling of light and lightness many times in connection with various experiences in prenatal life. The feeling signifies an increase of the energy of consciousness, which indicates that such a feeling resonates with our personal truth.

The places of the liveliest self are the *pituitary* and *pineal* glands.

When we are diligent and discriminating managers of thoughts, our minds are sound, and our lives strong.

Foremost, we have to be careful in managing our thoughts, since they consume our life energy and can crowd our mind's garden. Bertrand Russell shared similar ideas about his need to examine each thought and how, if he found a given thought bad, he threw it out as if it were a weed.

Where do thoughts come from? They originate in the brain and are formed by the mind using aware consciousness in examining the information content of the brain. The brain is a vast reservoir of life experience. This information and its different forms comprise the ingredients of thought formation. The fetus tells us that we need to pay special attention to thoughts coming from without: **Each being outside sends thoughts to me... expecting my life to carry their messages.**

How does the fetus receive the messages? The fetus communicates by telepathy. This requires an explanation.

Thoughts are accompanied by consciousness and thus can be regarded as quantum phenomena. Although their electrical charges are small, they nevertheless cause tiny ripples in the quantum fields of consciousness and can be received by the brain of another person, when they are open and tuned in. Being quantum entities, thoughts have quantum properties. How it works physically is still a mystery, but there is enough experimental evidence to consider telepathy as a real phenomenon. While we are thinking, a thought is a wave. When our consciousness collapses the wave, the thought becomes a particle, a decision, opinion, etc.

Telepathy as a transference of thoughts still does not tell us how the fetus in our prenatal story understands the meaning of thoughts, verbalized or silent, expressed by people who came to talk with its mother during her pregnancy. Those people would have been aware of the unborn child and might have imagined a picture of it, perhaps even its character and gender. Words elicit an image in our brain, an iconic form. If we accept the idea that our brain is prewired to recognize these icons, then like pieces of a puzzle put together, the meaning of a thought might be revealed in the composite.

An intuitive thought: neuronal cells are equipped to receive the icons much as the body cells can receive particles of food—via their receptors. The human mind is designed to process images, which computers with digital processing find extremely difficult to do and may never be fully capable of matching.

Is the life of thoughts unlimited? Until they are accepted by the self, thoughts do not exist as part of our life. However, they become so when accepted, and will empower us from that time on so long as we keep them alive by feeding them energy through our conscious attention. If we do not give them any further attention (energy), they will weaken, atrophy and die of starvation.

Apart from the thoughts coming to us from the outside and those based on the processing of information in the brain, there exist thoughts that well up from the deep levels of our unconscious, such as the intuitive thoughts. As an example, the fetus begins the poem *Thoughts* by saying, **I lie in a trough that will narrow, curve to the right as it takes me closer to the world outside.**

This is obviously its *view* of the upcoming birth.

24
Seeking Goals and Life's Design

Most of our adult life activities consist of journeys whose ends are goal- and purpose-oriented. On the other hand, in the life of a fetus, there are only a few cases when its journey could be termed goal-oriented. They are: finding a place to implant; starting the heart; finding a way to communicate with the mother; searching for an exit door to leave the womb and struggle to be born. In all of these cases, the unborn child is guided by the survival instinct built into the life force as part of the grand life design.

The method the fetus uses in finding the goal is known as trial and error. It is a method commonly used by all of us while learning new skills and overcoming obstacles. It is used also in scientific research, design and analysis of experiments and myriad other situations that present themselves in life as challenges. Entrepreneurial people are familiar with it, when they say, "If at first you don't succeed, try again."

In the case of the fetus, its search for a means of establishing communication with its mother was, on the one hand, a process of trial and error, and on the other hand, its success was preordained by life design. The outcome was also predetermined in the other four cases. In all of them, the need for repeated trials was led by the creative spirit of the life force, accompanied by the survival instinct.

After birth, the goals that we seek—while still generally motivated by survival—are led mostly by choice and free will. Their outcome is, therefore, not definite and straightforward. In postnatal life, we can be really creative and follow our dreams. Herein is the big difference between the prenatal and postnatal life: in the former, life follows mainly the Creator's design, whereas, in the latter, our free will and the creative spirit, among other factors, often play major roles. As a result, there is much higher uncertainty of outcome of our goals after birth. It may even result in chasing for *unreachable* goals, such as the quest of Don Quixote.

It follows from the fetus's description of how it succeeded in establishing a physical communication with its mother (in the poem *Knocking on the Wall*) that it is the child who is the initiator of the preparation for birth; it instinctively knows what is involved physically to reach it. The communication with the mother was achieved by knocking on the wall of the womb, and that caused reflex movements of her organs and muscle tissues engaged during birth. The expectant mother should use the opportunity to work with the child in training her internal anatomy for natural movement of the child through the birth canal. Each time the child knocks, she should focus consciously on the abdominal area around the place of the knocking and take time to relax and give way to the natural reactions of her body and psyche. I believe that this represents the most important step in preparation for delivery. The key role in this process is played by consciousness. Other preparations for birth that are being offered to expectant mothers in the form of various courses and exercises can be beneficial to them only if they do not divert their attention (through the mind) from the way nature intended childbirth to be, namely, based on the co-operation between mother and child.

24.1
Reaching Goals Through Anticipation

Much has already been said about the force of change in the analysis of the poem by the same title in the second part of the book. The theme of this discussion is the anticipation by the fetus of a change in its life that is coming up. The fetus sees the upcoming change as a translocation of its body (birth) that will occur in the near future. As was already observed, the fetus is aware of time only when it accompanies a change.

Location of a moving object in space has been defined in classical physics in terms of a four-dimensional space-time continuum. We will refer to it by one word—*change*. Our definition will include more than just a position and momentum of a moving body in space. It will include any change whatsoever, for example, physical, chemical, psychological, etc.

The fetus feels that everything outside changes, not only its position but that all things are also undergoing an inner change, too small to be experienced as a relocation in space. It feels that all changes are caused by an invisible force that permeates everything. The fetus describes it as the *force of change.*

There are two ways of dealing with life changes: (1) accept the changes that life offers us or (2) resist the changes that threaten or do not benefit us. At times, it is not clear which way we should go. In such a case, it is best to do nothing and wait until the situation clears up enough to make a decision.

The fetus normally trusts the life force and accepts life changes as they come. At first, the fetus feels sad when faced with the prospect of leaving the womb, a place that was a good home. It will miss the friendship with the tree (placenta) and all that it got to know and befriended there. Still, it will not resist the force of change, when its time comes. From that we could theorize that our life is directed toward a developmental goal. Co-operation with the life force gives us a feeling of self-confidence, satisfaction and fulfillment of life. There is no need to fret about the future of life, including death. Life safeguards its continuum, and nothing is wasted or disappears permanently.

24.2 Reaching Goals by Precognitive Dreaming

In the third example of the application of the method of trial and error, the fetus is preparing for its exit from the womb by trying to find an opening that will also signal the beginning of birth. The fetus thus determines the day of its birth.

To find the opening to the outside, the fetus has to reach deeper inside itself, into the realm of dream consciousness. There is a reason why this exercise could not be carried out during its waking consciousness. Finding the exit door from the womb is not a physical but a psychophysical exercise involving communication with the unconscious realm. The whole process may appear to us as a repetitive dream within which lies the solution to one of the most important life tasks. It is a precognitive, premonitory dream that predicts a crucial life event to take place. I believe that this kind of dream will also predict the death of our physical body and exit from the material existence.

Psychophysical changes, in which there is no input of prior knowledge, especially those that deal with important events and life stages, are usually presented in the form of a dream. In our case, the fetus enters a room in which it looks for an exit door. The dream repeats for many nights without success of finding the exit door. During the day, the energy of the fetus and the tension grow progressively stronger until, near the end, it can hardly stand it. During waking hours, the fetus practices the exercise of strengthening its neck described in the sub-chapter 21.1. After a sequence of many of these dreams, the fetus asks, **How many rooms must I still visit till I find the way out?** Finally, the dream reveals the solution. The fetus finds the opening and declares, **Tomorrow I'll be born.**

The process bears many of the manifestations of a quantum process in which the outcome has a high degree of *à priori* certainty.

Does this remind us of our adult dreamlike experience when, for example, we are in a city with many streets and buildings, trying to find a way out or looking for an address we cannot find before the dream ends? Such and similar dreams likely originate in the prenatal period. We find similar motives also in paintings of classical masters. It does not have to be a scene containing houses and rooms. Every repeated dream in which we are trying to find an exit from an important situation could be a reflection of a prenatal experience. In the same way as the unborn child searches for a door to exit the womb—knowing that it will open—we, at the end, also find the exit from a situation in the form of a solution.

Nature of Dreams: Dreams are a way our subconscious and unconscious realms communicate to us important and essential knowledge about our life, knowledge that we have suppressed during our waking state. A dream's physical nature is, in my intuitive view, a neuronal pattern in the brain that is created by the dormant consciousness to convey a message to us. To remember and be able to examine the information contained in the message, we need to catch it at or near the boundary between the waking and dormant states of consciousness. Our waking consciousness must be in the basic state *I am*—no mind or identity—to see the image before it identifies itself with it (accepts it as us). Our waking mind, with the aid of feelings, then interprets the image as a space/time event.

25
Birth

Birth is a key event in our prenatal life, second in importance only to conception. Conception represents our entry into life as an autonomous living being; birth represents our entrance into the world as a complete being. Death signals the discontinuity as a physical living form. Whether there is continuity in some other form of existence after death, we will learn when we get there. We will return to this topic at the end of the book.

Conception is directed entirely by spiritual forces and is—if we exclude the technology of reproduction—entirely natural, whereas birth is also influenced by people and is, therefore, not entirely natural. People are no longer entirely natural.

At birth, the natural, hidden world of the child begins to collide with the world of adults. Depending on the severity, this collision is not without some physical or psychological damage to the newborn. Today, we know of many disorders caused by birth, and more will be identified in the future. For birth to be natural (without harmful interference), there has to be complete harmony between the performance of the child and mother during delivery. An *unnatural* mother will not have a natural delivery. What do we mean by *unnatural*? There are many ways to be unnatural. One of the most common is a high level of stress fueled by fear.

We have stated that the child is the initiator and leading actor in the drama of birth. Using its body movements, the child tries to squeeze through the uterine opening to reach the outside. The birthing mother reacts to the child's movements by letting her organs give in to the pressure in a responding manner, thereby enabling the passage of the child. The process is similar to passing a stool. If she trained her muscles prior to delivery during the time the child was communicating with her by knocking on the womb wall, it will not be difficult for her to do so now. All the mutual movements of mother and child are unforced; they seem almost automatic. Her performance could be easier if first rehearsed.

It is regrettable that at the level of our civilization today, the natural harmony between the birthing mother and child has been weakened. As a result, the birth process frequently becomes a dramatic event. Birth is a holistic event that we can still observe in nature. It is commonly viewed (incorrectly) as a process in which the woman plays the principal role. Since the human birth is no longer holistic, we will divide its discussion into two parts: (1) the child's effort to be born and (2) the woman's effort to deliver.

25.1
Child's Effort to Be Born

The process of birth for the child begins with the establishment of communication with its mother by knocking on the wall of the womb as described in chapter 24. In the poems *Force of Change* and *Preparing to Leave,* we learned about the child's activities that include its preparation for birth, such as strengthening the neck muscles, knocking on the wall and raising its energy, accompanied by a feeling of change and searching for exit. Finally, by finding the *door*, the child is ready and sets the day of birth. When that time arrives, it signals to the mother its wish by pressing and knocking its head against the opening in the uterus. Its effort increases and becomes more emphatic until it reaches the peak of the child's tolerance. If the birthing mother does not co-operate with the effort of the child, it can lead to its exhaustion and feelings of hopelessness, even despair. Further, its struggle can bring on a feeling that its mother and the people outside do not understand, that it cannot do anything more to be born, and decides that its life cannot continue as is.

To give up living is the last stage in the impossible struggle to continue living. The child is ready to surrender the life it has experienced so far. However, it does not say that this is the end of its existence. We can see a similarity in the prey surrendering to the predator at the end of its struggle to live as an independent lifeform.

In our case, the feeling of dying appeared to the child as a separation of the conscious soul from the body, moving outside, finding a stream and dropping down on its bank to die, covered by fog. It shuts down its waking (aware) consciousness in the process. We will look at this event in more detail.

First of all, we have the conscious self/soul leaving the body. Right away, we should consider two possibilities: Was it a journey into (1) the real world outside or (2) the inner world of the child's subconscious? It may be difficult to find the answer.

Let us start with the second question first: the fetus knows about the outside through the physical movement of its mother. This knowledge, which may appear dreamlike, lacks detail and clarity. On the other hand, to answer the first question, the description by the child corresponds very closely to the existing landscape situation at that time of birth (end of February). It was a time of snow melting and high water flow in the creek, also a time for the arrival of the storks that nested regularly on the chimney of our small country flour mill. The accuracy of this description supports the first possibility, namely, that the conscious soul left the body and actually moved outside. When consciousness moves out of the body that is still alive, it maintains its connection with it due to the inseparability of the two quantum objects: the free-moving consciousness and the consciousness (energy) tied to the living body. The detachment of the aware consciousness (property of the soul) from the body is almost always described by people who have had a near death experience.

In Greek mythology, the river Styx symbolizes the boundary between the living and dead. Crossing the river signifies no return to life as it was. In our episode, the conscious soul stops and rests on the near bank of the river; it does not cross it. When it hears the call to come back, it wakes up (regains waking consciousness) and returns to the body to complete the birth.

25.2
Woman's Effort to Deliver

When a woman has doubts about being able to deliver the child naturally, the birth usually takes place in a medical facility with medical supervision and assistance. Even in such situations, complications could arise that can cause discomfort, pain, even injury to her and the child.

Our story took place at a time (close to a hundred years ago) when it was common, especially in a country setting, to conduct birth with the assistance of a midwife. Such was also the situation in our case. Unfortunately, as we learned from the description, the birth resulted in lifelong damage to the health of the child.

A stiff umbilical cord caused excruciating pain and shock to the abdominal area of the child. Twisting of the baby's head by the midwife during the passage of the body through the birth canal caused damage to the cervical vertebrae. The baby trained its neck to push and pull motion, not for a twisting motion. Because of the prolonged delivery, the baby went through out-of-body consciousness experience, which can be viewed as an attempt by the child to exit its life. In retrospect, this also became a learning experience.

The conditions surrounding birth have since improved, both for women and children as far as medical understanding and technical assistance are concerned. However, we must not give up in our search for a natural way to conduct this most important step into the world for the baby.

26
Pillars of Personality

From the biography of the prenatal child, we can form a picture of the fundamental traits of its character and behavioral tendencies that form the beginning of its personality. The word *personality* in our discussion will be used in its original meaning used by C.G. Jung as the state of realization of the individual's life potential at that time of their life.

Personality is constructed from a human being's experiences and reactions to the developmental events and growth. We have found that the important personality trends appeared already in prenatal life. We could observe others appearing shortly after birth. Because of their early appearance, we can say that they form the foundation of human personality. They also form the basic pillars of civilization.

One of the first expressions of personality is the feeling of independence, which we found in the poems *Ring of Independence* and *Mati*. The preborn's awareness of his autonomous and free existence is necessary to fully realize its potential. While independence in postnatal life may separate us from others, it also adds to the curiosity of others about us. Originality, which is always accompanied by individuality and independence, is often found attractive. For the full unfolding of our potential, we need freedom to be and freedom to do. The greatest gift a person can give to another—or a nation to another nation—is to acknowledge their inherent right to freedom. It should never be taken away by man.

Just as freedom is the basic necessity for the growth of personality of an individual, it is also necessary for the functioning and development of a nation, including its various groups and organizations. Both the citizen and the country require personal and political freedom for optimal development. Suppression of human rights of freedom of expression, movement, private entrepreneurship, as well as interference in the independence of other nations and countries, and politically motivated pressures directed by one country toward another, are pathological symptoms that disregard the right of freedom. For global civilization to move forward, the time has come to root out dictatorship, propaganda and wars in the same way as rooting out communicable diseases. To defend oneself against an attacker or occupant, to defend one's freedom and sovereignty is natural and necessary. Killing of innocent, defenceless people in a forceful act such as an unprovoked war is a crime against humanity. The number of victims determines the size of the crime. An excuse for killing innocent people as unavoidable (collateral damage) within the framework of a war is hypocrisy. The attacker, unfortunately, fails to realize that his act is a moral crime.

The merging of the reproductive cells and the conscious experience of conception is physically and psychologically the most fundamental, meaningful event of our life. It establishes the base for our personality. Its lasting influence is reflected in our tendency to seek closeness and become one with everything that interests us and is attractive. It results in our propensity to participate in life. In this tendency is rooted harmony and love not only for people but also the environment. Everything that life creates benefits from this interaction. It is remarkable that we do not have a word for it. Perhaps people did not have a need to talk about it.

Freedom and harmony alone, however, will not guarantee that our life will proceed in the right way. For that to happen, we need to experience life and seek the truth in our experiences. We have many examples of seeking personal truth in the poems: In the poem *Hungry Birds*, the fetus tries to help quiet a flock of hungry chickens and associates their feeding with its own food intake. In *Order of Life*, it wishes for everyone to have perfect order in everything as it has. In *Tree, Earth and I*, it tries to make its anxious mother aware of the tree of life as a source of an unending supply of life sustenance and joy.

The experience of pure truth in adult life is rare, but those who feel that moment learn that truth awakens (1) a feeling of enlightenment and (2) a wish and inspiration to help others reach the same. Truth reminds us of the unity of all life. The feeling of unity induces in us an extension of the feeling for that unity by caring for others. The statement "Love thy neighbor as thyself" is not an order; it springs from the depth of being alive. All that we call life is the same kind of energy that imbues and binds all that is living, even the nonliving. The three pillars of personality and civilization thus are:

freedom, love and truth.

If we view them individually in their order, they make sense. To be able to live fully, we need freedom. To participate in life, we need to make and maintain a contact with it. The easiest way to make and keep contact with life is to follow a path of least resistance which is a harmonious approach and love. Freedom and love, however, are by themselves not sufficient to keep us on the right track in life. For that to happen, we need to follow the path of truth. Truth is generated by following *Life's Order*, discussed in chapter 14. These pillars of personality lead to a successful expression of life. Natural systems behave similarly. An example is the flow of water or growth of trees.

What life gives us and we create, we want to share with others. This is simply logical. If life gives us something and we are part of it, it follows that we will naturally also give it. Each one of us is a link in an infinite and eternal chain of life, and therein lies our immortality.

Note on giving: Sharing something with others is only possible when we have what we want to share or give. For example, wishing someone good health while feeling its lack in ourselves will not help. However, if we truly have and feel good health, we are sending (sharing) a thought (energy) of that state and that, by extrasensory communication, can help a person. On the other hand, if we do not want a person to have something that we have, such a thought, will only harm us, since it will not find a recipient and may return to haunt us.

27
Reality

Suppose that we know nothing about the life of a prenatal child, except what we learned from biology in school. Curious, we still may ask, "Can we say something about the world in which such a magical, natural happening takes place?" Different images and ideas of such a world could come into our mind, but one thing is certain: the creation of such a complex biological system—which can function for almost a hundred years—would require an intelligence and knowledge of a highly superior and advanced kind. In our present state of capability, we can only dream about it. The good news is that we are able to dream about it because all of us already have been witnesses to the process of such creation and the world in which it took place.

Since time immemorial, people have been attracted to and secretly imagined such a world, moved by the belief that they would find in it answers to deep life questions, which would help them cope better with difficult times. Their intuition always was and is a correct one.

Below is a quote that has been attributed to the eighteenth-century German philosopher Novalis (his pseudonym), but its origin probably goes back farther in history:

> all that is visible clings to the invisible
> all that is audible clings to the inaudible
> all that is tangible clings to the intangible
> all that is thinkable clings to the unthinkable

This statement creates an image of a world of which only a small part is visible, similar to an iceberg floating in arctic waters. We perceive this *visible* part through our senses and study it with the faculty of reason in postnatal life. Science deepens and widens our perception and knowledge but has yet to discover the nature of the hidden world as far as life is concerned.

We can put forward a theory based on the above idea. Let us assume the existence of one world. We can talk about it as the world that is given, natural and *real*. Although we rose from that world, only a very small part of it is presented to our senses and intelligence to see. We all perceive this world the way it appears to us with our sensory tools. The world we live in and know as *our reality* is, therefore, the result of our perception, observation, research, thinking and creation. However, this world that we constantly talk about is in large measure only an image of the real world. We will call it the *apparent* or relatively real world. We can summarize the above statements into one:

All that is apparent clings to the real.

Let us illustrate it by some examples. Our body is a part of the real world, but the view of it from outside belongs to the apparent world. Nature is real, but our description and explanation of it are part of the apparent world. Analyzing the nature of life leads to the apparent world, but a true intuition about it has roots in the real world. The way we see ourselves, what we think about others and everything around us is mostly apparent, unreal. Only the conscious statement *I am* can connect us with the source of life and the real world. We can state that the key that opens reality is the basic consciousness, *I am.*

The conclusion that our sensory perception—and all that goes with it—is insufficient to get to know the reality of a living form is a result of separateness. If we did not feel separate from the real world, we would experience more of its reality. Let us be clear that what we mean by *separate* applies only to the living world.

The important thing to remember is that there is no firm boundary between the two worlds as there is no unanimity between perception and imagination. Moreover, the boundary between them is individual and changing. We all differ in the degree we feel the existence of the real world and to what extent we are willing to go in its depiction. It is important to realize that both the apparent and real worlds are entangled and remain interconnected by a mutual *clinging* relation (correlation?).

At this time, the reader may want to recall the poem *Mati* in which the embryo describes itself as different and displaced from its mother but, at the same time, feels its life connection with her. We learn that individuality does not imply separation from the source of life.

Let us clarify this point. When we move away (unaware consciousness) from our source of life energy in our psyche but remain connected to it physically by a channel (through umbilical cord), we are not separate. However, when our life support system is permanently cut, our physical life, as we know it, will terminate.

Is there a way of maintaining our connection with the real world during our waking consciousness? The way is the aware consciousness, otherwise our foregoing argument is faulty. We can start with the following exercise.

If you stand by a calm lake on a bright day, you may see in it, as if in a mirror, the image of a tree growing on its bank. Try to quiet your mind and gaze long at the image. Then, very slowly turn to see the real tree. If you repeat the exercise, very, very slowly and with full awareness and focus of what you are experiencing (all in the present) you may succeed, for a brief moment, in seeing the reality of the tree as you look at it. During that moment, you and the tree will unite. The form of the tree will disappear to your eyes, but not to your inner being. The life energies of you and the tree have united in a vibratory harmony, a resonance. This will take place at the molecular level and will be *seen* by consciousness in the head.

The exercise may appear simple, but the success for a beginner may not come easily. However, if you do succeed—you will be the only one to know that—your life will gain a new, wider dimension and an inspiration for further study of reality.

Like a quiet mind, a calm lake will produce a sharp image of the tree. Does its image in the water have anything in common with the reality of the tree? The light from the sun and sky illuminates the tree and is reflected by the lake to our eyes falling on their retinas, where it is converted into an electrical signal and conducted into the brain for visual analysis by the mind. This process and all its components are part of the real world, but its mind image does not tell us anything about the tree as a living form. It is only a reflection, nothing more. The sun disappears behind a cloud, and the picture, like everything unreal (phenomenal), vanishes. The tree on the bank and you remain. Two things can happen then. Either you perceive the tree with your senses and mind (an unreal life experience), or you can connect with it by means of the common life force (unite with it). Needless to say, in the latter case, it would be difficult for us to cut the tree.

At this time, we may want to contemplate our union with all of life, as discussed in chapter 10 *Energy-Matter Interaction*. It is difficult to express this union in words. We can only say that we feel our life connection. Normally, the union with all of life resides in our subconscious. All of us experienced the union in prenatal life. Infants and very young children feel this connection for a short time after birth. They, for example, experience every tree as a unique living being. They do not understand why people can talk about them *en masse* as trees, implying that each one in the group is like the other. To describe them as all the same tree, we are merely describing their form, the apparent world. To know them as individual living forms, they are part of the real world.

Even if we are not aware of the real world and see it only in an apparent form, the connection with reality is always available to us. A small sensation of pain in our body and we are back in our physical reality.

Where do we stand in this discussion when it comes to imagination? We are all aware of imagination, fantasy, illusion, etc. The human mind is endowed with the capability of forming images.

In certain cases, we can certainly take imagination to be a legitimate expression of image-forming ability and consider it a real function of the mind. For example, when an architect designs a house, they can imagine it *existing* in reality. They exercise, among many other considerations, their knowledge of distribution of space and matter with regard to movement of life. Their imagination, knowledge and skill will lead to the reality of a built house.

The situation is not as clear when we are imagining past events. We form images of our past experiences. These images in time become less sharp, blurry, degraded. When we recall them from memory, they may no longer correspond closely to those at their inception. Even the apparent reality has been altered. We are creating our own apparent reality as we go along in life.

> They said, "You have a blue guitar,
> You do not play things as they are."
> The man replied, "All things as they are,
> Are changed upon the blue guitar."
>
> —*Wallace Stevens, The Man with the Blue Guitar*

At other times, our mind is subject to random noise or delusional wandering. It is up to us to identify where we are leaving the region of apparent reality and entering illusion. What helps us in these cases is consciousness and reason. If our consciousness points to us that we have deviated from a true course in our life journey and are entering a place where we have nothing real to hold onto—where we feel like being in limbo or having lost terra firma under our feet—we are threatened and vulnerable. There are plenty of such dangers. Among the most precarious are states brought on by large doses of intoxicating substances such as alcohol and drugs, but they can also be caused in smaller measures by mass hypnosis and other less identifiable factors where our true self is not in control. Therefore, it is necessary to be always in close contact with consciousness and reasonable mind which are our safe means of maintaining contact with reality, even though it is only apparent.

Our senses and mind create a *mirror* in which we see an image of the real world. We have two possibilities: we can either (1) work with this image to pursue the knowledge of the apparent world and study it objectively with the traditional *proof* of things, or (2) we can unite with the object of our interest psychically at the level of life. For the sake of simplicity, we will limit our discussion to live objects. The form and other sensory inputs about a live object will disappear, and we will be communicating with the living entity at an elementary life level using our consciousness *I am*. The desire of most of the lower organisms is to become part of humans, and they are glad to enter the "conversation".

The more we occupy ourselves with the imaging and analyzing the real world and life, the more we distance ourselves from it. In time, our way will become habitual and seem real. This process of distancing from reality—we also call it alienation from nature—deepens with the progression of civilization and is accelerated by technological advancement. Some young people today find greater interest in the virtual reality of digital imaging than in a concrete life experience. A few years back, the attention of many young readers was held by the adventures and magic of Harry Potter. Even if a fantasy contains examples of high human values and character, it means little to us who are unable to experience them and see their values ourselves. Most of the time fantasy remains a form of entertainment and a temporary escape from reality. At the same time, we can find the greatest magic of all in the real world of nature and the universe. In contrast to fantasy, exploring nature brings us closer to reality. Fantasy is fleeting, but reality is eternal. Fantasy evaporates in sunlight like the morning dew, but the reality of nature remains a source of enjoyment.

Examples of the magical, real world events in nature include a blooming apple orchard in the spring, full of fragrance and industrious bees, and red apples in the fall; the flight of the monarch butterfly at the end of summer from as far as Canada to a particular valley in Mexico, a distance of several thousand kilometers; a maternal egg cell that sets out on its journey, recognizes and fulfills its mission to enable a new life on Earth... all these are examples of the spirit of the life force and its magic.

Currently, a lot is written and said about advantages of living in the present. We notice that everything around us constantly changes. We observe growth, changing weather, life movement in general, all the way to the molecular level. Changes involve space dislocations and deformations. Intelligence introduced *time* as a means of monitoring and keeping order of changes. Physicists defined space and time (space-time) as variables to track changes in the position of objects.

We will consider changes from the way we experience them as *life changes*. We can all agree that we can experience life fully only in the present—this is a common sense. What happened before the present moment is the past, and what will happen after the present moment is the future. But both the past and future are imaginary spaces and lives.

To recall our life in the past, we have to image it (imagine it) based on our memory. We are not really living it; we are living its recreation. Similarly, to envisage the future, we have to use our imagination. We can say with certainty, therefore, that we live consciously only in the present moment. This may be argued when we consider the influence of the past on our current life.

Despite all the talk about reality, we might ask a practical question: As long as our life appears successful and we are happy and content with it, why should we care whether it is real or not? One of the reasons is life's unpredictability. At any time, we can meet with a misfortune, illness, natural catastrophe or even death and be suddenly shaken out of our comfort zone, seeking answers and ways to cope. In serious cases, we may even feel that our world has collapsed or disappeared. However, it does not take a dramatic event to derail us. We have many reasons and opportunities to contemplate the purpose of life, seek explanations of its surprising happenings and cope with its insecurities that force us to think what life is all about. Simply, life is never completely clear to us, prompting us to seek advice and help. We may start to doubt the world we live in, even doubt our own life. For example, we live in a mistaken belief that we can maintain our state of being, even if life keeps convincing us that things are constantly changing. That is the main reason why we should seek the connection with the real world.

Contemplative people seek the real world to understand its nature. Some seek spiritual values and God, focussing primarily on life and its order. Others are trying to find and describe mathematically its physical structure and laws. Many are making an effort to penetrate the secrets of nature and uncover its metaphysical and biological laws. We should not forget those who seek, in the natural world, an inspiration for their creative work. They all are trying to bring the natural world closer to us. Others offer us their views and opinions about it. These characterizations of the real world may be interesting and useful but remain only notions and images. Each one of us has a unique impression of reality, and that also applies to this discussion.

27.1 Reality of Prenatal World

The prenatal child lives fully in the real world. It does not know any other. It is aware of using its consciousness (inner light). One way to get in touch with reality, therefore, would be to awaken prenatal memory. That may not be easy or even necessary. All young children have the ability to see the reality of living things. If we lost the reality in childhood, it may be very difficult to reclaim in adult life. Some of it may come back in old age. A good way to approach it is through intuitive meditation. Intuition can be increased if we recognize it and pay attention to it. In the same way that consciousness, combined with sensory perception, is the main instrument in creating and perceiving the apparent reality, intuition, combined with a clear mind, can bring reality close. An example of making contact with the real world is practicing unity with nature. This ability can be found in many native people all over the globe. They show us that they live in close relationship with nature but are unable to give us the knowledge of their perception of the real world. This is logical. We have to gain it through our own experience.

I believe that a newborn child is pure and innocent, a creature of God. It follows that it must have risen from a world that guarantees such a magnificent physical, mental and spiritual unfolding through creation. To imagine its beginning, we can transport ourselves to a realm of very fine energies acting on micro-particles of matter in which all life has its beginning (refer to the poem *Hungry Birds*). Such a state of elementary existence has a strong dynamic during which energy (spirit) and matter have their first meetings. Matter is activated by spirit (spirit, being energy, *knows* matter), and by its creative power, matter is altered. According to the poem, the elementary world is inhabited by elementary living entities that create the physical beginnings for all living forms on earth. Their substance also determines the position of that species on the evolutionary scale. Humans are given the most *refined* substance resulting in their highest position. All lower lifeforms look toward humans as their guides in reaching a similar high state of evolution and regard them as their benevolent leaders in life.

The real world with its mysterious Life's Order is perceived and accepted by the prenatal child with an instinctive trust and willingness to submit to changes that the life force brings on. When it senses the advent of its approaching birth, the fetus feels sad at having to leave its home and friends but says, **I cannot resist the force of change urging me on...**

The prenatal child submits and entrusts its life to the life force naturally, like the lilies Jesus Christ spoke about in the Bible (Matthew 6:28): "Consider the lilies in the field, how they grow..." It is this trust of life that most of us seek when it gets dark and foggy, and we cannot see the road ahead clearly.

Although we all went through the world of natural reality, we cannot prove its existence. The Christian religion talks about it as the Kingdom of Heaven, which is inhabited by the Holy Ghost. Science is trying to describe the physical behavior of this world mathematically by such theories as quantum mechanics and the string theory.

Despite all the unknowns, we can talk about the world and life in which matter works with the creative force of spirit as spiritual. Hence, the real world can be called also the *spiritual* world. The spiritual (real) world is sovereign to the apparent, phenomenal world. This is reflected in the common belief among people who have always believed in the existence of a higher power that directs their life. We all have innate knowledge of the spiritual state given to us in the prenatal period. All we need to do is become aware of it. Our tendency to look for it externally in religious teachings can help, but a sure way is to know it from our own roots. If we did not already have the prior knowledge of the spiritual life within us, we would not be able to admit its existence and seek its knowledge later.

A prenatal child accepts the world in which it lives as given, with a feeling of total trust and confidence. Its attitude toward life is based on submitting to the life force and accepting its effect. Faith in life and the world and the acceptance of it as it offers itself is the principal characteristic of the spiritual existence of the prenatal child. This is also true for us adults but only if we follow our personal truth: to be in the depth of our soul true to ourselves. There is a simple logic to it; if we believe in everything life brings and accept it as something that has a meaning for our existence, our life will unfold according to our faith and appear natural.

This is not a passive faith in our fate. It is a faith that requires our participation and becomes our psychic strength. However, faith in ourselves would not guarantee that our life would always be moving along the right track. Only truth will guarantee that. It is worth repeating the words of Jesus: "I am the way, the truth, and the life." (John: 14:6).

To have a clearer picture and understanding of the spiritual nature of a human adult, we can imagine the prenatal child as it is described here, turning instantly into an adult. How would such a person behave and act?

He or she would have all the characteristics described in the preceding chapters. They would have charisma and draw us to them by their natural personality. They would appear dignified, self-confident, sophisticated, unafraid and calm, seeming to us noble and real. They would look at everything happening around them from a higher perspective and deeper viewpoint stemming from wider spiritual consciousness and awareness of the relationships among things. They would act with the prudence that we associate with a person of high intellectual and psychic ability, regardless of their social standing. They would speak directly to any point in question and tell no jokes, yet have a sense of humor based on the natural joy of life. They would always live in the present. Conflicts would be resolved in their presence. If they walked by, people would turn their heads to follow, drawn by some invisible force. They would probably remind them of their own spiritual state that they are not consciously aware of.

Each one of us is capable of creating our *image* of a spiritual person. It is, therefore, hard to understand that newborn children often become puppets in the hands of their parents and are considered undeveloped, ignorant and dependent beings that need to be introduced to the outside world as soon as possible. This is because we as adults are unaware of their inner life and are unable to communicate with them at their stage of understanding. Then in their later life, those children spend a lot of time seeking something that they already knew but forgot, lost by ignoring.

Finally, we need to mention that the significant events and knowledge from prenatal life are not lost. They are stored in the vast realm of our subconscious and unconscious. Although this region is not directly accessible to our waking consciousness, it penetrates the conscious realm in dreams, visions, intuition, instinct and paranormal experiences. The mediator of this communication is our conscious soul. The unconscious contains the history of the past states of consciousness together with the creative work of spirit. In this regard, we should also mention the influence of Life's Order, which led to the creation of archetypes as fundamental life models. As the DNA is a blueprint for the physical form, archetypes and symbols are ideal models for our psyche. An example is the archetype of the relationship between the male and female spirits during conception (see chapter 9.2), which contains not only the gender selection and incarnation but, most importantly, the role of the selected incarnating gender vis-à-vis its silent spiritual mate.

Important events of our real life are not lost. They are filed in the region of the unconscious that C.G. Jung described as a neutral (indifferent) realm that influences our conscious life. Two ways in which information about past life can penetrate the present are: (1) through the continuity of the life force and (2) exploration of the unconscious region by the soul.

28

Roots of Religion, Arts, Mythology and Folklore

If we view prenatal life from a spiritual viewpoint, we can expect to find common elements, harmony and agreement with religious thoughts that are found in the major religious texts such as the Christian, Hebrew and Buddhist Bibles, the Quran, the Vedas, Tao Te Ching, etc. In the discussions in part 2 of the book, we have come across many of these similarities and agreements. Among the most prominent are the words of Jesus Christ: "I am the way, the truth and the life," which correspond to the *statements* by the prenatal child contained in the poem *Order of Life*, worth repeating here:

> **Everything I do, I complete... My life stays the same: to follow, remember the way, wherever I go, whatever I do, whatever I feel, whatever I learn... The journey is my way... to know who I am*.*

A close correspondence exists between Life's Order of the prenatal child and the Order of Nature issuing from the Tao. Figure 7 shows the Chinese character of the Tao. It consists of two parts: the upper part is the radical for *head*, and the lower part is the radical for *moving on.* Together they signify *Head moving along a path.* We can, therefore, say that the statements "I am the way" (Christ), "Head moving along a path (The Tao), and "Journey is my way" (prenatal child) express the same idea about the dynamic of life. We can go further and say that they all have their origin in prenatal life and before.

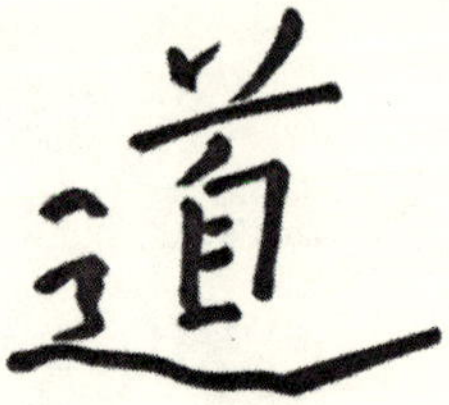

Figure 7. Character of the Tao

A similarity to the Buddhist nirvana is referred to obliquely in the poems *Place of Silence*, *Wellbeing* and more directly in *Prologue*.

The symbolism of the Dancing Shiva in Hinduism and the human heart described in the poem *Flame and Friendship* is apparent.

Bhagavad Gita, the sacred book of Hindu teachings, emphasizes three major paths (yogas) to reach the state of *atman* (the highest consciousness of universal being): *Karma* yoga, *Bhakti* yoga and *Jnana* yoga. We can take them to be identical to our pillars of personal freedom, love and truth.

As described in chapter 26 *Pillars of Personality*, one of the main character traits of the prenatal child is a feeling oneness with and compassion for all life. We encounter this attitude toward life in all major religions. However, we do not have to resort to religion in order to seek life's spiritual truths. Each of us has sacred life teachings from prenatal life given to us. We could call them our personal bible. Christ was fully aware of his divine origin from birth and built on it his whole spiritual journey, unlike most of us who have forgotten our divine origin (see also the discussion of spiritual embodiment in chapter 9.4).

Arts, primarily writing and painting, contain an abundance of hidden references to prenatal life. In literature, it is mainly poetry (especially the writings of old masters and religious figures from the medieval period) where we can find rich, hidden references to prenatal life and beyond. In this book, we mention many examples of ideas of the Persian poets and Sufi leaders Rumi and Hafez. Their poetry contains ideas about the origin of life and consciousness that agree with or are similar to those presented in this book.

Apart from religious writings, prenatal life is a cradle of a wide variety of mythological symbols, customs and traditions. We have brought up many of them in part 2 of the book. Interested readers may find many other examples from their own lives.

Among the best known in the Western world is the tradition of celebrating Christmas with a lit-up tree. In Central Europe people still call the gifts put under the Christmas tree gifts from little Jesus. In our explanation, the Christmas tree has its origin in the human placenta, lit up by energy-charged food particles. The birth of Jesus thus takes on a wider meaning of celebrating every newborn child.

It would be an impossible task to compile a comprehensive list of all of mankind's references to prenatal life, life's origin and meaning—even at a layman's level—found in religious writings, mythology, arts and customs. It would require people who themselves possess that memory to recognize such content in the sources.

29
Prenatal Life—Summary

The most important insight we gained in prenatal life is the realization that this period takes place in a world in which life unfolds with the precision and finesse of a very high life order. We spoke of this world as the real or spiritual world. We referred to the propelling force of life as the life force and its creative energy as spirit. The most important insight we gain in prenatal life is the realization that this period takes place in the real world of life. We called the process of life—created by the life force—growth. Growth is the result of the interaction between energy and matter.

The result of this creative growth is the most sophisticated biological system ever designed, namely the human body. We should keep that in mind whenever we discuss prenatal life. On the basis of experience of prenatal growth, most of us would not want to entrust such complex development to the whims and uncertainty of the apparent world in which we live after we are born. The prenatal child is well protected against its influence. Also, its psychic development, which accompanies and is firmly connected with the physical, is governed by the highest laws of the real world and enjoys a similar level of protection. All that has been said so far is not a product of imagination. Rather, it is a description of reality "seen" by intuition and consciousness.

In this evolutionary phase (an abbreviated rendering of evolution) the human being rises from the depth of the natural or essential world that embraces all of the past, present and future, from the world of infinite existence and truth. At the time of birth, the human being is a perfect biological creation ready to apply and continue this truth and knowledge of life. The fact that the child almost never succeeds in maintaining its prenatal knowledge of life is a result of it being unable to survive by itself. Survival is its first need. It takes a long time before a young adult can stand on its own feet. When they finally enter the stream of life, their effort is directed toward building a career, starting a family, etc. Life after birth is governed by different laws than those in prenatal life. In prenatal life, we participate more as observers and passive *recipients* of life, whereas in postnatal life, we become active *earners* of life.

There comes a time, mostly in the second half of our lifespan, when we suddenly begin to ask questions about the purpose of our life and what we still need to know to fulfill it. We are often reminded of it through a sudden, psyche-shaking episode. We begin to search for values that last, the spiritual values. Unfortunately, we often seek an understanding of the spiritual state outside in the world we know, the world with which we are immediately connected and familiar. Our search there will be long and difficult. The most direct and proven way is to awaken the spiritual values with which we came into the world—by directing the search within.

In a biblical story, Nicodemus asks Christ about the Kingdom of God (John 3:1–10). Jesus answers that the Kingdom of God will admit only the one who is *born* again. Nicodemus then asks how one can do it—surely not by re-entering the womb of one's mother and being born again? Jesus answers that it means a rebirth by spirit and water, the principal dynamic forces in prenatal life.

I think that this episode clearly points toward Christ's advice that the one who seeks God must awaken the spiritual state they had in their prenatal life led by spirit (energy) and water (moving substance). Christ thus states that our prenatal life is the Kingdom of God.

The main reason for becoming conscious of and maintaining the spiritual state is to become aware of a higher (divine) and wider view of relationships among things and people, which leads us to be more successful in dealing with life's difficulties. To work with spirit does not require any special schooling and preparation, only a conscious awareness of spirit energy.

We could say that the spiritual state that the child experiences before birth as described in this book and that offered to us by religious teachings have much in common, despite their seemingly disparate explanations. Life force, consciousness, spirit, soul and love are all the same kind of energy.

What are the major examples of prenatal knowledge that Rumi calls "wisdom beyond anyone's learning?"

We can begin by listening to people describe certain occurrences in their lives that influenced them profoundly, for example, in their work, behavior, thinking, etc. If we accept the prenatal story presented here as believable, we are struck by the similarity between many of the prenatal life events and those from our adult life. For example, we can compare the cellular phase of our biological beginning (a) with the life of an adult (b):

(a) A mature egg sets out on a journey into the world. After some time of traveling, it finds the purpose of its mission. On this journey, it meets a cell of opposite gender (sperm). These two cells experience attraction, their spirits and bodies unite and agree on the form of living together. They find a place and build the body.

(b) A young mature person leaves his/her home and enters the world to seek work and pursue a career. In life they meet a person of the opposite gender. They fall in love and decide to live together. They find a place to settle down and build a house and start a family.

On the basis of this remarkable similarity of the life journeys (a) and (b), we can assume that the pre- and postnatal periods are related and seek their connection. The first event takes place in the real world ruled by spiritual order, the second in the apparent world ruled primarily by the worldly order. If the two journeys are correlated, conception becomes a model for the man/woman relationship and creation of new life. We can admire the genius of creation and the intelligence that gave us an opportunity to experience the way of the spiritual Order of Life *before* we enter its outer world version.

In postnatal life, we put into practice what we learned in prenatal life. This is in agreement with the idea, advanced earlier, that we should seek the understanding of the origin of a manifested event before we draw any conclusions about it—in our case understanding the child before analyzing the adult.

In prenatal life, we followed consciously the development of our body and its major organs, including their functions. Through growth we gained knowledge of physical health. We learned that, in food, we accept the living substance (body) of Mother Earth and give it a home in our body.

Food contains life energy from the sun. Our awareness of life energy is our life consciousness. Consciousness enables us to monitor and regulate life energy in our body, thus maintaining its health (see discussion of consciousness in chapter 5 and 7). This represents a not very well known, yet simple and efficient method of healing an organ, where energy deficiency is the cause of the ailment. Eastern methods of healing, such as acupuncture, are based on the idea of balancing body energy but are likely to be less efficient than consciousness in targeting a specific organ.

Every part of our body requires our attention and acknowledgement to maintain wholeness and health. If we do not give every organ or a part of our body sufficient attention—i.e., if we do not irradiate it with consciousness (give it love) and do not make sure that it continues to be a wanted part of us—the neglect may cause it to weaken, even become sick. To heal a sickness should always include the help of conscious awareness.

The heart is the most important organ of our body (see chapter 15). We ought to know its physical and psychic roles well. For a healthy heart, we need, first of all, a good vitality of the spark (see the poem *Flame and Friendship* and its analysis). The spark is the energy and consciousness that we receive from the sun. It manifests in the energy and "sunny" disposition of the individual. The exuberance and will to live is a joy we get from cultivating optimism. In short: strong spark for healthy heart.

The most important psychological role of our heart is as a starting point of every action. Every task, every action requires for its execution a decision on our part. The decision may involve courage and a friendly approach, the very ingredients that our heart can supply. It happens quite frequently, though, that our mind sneaks in before we have a chance to involve the heart and takes over. While a reasonable mind plays a key role in many decisions, a friendly, loving attitude can make every task easier. In the same way, fear (lack of courage) can make every job seem difficult.

A prenatal child uses its heart always as a starting point of a physical action. In the life of an adult, the heart's psychic powers become prominent as well. There is a saying: In a conflict between heart and reason, heart always wins.

Consciousness, a faculty of the self/soul, plays an important and unique role in the cognitive aspect of prenatal life. It is the child's unique way of communication with its inner and outer surrounding, including its mother. Consciousness, as the awareness of energy, follows every energy-consuming process. It is always present at the beginning of every life journey or task as the inner light (energy). That may include every thought, talk, walk, every feeling and bodily sensation, every sensory input, every physical action, every memory recording and retrieval, every output from the hidden realms of the unconscious through intuition—simply everything that unfolds as a conscious linear sequence of a life's experience. Consciousness opens the door to let us see and know life's reality in the prenatal period.

After birth, consciousness is directed to the outside world where it accompanies mainly sensory inputs and mind. Slowly, the prenatal way of perception is displaced and replaced by sensory input analyzed by the mind. The direct conscious communication with the (hidden) real world is greatly diminished and lost.

Experiencing the flow of life and its various aspects generates our life journey. Journey is the true way of living. With the help of consciousness and intelligence, we gain knowledge of what holds our interest and inspires us, that which is important to our life. We could therefore say that *life is a journey of consciousness*. We can know only that of which we become conscious. It follows: more consciousness, more life. Wider consciousness enables us also to see a wider dimension of a life event and thus become more aware of the relationships in a given moment, a path to greater understanding. I agree with the idea that the majority of our misunderstanding lies in seeing only a part—each of us usually a different part—of the picture of a situation. The fable of blindfolded people and an elephant is a good one.

In prenatal life, we became aware of and experienced the truth that life follows an order which is accompanied by the best feeling of being. The level of intensity of a feeling in a prenatal child is a measure of the level of truth the feeling is associated with. Where and how did this state of being originate? I believe that it began at the time when life started, when a proto-life absorbed and reacted to the light of the sun. Since it became alive, according to our definition, it also gained the awareness of being complete (*I am*) and with that a wish to preserve that state by replication, the feeling "I am complete, you can all be like me."

Contrary (or complementary) to Richard Dawkins's belief in the life's dominance of the selfish gene, just as strong an argument can be made about the presence of the *sharing* gene. The selfish gene is a sign of incompleteness (wave), an as-of-yet lack of knowing the truth, whereas the appearance of the sharing gene signifies the realization of the truth (particle). Any time an organism reaches a higher step of evolution and feels complete in a new advanced state, it feels a desire to share it with others, so that they too can reach the same level of evolution. This follows from the law of unity of all life. We have seen that this penchant for sharing permeates the whole life of a prenatal child. It is a property of the real world ruled by the spirit of life's unity. On the other hand, Dawkins's selfish gene of the apparent world has resulted in a disparity of wealth, exploitation of life and environment, destructive acts, including wars, etc. We conclude, therefore, that the selfish gene is regressive and the sharing gene dominant. Evolution confirms that. If we look at them as complementary, it appears that civilization has moved in the direction and dominance of the sharing gene.

The prenatal child's greatest discovery is Life's Order. We can call it greatest because this state is felt by it as the perfect state of being. It is impossible to describe the feeling in words. One can only circumscribe it by terms such as a feeling of completeness, perfection, overwhelming beauty, clarity... there is nothing that can be better. The closest I have come to expressing it is the *divine* state. In religious literature, Taoism and Christianity come closest to describing this state.

While it is impossible to express the perfect state of being in words, we can consider the way it manifests in life. We can picture life as a linear sequence (chain) of short and long journeys, each begun and brought to an end, each yielding a life experience, filed in a genetically provided place in the brain and added to the previous whole. Everything is a journey: a thought, laughter, talk, a walk to a grocery store, sleep, vacation trip, writing an essay, learning to drive a car, etc. One journey lasts a lifetime. A journey may be further subdivided into a series of sequentially occurring events (tiny *journeys*). Life's Order requires that every journey reach its end before a new one can begin. A journey that is not finished or terminated will not yield a life experience. Unfinished journeys clutter up our mind, since some of the mind energy continues to be devoted to them.

Along a journey, we use energy and create growth. At the end of each journey, we harvest its fruit, which is the value of that particular life experience to our life. Most experiences, especially the short ones, may not yield an important value, one that we would want to keep (make part of us). However, those that we like and wish to retain will add to our personal truth. Experiences gained in this way follow Life's Order, contribute to our mental and spiritual growth and knowledge and bring about the feeling of the state of perfect being. With this feeling, ideally, we also will want to die.

In prenatal life, we learned that the reality of life is contained within the experience of a journey. Anything outside of our experience of life is not really us. One may say, "What about all the learning we receive using the mind in school?" Thinking is also a journey; therefore, it is part of our life, but by itself, it does not generate new knowledge of life or personal truth of who we are unless we find the truth of it ourselves.

The closer we approach our core, the more intense will be our feeling and desire to know the complete truth of who we are. It is because we are approaching our starting point, our home—the Source of all being.

Truth will often come unannounced, but it will always awaken in us an ecstatic feeling of intense light and freedom, followed by a sudden sense of relaxation of tension. At that moment of truth, we touch our primal boundless *I* or *Soul* and the very source of life (light) that we associate with God. In this case, we could talk about universal truth as a manifestation of a Godlike state. The ecstatic feeling of the universal truth will always be accompanied by a thought and feeling to share it with others, to help them reach the same level of awareness. This follows from the unity of life. It happens often that people arrive at a similar or the same experience of personal truth. In that case, we can talk about common truth. A refined form of common truth arises out of what Carl Jung called collective unconscious in the form of archetypes. Universal truth emanates from the real world, such as the prenatal and early postnatal periods.

At the beginning of life, during conception, we learned that the newly created life unit sought its identity and knowledge of its life role. It is very important for us to realize that, at every moment, our consciousness is identifying with some definite role that we play in life. You could say that I am identifying myself at this moment with the role of a person trying to describe the meaning of prenatal life. Such an explanation or definition would probably be sufficient for the outer world, but it would be insufficient for us to comprehend what takes place in my inner world and from where I draw my ideas. For that we would require long explanations and, in the end, the words may not be adequate to describe it.

Our true identity and all the roles that issue from it form the essence of our soul that reaches far into the past. We should never minimize it or take it superficially. We should never do anything that hurts our soul.

We should be aware also of the origin of our identities. Thousands of new cells in our body are born every moment. These new cells are psychically empty and are seeking their identity through a connection with our body. They find it in the content of our feelings and sensations—our psychic environment—at that moment (which is where the energy is). Every cell thus partakes in our life as it is expressed in our roles, actions, behavior. It is therefore crucial that we welcome the new cells into our bodies by living our lives as well as we possibly can. This thought ought to be part of every school child's education.

In prenatal life, we get to know the life force that carries us forward. We become aware of it on the basis of its action and the effect it has on everything. We have called it also the force of change. The awareness of the life force, a flow of energy which the prenatal child feels directly and of which adults may be aware intuitively, awakens in us an exuberant feeling that life unfolds "the way it ought to."

A countryman once told me that when he was a little boy, his grandmother kept telling him, "Jan, I would like you to believe in everything that's happening." He took his grandma's advice to heart and discovered, later in life, that everything was indeed happening according to his belief.

The life force we have in mind as described above has a transcendental nature. We could call it the energy of design and creation. This energy is often felt by us as causing a change, something like the background energy the Tao is sometimes described to represent. One could call the life force also the force of change.

The feeling of the existence of à priori energy of creation (Tao) makes us trust life. As we cannot push the river, so we cannot push life. Everything has its own natural flow. At the same time, however, modern life, particularly in the West, is pressured to move faster than a natural flow. Modern life seems to be under pressure to pack in many activities, often extreme performances. As a result of the hurried life, we cannot give our work and the various activities the time they deserve. The result of which is that our lives becomes shallow. We become surface feeders demanding quick solutions and satisfaction. Technology offers us ever-widening opportunities, easier ways of doing things and more ways to experience life, but all that robs us of life's deeper experience. Having more opportunities in life does not necessarily lead to more success. In the same timespan we may dig many shallow wells without finding water or one deep well that does. Also the life force—the mighty, omnipresent and omnipotent power—remains not fully utilized. For that reason, life becomes more difficult. With many options and experiences our life may appear richer, but in reality, we have a lesser, more complicated life with a weakening consciousness. Our behavior becomes more automatic, robot-like.

Is there a remedy? Yes, a simple one. We could start by ceasing to buy—for example, for one year—all the new versions of entertainment and communication gadgets and be satisfied with what we already have.

This would give people a chance to consolidate their past investments and improve their skills. Those trailing will have a chance to catch up. The money targeted for purchases of new models can be redirected toward other, more useful purposes. There would be some slowing down and relaxation. The runaway horse of technology might be slowed down or halted, at least in one area, temporarily. To be fully effective, the proposed measures would have to be applied selectively, where most needed.

One of the very central discoveries from the prenatal period is the tendency of the prenatal child to wish others to have the same quality of life it has because it feels that it could help them better their lives. It cannot give them what it has, but it wishes them to become aware of those qualities in themselves. The *Poem* gives many examples in which the fetus longs to help its mother and others to have what it enjoys and considers good in its life. It wants to help also other organisms and forms of life to a fuller and better life. This tendency springs from the feeling of "I have something that's good for me. You can have it too by becoming aware of it. I can help you if you want." This proves again that life is one, and the forces that move it forward try to maintain a balance and wholeness regardless of individual ambitions that tend to break it up. The key lies in consciousness.

The knowledge of life from the prenatal period is available to everyone, but not everyone is willing to retrieve it by awakening its memory. There is another way, less direct, to learn about prenatal life, and that is by simply becoming aware of what one truly is. It seems simple, but it may be even more challenging—and not as reliable. It is very difficult to awaken past states of consciousness if one does not, at the same time, become aware of their circumstances. However, I do believe that future research and consciousness-awareness will show that the application of the spiritual way in life is easier, more economical and productive than any other way. It is natural.

At this point, it might be useful to remind ourselves what we mean by spiritual state. As we have defined it, spirit is the creative energy, a constituent of life force within man. Spiritual state is the actualization and manifestation of this energy. We have shown that spirit has been with us since the beginning of life. Why not use it?

There is a popular conception that the life before birth is a "walk in a rose garden" where all the needs of the developing child are met, and its worries about the future are none. In reality, it is not like that. We saw in the *Poem* that the unborn child has many challenging tasks to perform as part of its development. It has to face bothersome situations originating outside of it. Among the most difficult developmental challenges is the implantation as an embryo. A large percentage of the embryos expire, unable to implant. Another major and difficult task is establishing communication with its mother. Ultimately, the birth process represents the biggest physical challenge which may result in near death experience as was the case in our story.

How does the prenatal child view the threat to its life? In our story, this feeling occurred when the child struggled in carrying out a life-dependent task and reached a critical threshold of *life-or-no-life* (to be or not be) in its struggle. The prenatal child described the possible end of its life as **I cannot be (the way I am)**. We should note that "I cannot be" implies only that the struggling child would *not be able* to continue to be the way it is now and says nothing about any form of existence beyond that. In one case—the birth trauma—the self/soul moved out of the body and waited, while its waking consciousness went to sleep.

We can thus conclude that that the fetus viewed death as a change of its state of being. In the language of quantum mechanics, we could think of it as the collapse of the wave function of waking consciousness. Since we do not see it, we are really not sure what the *particle* would be or whether it was a complete collapse of the wave function of the waking consciousness, or only a temporary discontinuity as in the case of the birth trauma.

In the discussion of prenatal life, its nature and effect on our postnatal life, we have to include the huge health benefits that its awareness could bring to our life after birth. The memory of the (potentially) perfect growth and state of health remains in our subconscious. The awakened memory alone can help in solving our health problems in adult life.

Conception is prenatal life's most significant moment. It represents meeting and unification of the masculine and feminine spirits. At the spiritual level, a prenatal child is an androgynous being.

With increased health, we get to live longer. I estimate that by reawakening the memory of my prenatal life my personal life gained at least seven extra years of life.

Postnatal life

Prenatal life is a period of pristine growth and true experience of life. A newborn child expects to continue to live that way after birth. The reason why its goal is generally unattainable, must be blamed on the circumstances and condition of the world it enters. In my view, this is the result of the fact that the evolution of life on Earth has yet to reach a state that will enable it to happen—according to the law of life and the Tao that we discussed earlier: "Nothing happens until it *can* happen." Under these circumstances, the child has no other choice but to follow the way dictated by its social and physical environment. Still, in every newborn child, the ideal is present as a potentiality.

30
Whole Life Journey

The main thread of this book has been the concept of life as a journey. A life journey is characterized by its continuity, contiguity and content. In this chapter, we will examine the whole life as a journey. The life of every individual is unique. The majority of human journeys may appear ordinary or too personal to be noticed. Some become better known, but only very few reach a universal appeal and importance. Yet every life journey is as important as another, on an individual basis as well as in the universal scheme of things.

It would seem only natural that a life journey would have a long and rich mythological history. A prominent kind of life journey in mythology is the so-called *Hero's Journey*, described by Joseph Campbell. According to Campbell, the journey of a hero has three main parts: (1) the hero suffers a *separation* from life; (2) the hero sets out (departs) on an adventurous journey (*initiation*) that takes place in both the apparent life as well as in his inner hidden realm of reality. During this phase, he discovers the fruit of his journey (*boon*), which not only resolves his quest but also benefits mankind; (3) the hero returns to deliver the boon.

Can we identify in this book a journey that would qualify it as a hero's journey?

A physical separation occurs at birth. A newborn child (*hero*) undergoes a separation through birth and sets out on a life long journey to deliver the boon—his or her life work—to benefit mankind. However, while birth can be considered a separation physically, it is not a life separation. It is only relocation in space when we look at it objectively from without. It may be of interest to review the end of the poem *Into Light and Space: *A small regret enters my head to return where I came from, but ecstasy turns me forward. I am born!** The newborn child expresses a temporary longing for the womb it left, but the feeling is quickly superseded by the elation of being born. A parting such as birth is only a physical separation and relocation in space for the child. It is overcome when the baby and mother are reunited. It is part of a natural life event, not a real separation from life. The separation comes when the child is unable to continue the way it knows as its life. If as an adult, that person reconnects with real life by awakening their prenatal life memory, the separation from the real life is bridged. They have discovered the boon to give to mankind. Under those circumstances, that person's journey can be called a hero's journey.

A sounder way to view the events described in this book is to see it as the author's *Life Mission.* The concept of life mission was introduced in chapter 20. The Hero's Journey is a mythological phenomenon that is usually nested as an episode within life. The Life's Mission has a unique structure and spans the entire life. A life's mission may still contain the same three basic steps as the hero's journey—separation, departure, initiation and return—as a subset within the overall mission.

To fulfill a mission, the individual journeyman has to complete and deliver the object (boon) of the mission. Unlike a hero's journey, the steps or signposts of a life's mission appear to have no particular order or sequence of happening. Rather, a life's mission is subject to a higher, mystical order. Some people may refer to their life mission as destiny.

The foregoing lists the major steps in the author's personal life mission, which were necessary to carry it out:

> 1. Shortly after my difficult birth, I view—over a period of several weeks—a replay of my prenatal life. It is like watching a movie. I am very interested in what I *see* and am grateful to my mother to be left alone and have time to witness it day after day.
>
> 2. As an infant of six months, I am separated from my mother—against my will. This is the major traumatic

episode in my life that eventually caused me to put my mother and life as a nursing infant out of my mind. As a result of what is, for me, a traumatic separation, I shift my consciousness from the right to my left brain, where I find images of life that appear interesting for me to follow. This helps me to distance myself from the trauma.

3. At the age of four, I become aware of having a message for people around me. The message is to help them become more aware of themselves, thereby making their lives better.

4. As an adult, I live a stressful life marked by psychosomatic illnesses arising from my infant trauma—by now unaware of its origin and cause. I turn to science as a way of life and search in it for the understanding of my condition.

5. At the age of forty-six, the death of my neighbour in the middle of the night shocks my psyche, shatters my defences, and causes an explosion of my fear of death. Eventually, it forces me to face my own psychological death as an infant of six months (Step 2). It compels me to face the truth and becomes the call to action to deal with it.

6. Over the next decades, I grapple with the task of re-acquainting myself with the death-stricken infant inside me. In the first few years of the integration, the feelings are very heavy, accompanied by difficulty functioning in my personal life and career, mental upheavals and a fight for my own sanity. Gradually, the intensity of the breakthrough subsides as I begin to learn more and more about the trauma of my infancy and come to accept it. Some illnesses that were part of that distress begin to disappear. Eventually, I become aware that, to

heal my break with the unity of life, I need to awaken the memory of the time when I was still united with it. That leads me to a time prior to six months, which holds the memory of my prenatal life that I replayed after birth (Step 1).

7. As I slowly unravel my early postnatal memory and record it in the form of a daily journal, I have a daytime vision in which I am being sent, together with some others, to a place on Earth to carry out a teaching assignment whose nature is not known to me. When I object that I am too young and inexperienced, the man in white who selects me agrees with me only in part and assures me that I have just enough ability to carry out the assignment.

8. At another time, I and some others are flying through space at an enormous speed. We have no bodies, just consciousness. Suddenly, I see a beautiful little valley in bloom below me, peel off from the group and drop down. (I was conceived approx. May 25, 1924 in a highlands valley in the former Czechoslovakia.)

9. At the age of sixty-four, I publish my first biography of my prenatal life in the form of an epic poem with the title *Journey into the World – My Life before Birth* and begin to talk about the topic of prenatal consciousness and life. In 2001, I move to my birthplace in the Czech Republic to reconnect with my childhood roots. There I write a three-part book in the Czech language titled *Forgotten Truth – Life before Birth* and lecture extensively on the topic in many cities of that country. At the end of 2010, I return to Canada to write this major work in English.

A cursory view of the steps may suggest that they could have been chance happenings, but a closer and deeper examination would rule it highly improbable, especially in view of their definite journey-like sequence and the other-worldly episodes in Steps 7 and 8. We would be more prone to accept the idea that this journey has been directed by a higher mysterious intelligence.

> The Divine Creator had etched
> every moment of your existence
> no artist ever could
>
> —*Hafiz* (*translated by Daniel Ladinsky*)

We need to be cautious here, too. When we are dealing with a vision or daydream similar to those described in Steps 7 and 8, we should examine first whether it might have been a recollection of an actual, forgotten early life event. When a past event in our life is recalled, it may often take the form of a vision or dream, since our mind is unable to connect it to a real happening.

This would have been the case in Step 7, since I do recall as a very young boy walking into our small flour mill one day where my father was talking to a man. My father was always covered with flour and appeared to me to be wearing white clothes. I remember him talking to that man and saying something about me growing into an important person of knowledge one day. It was my father's vision for me then.

Can this actual occurrence have anything in common with the daytime vision in Step 7? The content of both is similar, except that in the daydream I am the last one in a group to be selected. There could be a similarity, namely, my father might have had in mind a *select* group of important people. Thus, the possibility of turning a forgotten experience into a vision (Step 7) cannot be discounted. I find no real occurrence in my past similar in content to Step 8.

Personally, I continue to be intrigued by the sequence of the events in my life journey. It resembles a play of nine acts. Everything happens for a definite purpose and at a proper time. I wonder if someone could have written a different or better scenario to deliver the memory of a prenatal life to the world.

People often asked during my public talks how I was able to remember my prenatal life. The true and clear answer came to me only at the time of the present writing: I had to have had an opportunity and time alone as a baby to watch the *movie* of my prenatal life shortly after birth. This established its memory record in the brain.

It leads me to suggest to parents of newborn children to give their babies time to be alone when awake. If it has no distractions in the form of toys, the infant may use that time to replay the memory of its life before birth. This is natural. Such babies must not be talked out of their memory as they grow up.

We may also note that within the above nine-step life mission we can identify three steps that would form the classical hero's journey: Steps 5, 6 and 9. This may lead us to suggest that the hero's journey is a subset of the life's mission. We cannot even exclude the possibility that life's mission is further a subset of a higher, more inclusive life journey, if we consider the whole evolution of life on the planet and call it *Life's Evolutionary Journey*. Such an idea would underscore the role of creative process in life with an implied order.

Many of you may be curious to know if I consider my life mission a divine act. It would be hard not to think of it that way. However, this does not make me a special person, only a person with a memory. I will throw some light on it in the next chapter.

Ego's Journey

To make our discussion about life journeys complete, we need to mention another kind of journey, just as frequent and rich in mythology as the Hero's Journey. I will call it the *Ego's Journey*.

The ego's journey, like the hero's journey, starts with a separation from life. In early childhood, a child suffers a break in its unity with life and the world. It survives the trauma and makes a decision: "I must always get what I want, I will show you." That decision continues into adulthood. The individual lives a life according to the inner dictates of his powerful ego. Unable to collapse their life journey (a quantum event), they cannot reap important truths of life and remain unconscious about them. They excel in many ways: They develop a feeling of infallibility. Only they, their way, family, culture, etc. is valid. They pursues fame, power and wealth and never have enough. They become an autocrat, dictator, warrior for their own causes. Their egomania is pathological and can reach dangerous proportions.

In the wide region of life, bordered by ego and hero, all of us journey somewhere.

31
Contemplating Exit from Life

As we approach the end of our life, many of us might have thoughts such as: "What happens when my body dies? Is there something that survives the death of my body? If so, how do I exit from this life?"

Knowing why and how we came into this world might help us to know the exit from our life. There is a saying in my native land, "As one enters the forest, so one exits." Let us start with an example. The ovulating egg in our story began its journey with the desire to drop into the world below. After it did and journeyed, it began to wonder what the purpose of its urgency was, and discovered—by looking into its DNA—that it was to deliver the sacred human form (egg's image of its DNA) on time. That was the actual purpose of the life journey of the egg. In the process of merging with the sperm during conception, the egg lost its identity, but its innate gender spirit—vested in the feminine form— remained and played, as we saw, a key role in the determination of the gender of the new human being.

If we compare the elementary journey of the egg with a whole life journey and ask the question at the end, "What was the purpose of my life journey?" the answer might be similarly, "To deliver its content."

The content may be thought of as the result of our life's work in the broadest sense of the word. However, that would not be the whole story. The egg describes its "cargo" as a sacred human form. Accepting the sacredness of human life—as we generally do—we would expect it to be reflected in our human work. How would we judge it? The answer might be that our work is being judged by the contemporary life now, but it will be judged mainly by the life that will follow. Thus, we can expect to have, just like the egg, a life as a spirit (life after).

In the same way as the spirit of the egg plays its role in the creation of a new life by forming a union with the sperm, our adult spirit—vested in our life's work—enters into a union with spirits of those who come after us to continue the creative process of the growth of human civilization. In that, too, lies our immortality.

> One night, a dying star
> came to God with a cry:
> "Why am I born so bright
> if I am to die?"
>
> God smiled:
>
> "My beautiful star,
> you were born
> so that one night a child
> will look into the sky,
> catch your sparkling light
> in which you live forever."
>
> —*anonyma*

Both the matter and energy in our body are indestructible. After death, the body matter with its unaware consciousness will dissipate into the environment. On the other hand, consciousness (energy) can move out of the body (as discussed in chapter 25 *Birth*). We can imagine it as a ripple in the quantum field of universal consciousness. In the story of birth, the carrier of that energy was the soul/self. It is, therefore, theoretically possible for that to happen also at the time of death. Like the out-of-body journey of the birthing child, it would require a *conscious* decision by the dying person to leave their body. Since many deaths, as we know, are willed, this may be a way. Many people might not want to survive, facing the uncertainty of existence in another domain. All this is hypothetical, *intuitive science*.

Intuitive science is not science fiction. Intuition comes from the unconscious realm, which is our natural and spiritual domain, whereas science fiction is mainly a product of the mind (science and imagination). Most scientific breakthroughs come via intuition.

Epilogue

I journeyed into and
through the World
and returned to contemplate
the start of life on Earth...

I came to Earth
with a mission:
to shine light
on life before birth.
I studied science and love
and fell those two could
know each other better.

My main tools have been:
awareness of energy,
awareness of matter,
awareness of the light
of my heart and
my reasonable mind.

As my mission nears the end,
I ready myself for the time
when my body dies.

My life is starlight
—a universal force—
I plan to use it to unite
with my divine Source...

My soul's light body
will forever be visible
to your consciousness "I am"
in which I have never left you.

Acknowledgements, Credits, Gratitude

When we accomplish what we set out to do in life, see it as a whole and reflect on it, we become aware that we did not do it alone; there were *others*, visible, invisible, who resonated with and influenced our work. Thus we are led, naturally, to acknowledge them, give them credit and express our gratitude.

I would like to begin this impossible task by thanking the sun that gave me light and life and the living earth for her substance that enabled my life. I thank my parents and the generations past, human and nonhuman, that brought me to this point in life and countless others for their support along the way.

In this verbal account of my mission, I acknowledge and give credit to those whose thoughts resonated with mine and inspired me to carry on my search: the ancient Persian poets J. Rumi (in several translations by Coleman Barks, Harper One) and Hafez (translations by D. Ladinsky, Penguin Group); the Czech poets J. Neruda, J. Vrchlicky and Nobel laureate Jaroslav Seifert; the British poets W. Blake, W. Wordsworth , A. Pope; the American poets W. Whitman, E.A. Poe and many, many others.

I acknowledge and give credit to great artists who brought joy to my soul, such as classical music composers but also folksong musicians and dancers.

I acknowledge the influence of the great religions: Christianity, Hinduism, Buddhism, Islam and the world of mythology.

In particular, I acknowledge and credit scientists for opening my reasonable mind, thus providing the means for my living: mathematicians, physicists, biologists, philosophers, cosmologists, psychologists, and other scientists and technologists.

Finally, my deepest gratitude belongs to the heart of my mother, which awakened my sleeping heart when I was an embryo only a few weeks old, an act of consciousness whose light has been my faithful companion in the womb, life after birth and a universal connection.

With a tear in my eye, my gratitude to all.

Jaroslav Vlcek
West Vancouver, BC, 2016

Brief Biography of the Author

Jaroslav Vlcek (1925–), B.Sc.F., M.A.Sc., D.Sc., was born in a highland valley in Czechoslovakia. He spent his childhood mostly walking alone and exploring the nature that surrounded him. He loved trees and communicated with plants. His way of learning was challenged, however, when he began attending the village school. "School took away my way of knowing nature," he felt with sadness, but his interest remained and led him to a lifelong academic career. It started as a student at the Technical University of Prague, but was interrupted when he was expelled from it as "not suitable for higher education" by the newly installed Communist government. "That was my lucky moment," he says because it forced him to leave his country as a political refugee. His first experience abroad was landing as a 25-year-old immigrant in Canada. His first job was cutting trees in a northern forest in meter deep snow and -20°C temperature. "The healthiest job you can have," he says, "working, eating and sleeping." After a few years of doing odd jobs, he returned to his university studies and academic pursuits that eventually lead to a career as a professor at the University of Toronto. He taught and did research in remote sensing and image analysis of the earth's surface as a member of the Departments of Applied Physics, Civil Engineering and the Faculty of Forestry.

After retirement, Dr. Vlcek started his second career that began by having to take a deep personal journey into his early life. “It was much harder work than the one at the university,” he said. His deep inward search led to reviving his prenatal memory. That resulted in the first self-published biography *Journey into the World – My Life before Birth*, ELF 1978. In 2001, he returned to his native country to reconnect with his roots and to write a three-part book in Czech, *Forgotten Truth: Life before Birth*, Ticha Byzanc 2008. He lectured on this subject in many cities of the country. In 2010, he returned to Canada to deliver the fruits of his life’s mission in the current book at the age of ninety-two.

Jaroslav Vlcek strongly believes that to know anything fully, one must know its origin. He considers life experience and its memory to be the cornerstone of the knowledge of life. He considers his conscious prenatal experience and the intuitive theory of the beginning of life on earth to be the most important contributions to human knowledge: *Conscious, ergo sum—Conscious, I am.*

CPSIA information can be obtained
at www.ICGtesting.com
Printed in the USA
LVOW07s0539221117
557238LV00001B/1/P

9 781460 285046